NOVELS OF DISPLACEMENT

NOVELS OF DISPLACEMENT

FICTION IN THE AGE OF GLOBAL CAPITAL

MARCO CODEBÒ

THE OHIO STATE UNIVERSITY PRESS

COLUMBUS

Copyright © 2020 by The Ohio State University.
All rights reserved.

Library of Congress Cataloging-in-Publication Data
Names: Codebò, Marco, 1952– author.
Title: Novels of displacement : fiction in the age of global capital / Marco Codebò.
Description: Columbus : The Ohio State University Press, [2020] | Includes bibliographical references and index. | Summary: "Analyzes how contemporary novels—specifically Bernardo Carvalho's *Nove noites,* Daniel Sada's *Porque parece mentira la verdad nunca se sabe,* Zadie Smith's *White Teeth,* and Mathias Énard's *Zone*—resist displacement and offer a redemptive vision for the place of the novel for the future"—Provided by publisher.
Identifiers: LCCN 2020010473 | ISBN 9780814214473 (cloth) | ISBN 0814214479 (cloth) | ISBN 9780814278413 (ebook) | ISBN 0814278418 (ebook)
Subjects: LCSH: Displacement (Psychology) in literature. | Globalization in literature. | Fiction—History and criticism—20th century. | Fiction—History and criticism—21st century.
Classification: LCC PN3352.G56 C63 2020 | DDC 808.3/9353—dc23
LC record available at https://lccn.loc.gov/2020010473
Other identifiers: ISBN 978-0-8142-5602-2 (paper) | ISBN 0-8142-5602-3 (paper)

Cover design by Derek Thornton
Text design by Juliet Williams
Type set in Adobe Minion Pro

*To the memory of my teachers: Alessandro Bima,
Adriano Guerrini, and Edoardo Sanguineti*

CONTENTS

Acknowledgments — ix

INTRODUCTION — 1

CHAPTER 1   De- and Reterritorialization in the Age of Global Capital — 29

CHAPTER 2   The Novel between the Cloud and the Earth — 47

CHAPTER 3   Epistemic Displacement in Bernardo Carvalho's *Nove noites* — 73

CHAPTER 4   On Places, Hyper-places, and Agency — 91

CHAPTER 5   Lost in Space: Daniel Sada's *Porque parece mentira la verdad nunca se sabe* and Zadie Smith's *White Teeth* — 115

CHAPTER 6   Symptoms: Mathias Énard's *Zone* — 149

POSTSCRIPT   On Records and Errors — 171

Works Cited — 181

Index — 193

ACKNOWLEDGMENTS

This book would not exist had it not been for the many conversations I have had the pleasure to entertain with colleagues and friends over the course of the last five years. I would like to thank them all for their contributions: Nando Fasce, Manlio Calegari, Vittorio Coletti, Jorge Rosario-Velez, Sandy Waters, Lugi Ballerini, Beppe Cavatorta, Francesco Ciabattoni, Carol Viers, Alessandro Carrera, Tom Harrison, and Catherine Nesci. I am particularly thankful to the first scholar who read my manuscript, my elder daughter Agnese, who has been an enthusiastic proponent of this project from the outset. My warmest thanks go to my younger daughter Carlotta for sharing her remarkable knowledge of popular culture with me. I am deeply grateful to Václav Paris, my son-in-law and a gifted scholar of Modernism, who kindly read the manuscript and assisted me with a precious note on James Joyce.

My prose would never have met the standards required for a scholarly publication in English without the invaluable professional assistance of Bridget Pupillo, who edited every single line of every single draft of this study; I warmly thank her for her skills and dedication to bringing forth this work.

I am greatly thankful to Claudette Allegrezza, the accomplished librarian in charge of the Interlibrary Loan at the Davis Schwartz

Library, Long Island University, Post Campus, who found and delivered all the books and articles that my insatiable research required.

The Ohio State University Press provided me with the ideal environment for turning my essay into a published work. I am profoundly grateful to Ana María Jimenez-Moreno, who strongly supported my project throughout all the stages of publication and made an extremely helpful revision of the manuscript.

For years, my wife Giulietta had to cope with my desire for seclusion and frequent bouts of absentmindedness. For her uninterrupted love and support, despite these circumstances, I thank her from the bottom of my heart.

INTRODUCTION

In this book, I investigate a cluster of contemporary novels that I shall describe as "novels of displacement." Displacement belongs to the category of moods or frames of mind that shape the manner in which things matter to us.[1] Moods determine the way we open up to the outside: they are "essential to a sense of the kinds of significant possibility that the world can offer up for us" (Ratcliffe 158). Displacement, in particular, is one of those moods (like its opposite, emplacement) that inform our attitude toward the territories we inhabit and, in so doing, decisively affect the development of our subjectivity. Indeed, if living means experiencing things, then our disposition toward the sites where we meet with things, aka places, structures the way we project ourselves onto the world. Displacement becomes our mood, thus taking control of this disposition, when external, superior powers gain control of the places in which we live and work. As our own agency is overwhelmed, we fail to establish meaningful relationships with our surroundings. Indeed, displacement consists of a diminishment of our agency and a correlative loss in meaning affecting the objects that coexist with us. I

---

1. Moods constitute "specifications of affectedness, the ontological existential condition that things always already matter" (Dreyfus 169).

believe that displacement represents the prevailing mood of our time, the age of global capital.

As described in this book, the era of global capital began in the early 1980s with the progressive liberalization of capital movements, financial transactions, and stock markets in the wealthy countries of the Western hemisphere as well as in East Asia, Australia, and New Zealand. Four decades ago, certain capabilities, tools, and institutions that had been built in the years following the conference of Bretton Woods (1944) reached a "tipping point" and "became part of a new emergent organizing logic leading toward the constituting of a novel assemblage of key components" (Sassen, *Territory, Authority, Rights* 18).[2] While in previous stages of capitalistic growth, "that logic was geared toward building national states," but today it is "geared toward building global systems inside national states" (Sassen, *Territory, Authority, Rights* 17). The current phase of capitalism differs from other international expansions of capital in that it is the first globalization in history tailored to downsize the role and prerogatives of the nation-state as a player in the market.

In 1977, roughly at the same time in which the age of global capital began, a new technology started to take shape. In that year, Alan Kay and Adele Goldberg published a paper, "Personal Dynamic Media," which can be considered the harbinger of the technological developments that have informed our time. In their essay, Kay and Goldberg outlined their vision of "a personal dynamic medium of the size of a notebook" that could function as a metamedium, able to integrate "*all other media*" (393, emphasis in the original). In the following decades, the development of computer software turned Kay and Goldberg's vision into reality. It is indeed software that transforms computers into metamedia, by encoding the analog language of traditional media into the digital code of computers and then recoding the latter into an analog signal compatible with the human user's sensory apparatus

---

2. In Sassen's book, the entire fourth chapter, "The Tipping Point: Toward New Organizing Logic," displays her deep insight into the dynamics of globalization. Sassen discusses how certain foundational realignments inside the State, in particular the United States, were instrumental in establishing capital's global organizing logic. Her discussion helpfully illuminates the evolution of nation-states, supranational organizations, and finance in the period of time spanning between the end of WWII and the 1980s.

(Manovich, ch. 2). As the invisible, operational layer that makes the computer-human interaction possible, software constitutes an indispensable component of the capital-driven machine that is presently running the planet.

In the age of global, software-enabled capital, significant innovations affect the political, epistemic, and technological environment in which individuals operate and societies are built. These transformations comprise, but cannot be limited to, the rise of international financial institutions (e.g., International Monetary Fund, World Bank, World Trade Organization) and nongovernmental organizations to the status of competitors with the nation-state on the planetary stage; the establishment of a small cluster of supranational financial corporations as the directional center of global capitalism; the advent of the digital, relational database as a storage system for public and private records; and the development of software-based technologies for executing an incredibly vast array of operations related in some manner to the production of culture, such as writing, drawing, watching films, calculating, mapping, mailing, as well as making, recording, and listening to music, to name just a few.

As a consequence of these world-historical processes, the inhabitants of our planet, as well as the artifacts of their material and intellectual production, undergo a type of mobilization the likes of which has never been seen before. Migrants crossing national borders, flows of surplus value internationalized through the channels of global finance, assembly lines outsourced to cheap-labor countries, language shifting from digital documents to social networks, data moved across digital platforms, artistic products bouncing through disparate media: the list of persons, objects, and signs that are set loose by the initiative of global capital and/or the utilization of software could go on forever. This universal mobilization seems to hamper or utterly negate the practice by which human beings define themselves in relation to the places in which they live and operate, thus presenting a threat to the very possibility that place and subjectivity might relate to each other. As I will discuss in chapter 4, this threat achieves its goal when mobility results from coercion.

There is nothing new in this coexistence of conflicting impulses, one aiming to empower people by enhancing their ability to move and the other intending to disempower them by cutting their roots in the territories where they operate. The current time is simply the latest stage in the development of modernity, a contradictory age based on constructive destruction. In *All That Is Solid Melts into Air,* a book that has been influential in my own approach to the modern age, Marshall Berman describes modernity as a maelstrom of energy in which building and demolishing live side by side: "To be modern is to find ourselves in an environment that promises us adventure, power, joy, growth, transformation of ourselves and the world—and, at the same time, that threatens to destroy everything we have, everything we know, everything we are" (15). In this book, I focus on the destructive component inherent in the latest development in modernity, or the downside of today's universal mobilization. This destructive component manifests itself as an erosion of the connections between place and subjectivity.

Bringing this component to the fore, I believe, is necessary to counter a current, mass phenomenon: the oversimplified, unconditional support to the mobilization enchained by global capital. Albeit largely majoritarian, this attitude is not helpful in making "ourselves at home in this world" (Berman 348). In the current age, what can bring us home is only an inclusive, "Both/And" approach, able to take into consideration not only the evident benefits of the present widespread mobilization for the human community at large but also the human suffering that accompanies this process, in particular, when mobility results from pressures (or the downright use of force) on the human subject by external, powerful agents. By casting light on this suffering, this study aims to foster a more sensible approach to present-day mobilization and its effects on our lives. The objects analyzed in this book—novels—determine the limits of its contribution, which is strictly contained within the field of analysis and comprehension. Novels are not necessarily intended to change the world, but to aid in understanding it, as this study also hopes to do.

Negative Deterritorialization, Agency, and Displacement

The world-historical processes that I have outlined so far can be defined by one, encompassing term: deterritorialization. A concept elaborated by Gilles Deleuze and Félix Guattari, deterritorialization consists in "the movement by which 'one' leaves the territory [. . .] the operation of the line of flight" (*Thousand Plateaus* 591). The persons, things, and words that have been deterritorialized in our time have indeed left their traditional territories, be they countries, national markets, or original texts. We cannot be satisfied, however, with the simple observation of the frequency and the dissemination of today's deterritorializing movements. Contemporary deterritorialization must be probed in two directions. To begin with, an analytical effort is required in order to understand whether or not this deterritorialization is accompanied by a reverse movement toward reterritorialization. Second, the power relations underlying the operations of the subjects involved in present-day deterritorialization are to be uncovered. In particular, when human actors are directly engaged in deterritorialization—for example, migrants who cross borders or workers moving from Fordist factories to digital platforms—it becomes imperative to ask who controls these movements, who are the agents, and who the patients in today's deterritorialization.

In their discussion of deterritorialization, Deleuze and Guattari introduce the concept of "negative" deterritorialization, or deterritorialization "overlaid by a compensatory reterritorialization obstructing the line of flight." They go on to say that "anything can serve as a reterritorialization . . . : one can reterritorialize on a being, an object, a book, an apparatus or system" (*Thousand Plateaus* 591). Reterritorialization does not signify a return to the original territory. Rather, it reformulates the relations between the components of an ongoing deterritorialization (592). The tendency to counter a deterritorializing movement with a motion in the opposite direction appears to be capitalism's distinctive trait.[3] For example, as Deleuze and Guattari argue again, during the historical phase that precedes the present age of global capital, while the "capitalist machine" deterritorializes the flows of production in order to extract surplus values from them, "its ancillary apparatuses, such as government bureaucracy and the forces of law and order, do their utmost to reterritorialize" (*Anti-Œdipus* 35). It is this reterritorialization of bureaucracy and the law that the present-day, deterritorial-

---

3. Claire Colebrook argues that capitalism hosts a "deterritorializing tendency to open any system on to exchange and interaction" and, at the same time, "arrests its tendency to produce and open flows by quantifying all exchange through the flow of capital" (65).

ized flows of value, people, and production counter. These flows escape from all the territorial apparatuses of control, including, for instance, the factory, the hospital, the prison, and, most importantly, the State. In our time, as Pierre Dardot and Christian Laval argue, "States are increasingly submitted to the iron law of a globalized dynamics that largely eludes them" (283).[4] In the realm of financial circulation, today's deterritorialization liberates enormous movements of capital from the constraints of the national market. In the production sector, the current deterritorialization transforms control over the workforce from a factory-based, temporally limited (8 hours a day, 40 hours a week) practice into a 24/7 operation free from any territorial limit.

As for the existence of reterritorializing movements in the present phase, the answer is affirmative: reterritorialization does indeed happen today, as software becomes the immaterial stratum on which global capital reterritorializes. Doreen Massey aptly clarifies the role played by software in the internationalization of finance and services: "Little of this [the internationalization of finance and services] would have been possible without new technologies of communication, of image-processing and transmission and of information systems" (159). Software-enabled capital has unshackled itself from the nation-states and their territorialized instruments (national markets, national currencies, state-based regulations, borders, and customs). Today, as software makes global circulation and exchange possible, global capital gets rid of the old, state-based territorialization and adopts a kind of planetary reterritorialization in which the Earth becomes a single, massive territory formatted through electronic instruments. Last but not least, software also allows for a shift in the governance of the workforce, whereby workers' confinement in a delimited location is replaced by remote, ubiquitous surveillance.

Let us consider, for example, the wristband for which Amazon won two patents in January 2018. It is the tracking device mentioned by Ceylan Yeginsu in the following rhetorical question: "What if your employer made you wear a wristband that tracked your every move, and that even nudged you via vibrations when it judged that

---

4. Unless otherwise noted, in this study, translations from foreign languages are mine.

you were doing something wrong?" If one considers Amazon's overall approach to the management of its workforce, then the implementation of the practices mentioned by Yeginsu appears to be more than a mere hypothesis. As Sam Adler-Bell notes, "Amazon has built a vast logistics empire by subjecting its workforce to extreme forms of technological discipline—designed to keep workers isolated, fearful, and maniacally productive." In this context, Amazon's wristband would be just the latest and most advanced tracking tool made available through software-based technology. What matters in this discussion is the deterritorializing changes in labor management that such technology determines. In the analog world, in order to keep workers in check, management had them inhabit a certain territory, that of their station along the assembly line or their desk in an office. Nowadays, software allows for a new, deterritorialized control, not in the sense that it is deprived of a territory for its operations but in that it opens every territory to the controlling gaze, bathrooms and even bedrooms included. In the age of global capital, immaterial striations replace the analog, visible striations—the foreman's eyes, the walls of the cubicle, the gate, the clock—that formatted the working space in the territorialized companies of the paper age. The two reterritorializations I have described, one in the field of circulation and the other affecting workforce management, unfold on different scales, global and local, respectively, but follow the same pattern: spaces formatted through hard, material instruments are deterritorialized only to be reorganized by means of a soft, immaterial reterritorialization. This movement nicely fits Deleuze and Guattari's negative deterritorialization, with software acting as the system on which the entire process ultimately hinges.

On the basis on the above considerations, I can now answer with reasonable certainty the question regarding where agency is situated in today's negative deterritorialization: it lies in the hands of global capital. This is not to say that agency is not spread around during the deterritorializing process. It does not imply, for instance, that a person who moves to the metropolis in search of a better life is deprived of intentionality, as if he/she unconsciously acted under the guidance of a remote, almighty authority. With the notable exception of the unfortunate individuals who, in the twenty-first century, are working under a regime of neoslavery, we are all still agents who intentionally carry out our actions.⁵ However, as will be discussed extensively in chapter 1, only global capital possesses a panoramic knowledge of the entire context in which our movements take place. Since wide-ranging, comprehensive knowledge represents the condition for full agency, in the current context only capital can behave as a thoroughly informed agent whose movements are not conditioned by factors outside its control.⁶ What we are witnessing in our time is a capital-induced, negative deterritorialization.

Present-day, negative deterritorialization leads to displacement, the mood that represents the key concern of this study. For us as human subjectivities on the ground, displacement stems from undergoing an evident loss of agency in our experience of being in the world, and from becoming aware, at the same time, that this loss is rooted in processes whose goals remain obscure and whose ultimate agents continue to be anonymous. Displacement originates in the ambivalent character of this capital-driven, negative deterritorialization, in its countering the liberation of people and resources from territorial authorities such as the State with new forms of striation of the spaces inhabited by human subjects. Indeed, for the latter, the loss of existential reference points after leaving a territory quite often is not accompanied by a gain in personal freedom; in many cases, it may even lead to new, more sophisticated forms of oppression. Novels of displacement narrate the mood that originates in this context.

Contemporary displacement appears to be significantly different from Homi Bhabha's unhomeliness, as theorized in *The Location of Culture* (1994). Unhomeliness is the condition of those displaced subjectivities who occupy a minoritarian discursive position outside the great narratives of nation, gender, race, and class, and who can turn their very externality into a platform for writing histories of resistance.⁷ What

---

5. On intentionality as a decisive component of agency, see Markus Schlosser: "Usually, [...] the term 'agency' is used in a much narrower sense to denote the performance of intentional actions" (2).

6. Even here, there should be a noteworthy exception: the environment, which clearly lies outside of capital's control.

7. Ironically, the very idea that being an outsider provides unique insight into oneself, as well as the society from which one is marginalized, lies at the root of Western culture, the target of the narratives of resistance that Bhabha theorizes. As Arnold

separates present-day displacement from Bhabha's unhomeliness is the crucial, albeit short time (essentially the decade straddling the end of the twentieth century) in which capital-induced negative deterritorialization definitively outshined one of the Western hegemonic narratives, the nation, while simultaneously becoming the sole true great narrative of our age. The title of this narrative might well be *Empire*, as in Michael Hardt and Toni Negri's theory, or Google, or even Amazon (were it not for Alibaba). Negative deterritorialization deprives place of sense. Hence, the minoritarian in-betweenness of the 1990s becomes the majoritarian displacement of the 2010s: the condition of those who lose their place without even having to depart from it. Put another way, today's displaced subjectivities are situated in an outside that does not lead to any inside, as it does instead in Bhabha's metaphor of the interstitial space behaving like a stairwell between two floors in a house (4). To the contrary, contemporary displacement is pure outsideness, stairs leading to other stairs. In this context, the diminished agency that defines today's displaced subjectivities prevents them from feeling Bhabha's "compulsion to move beyond" (4). It also precludes the use of our deterritorialized spaces as the "terrain for elaborating strategies of selfhood—singular or communal—that initiate new signs of identity" (1). For the time being, what remains is a mood—displacement—and the novel's ethical commitment to narrate this mood.

At the Root of the Novel's Territoriality: Balzac's *Comédie humaine*

The negative deterritorialization that is shaping our living environment threatens the epistemic foundation of the novel. In particular, it challenges the novel's ability to represent the human being as a subjectivity operating within a given society. One of the pillars of this capacity is the novel's territoriality. Indeed, the novel has been a territorial cultural form for two centuries, starting from Balzac's groundbreaking work. Balzac, I affirm, was the first novelist to fully develop the novel's

---

Hauser wrote, at the dawn of Western civilization, it was as a minority surrounded by foreign populations that the inhabitants of the Ionian colonies on the coastline of Asia Minor (in the seventh century BCE) learned how to construct their own identity and to appreciate philosophical and cultural differences among various peoples (71).

potential as a territorial marker for both the nation-state and the bourgeois family. In so doing, Balzac incorporated territoriality into the novel's defining set of traits. Now, however, a territorial genre like the novel must survive within a context in which the territorial formations narrated by Balzac have been targeted by a deep deterritorialization. Discussing the Balzacian novel as the archetype of the novel's territoriality helps to assess the difference between our time and the age in which the tools for the novelistic representation of territoriality were forged. Understanding this difference is key to the apprehension of both the novel's difficulties in today's environment and the role the novel of displacement could play as a possible solution to the problem.

Among his contemporaries, Balzac demonstrated an unparalleled comprehension of the relation tying the novel to two territorial(-izing) entities: the nation-state and the bourgeois family. To accomplish this feat, Balzac took advantage of his own experience: living in a nation that, with the Revolution and the Napoleonic Code, pioneered the construction of the modern nation-state and the crafting of advanced legislation concerning the family. Even though almost two centuries separate our time from Balzac's, his narrative rendition of territoriality still matters to us in the age of global capital. It does so because it is based on Balzac's dynamic understanding of his epoch: a historical phase characterized by an extraordinary sequence of deterritorializing and reterritorializing processes, forerunners to those occurring in our own age. Living through the Bourbon Restoration and the July Monarchy, Balzac had firsthand experience of the reterritorialization that followed the sweeping, deterritorializing changes brought about by the French Revolution. In his fiction, he captured the very essence of this twofold process by narrating the rise of the bankers and profiteers who turned financial capital into a driving force in French society.

Balzac expounded his understanding of the connection between territoriality, the family, and the nation-state in *Physiologie du mariage,* an essay that constitutes a nonfictional epilogue to *La Comédie humaine.*[8] While *Physiologie* primarily focuses on the oppositional con-

---

8. Balzac wrote an initial, unpublished version of his *Physiologie* in 1826 (*La physiologie préoriginale*), three years before publishing *Le dernier Chouan ou la Bretagne,* the first novel he signed as Honoré Balzac (*Comédie* 11: 1732, 1739). In December 1829, he published the version of *Physiologie* that would become part of

flict between marriage and desire, it also makes frequent, important diversions into another antagonism, that of the struggle between individual desire and the will of the nation-state. By narrating each of these two conflicts as a metaphor for the other, the text creates an exchange of tropes that plays upon a trait shared by both the nation-state and the family: territoriality.

In *Physiologie du mariage,* and in the entire *Comédie humaine* for that matter, marriage is a male-managed institution. Marriage is based on the husband's absolute control of a territory—the home—that must be meticulously reconnoitered and delimited. The obvious reason for the husband's mastery of the domestic space consists in his wife's residence within that space; as Catherine Nesci crisply notes, in Balzac's *Physiologie* "the wife is the object of military cartography" (196). Balzac provides the sociological data that justify the exercise of such an intrusive practice. According to his calculation, 400,000 desirable married women live in France. They belong to the wealthy upper class, which has enough leisure time to cultivating its tastes and manage its pleasures (934). These women face an Army of one million bachelors of the same class, whose only preoccupation is persuading them to betray their husbands (940). The latter are completely oblivious to this potential for betrayal. Husbands arouse their wives' sexuality in the initial honeymoon period of their marriages. However, because of their erroneous lifestyle, they are unable to keep the flame of pleasure alive. These men dedicate far too much time and energy to business and show too little consideration for their spouses, above all for their sexual desires. It is at this point that Balzac enters, in the capacity of a marriage counselor. His task is to advise husbands on the best way to restrain their wives from infidelity. Husbands, he writes, must become experts in the "high politics of marriage," an art that follows in the footsteps of one of the founders of modern political science, Niccolò Machiavelli: Balzac's *Physiologie du mariage* itself is a sort of "breviary of marital Machiavellianism" (996).

The language of politics suits a discussion on marriage because rulers and husbands share one chief preoccupation: how to control the territory in their care. As Nesci correctly observes, "Since the practice

---

La Comédie humaine in 1846 (*Comédie* 11: 1746, 1753). Thus, while the actual writing of *Physiologie* is chronologically situated at the beginning of Balzac's authorial career, its publication marks the conclusion of Balzac's *œuvre*.

of marriage is the same as the practice of politics, both share the same goal: to hide the power relations so as to prevent the 'Other' from really empowering him/herself" (130). Appropriately, the husband's primary task is to exercise rigorous supervision over the family home and its boundaries in particular:

> Starting from Meditation 8, philosophical discourse turns into panopticism as a disciplinary practice. The husband climbs to the rank of master in technology. In order to preserve his happiness and honor, he must rule over the marital space, measure his wife's time, as well as give a direction to his submitted wife, this white page on which the masculine subject is going to imprint his trace. (Nesci 195)

Indeed, Balzac's husband is running a disciplinary facility, which is consistent with the role fathers played in the nineteenth-century European family: "In civil society, Bentham's panopticism relies on the sovereign gaze of the father, the master in the name of God's will and human reason" (Perrot 82). In the chapter of *Physiologie* titled "On Apartments," Balzac argues that the family home must be separated from all the other buildings, must be built in between the yard and the garden, and must have smooth walls entirely free of cavities. Further, in the wife's quarters, an iron grid must be fixed inside the chimney to prevent intrusions from above. As for the concierge, the ideal is an elderly male servant who pledges absolute loyalty to the head of the house. Through his daily vigilance over the main entrance, or "the custom" in Balzac's language, the concierge must make sure that no external threat can infiltrate the home (1038–50). If a lover does indeed appear in the conjugal space in spite of the husband's defensive measures, then comes the time for police methods. "An Essay on Police Methods" is the title of the meditation dedicated to the management of marriage when a wife's affair has become a concrete possibility; it includes sections whose titles reveal their contents: "On Mousetraps," "On Mail," "Spies," and "On the Budget" (1090–107). For example, regarding traps, Balzac narrates the story of a husband who falsely affirms that the man he suspects to be his wife's lover intends to fight another man in a duel over a danseuse of the *Opéra* (1094). From his wife's sudden indisposition, the husband realizes that the man he suspected is indeed her lover. As for the mail, "the man who does not see when his wife writes a letter to her lover or when she receives an answer from him is an incomplete husband" (1096). The budget, finally, becomes a veritable issue when a woman has an affair. In that situation, unable to cope with her monthly allowance, a lady "prostitutes herself with her husband" (1104). The latter is helpless because "nature endows women with treasures of seduction." As an alternative, Balzac suggests that the husband put his wife in charge of the domestic finances: an increase in the house expenses will tell the husband that an affair is going on (1105).

Balzac's imaginary husband represents a case study in territorial behavior. Writing within a conceptual frame inspired by the idea of territoriality as a state-inspired practice, Robert David Sack lists ten tendencies that can aid in defining territoriality. Within this inventory, the following three tendencies are to be considered "logically . . . prior":

1. Territoriality involves a form of *classification* that is extremely efficient.
   . . .
2. Territoriality can be easy to *communicate* because it requires only one kind of marker or sign—the boundary.
   . . .
3. Territoriality can be the most efficient strategy for *enforcing* control, if the distribution in space and time of the resources or things to be controlled falls between ubiquity and unpredictability. (32, emphasis in the original)

Balzac's suggestions for husbands (to classify all the rooms in the house, to establish firm boundaries, and to act territorially in order to control an elusive wife) correspond precisely to Sack's three logically prior territorial tendencies.

Balzac considers marriage the keystone of society and believes that his duty is to fortify the marital institution by placing his own knowledge of the intricacies of social life at the service of the unskilled husbands of his time. Preserving marriage is an extremely serious business, as becomes clear when Balzac argues that a strong analogy likens managing a woman to governing a nation. "Should not a husband's policies," he rhetorically asks, "be more or less those of a king?" (1016). Here, in order to make the husband's role abundantly clear, Balzac utilizes a metaphor, the second term of which is the head of a State. The metaphor works because its two terms share a common condition: vying with a recalcitrant subject. In the case of the husband, it is his wife; in that of the king, his people. Since everyone, or at least all the members of the social elite who constitute the ideal readers of *Physiologie*, knows what it means to be king (in terms of duties, governing techniques, and political goals), Balzac's metaphorical likening of a husband to a king aims to clarify the former's condition by using the latter as an easy-to-grasp example.

As the text progresses and readers become expert in the art of keeping a wife in check, they come to realize that the metaphor could also move in the opposite direction. Readers could learn meaningful information on the art of governing a State by first observing a husband trying to hold sway over his wife, and then applying the same expectations to a king ruling over his country.[9] When readers conduct their reasoning along these lines, a new type of knowledge presents itself. The premise of this knowledge lies in the definition of marriage that we can glean from *Physiologie du mariage*: marriage consists in the management of an economy of desire in which the enjoyment of the object providing pleasure (aka the wife) must be reserved for one subject, the male head of the family, and forbidden to others, his male competitors. Policing the domestic territory and controlling its boundaries are instrumental to the establishment of the husband's power over his home and its inhabitants. If this definition of marriage can function as a metaphor for political governance, then the state's business consists in administering an economy of desire that rewards its deserving subjects and punishes those unworthy ones, while keeping foreigners outside of the country: the state's ability to exercise forceful jurisdiction over its whole territory, starting from the control of its borders, appears to be essential to its success as the sole administrator of its sub-

---

9. Balzac's grasping of the similarity between the head of the family and the head of the State is solidly rooted in the tradition of French political thinking. As Michel Foucault argues, for political thinkers writing during the Ancien Régime, a deep affinity tied the government of the household to the government of the State. Toward the end of this epoch, for Rousseau, "to govern a state . . . means exercising towards its inhabitants, and the wealth and behaviour of each and all, a form of surveillance and control as attentive as that of the head of a family over his household and his goods" ("Governmentality" 92).

jects' desire.[10] Hence, Balzac's reversible trope yields a decisive gain in knowledge: understanding the true purpose of the State and the instruments necessary for achieving its goals.

Since, as Nesci notes, "the narrative program of *Physiologie* implicitly sends the reader to the doorstep of *La Comédie humaine*," the latter indeed represents the novelistic rendition of the principles elucidated in *Physiologie du mariage* (185). In *La Comédie humaine*, society is dominated by the search for *plaisir*, a broadly encompassing term that signifies the joy one may obtain from a vast range of intellectual, social, and physical activities: engaging in stimulating conversation, throwing a successful party, strolling on Paris boulevards, buying beautiful furniture, and so on. Consistent with *Physiologie*, at the pinnacle of the various types of *plaisir* stands gendered, male-oriented sexual pleasure. For the male subjectivity, other *plaisirs* are not only less intense but also hierarchically subordinated to sexual pleasure. In addition to bestowing joy upon their pursuers, these inferior *plaisirs* are instrumental in constructing situations favorable to the fulfillment of the sex drive. This occurs, for instance, with the pleasure of making money. Although the drive for wealth structures the plot of innumerable story lines, becomes the object of endless conversations among characters, and represents one of the favorite topics of commentary by the omniscient narrator of *La Comédie humaine*, at the end of the day money serves as an instrumental means to satisfy the male eros. In *Splendeurs et misères des courtisanes*, the most affluent character in Balzac's novels, Baron Nucingen, a ruthless banker who has accumulated enormous wealth through a mix of legal and fraudulent systems, wastes millions in order to satisfy his senile passion for Esther Gobseck, a woman of astounding beauty. However, as she limits herself to the role of courtesan to the Baron (while choosing Lucien de Rubempré as her lover), Esther can deliver pleasure only in the form of a commodity.[11]

---

10. In 1978, in a lecture on governmentality delivered at the Collège de France, Foucault arrived at a similar conclusion: "To govern a state will therefore mean to apply economy, to set up an economy at the level of the entire state, which means exercising towards its inhabitants, and the wealth and behaviour of each and all, a form of surveillance and control as attentive as that of the head of a family over his household and his goods" ("Governmentality," 92).

11. In *La Comédie humaine*, there is no doubt that female desire, too, becomes the object of fictional representation. However, in Balzac's world, female eros can become socially acceptable only if channeled through an institution—the patriarchal

In *La Comédie humaine,* the political formation that imposes a system of rules, rewards, and sanctions on its subjects' competing desires is the nation-state that emerges out of the French Revolution. In the first half of the nineteenth century, this State becomes a key factor of social and political stability by functioning as the centerpiece of the reterritorialization that followed the Napoleonic Wars. As the key agent in this process of reterritorialization, the nation-state counters the opposing tendencies that are simmering throughout Europe in the three decades leading toward the continental Revolution of 1848. By describing the surge and the management of the very same desire on which the State is attempting to impose its order, Balzac's narrative project takes on a political dimension. As a symbolic form standing for both the nation-state and the bourgeois family, the Balzacian novel relates to these territorial assemblages in a deeper sense than by simply functioning as their narrative representation. In actuality, the Balzacian novel manages the territory of the State and that of the family, side by side with the head of State and the husband, respectively. It does so by transforming precious knowledge into narratives, thus allowing for its circulation as usable, formatted information. It shows, for example, how to prevent one's wife from having an affair, to discover a lover hidden in a closet, or to arrange an advantageous marriage; it also delineates the French national borders, narrates key events in French history, and demonstrates how certain classes can be trusted while others are to be kept in check (the former are deserving subjects, the latter unworthy ones). As an integral component of both the bourgeois family assemblage and the nation-state assemblage, the Balzacian novel is not merely narrating territorial practices: it is carrying them out. In so doing, the Balzacian novel proves itself to be territorial, born and bred.

Balzac transformed the novel into a constitutive agent within the broader nation-state project. Understandably, an operation of this kind took place in France, a country that had first lived through the founda-

---

family—that is geared solely toward the satisfaction of male desire. Balzac narrates several stories in which marriage survives only because either one or both of the spouses are involved in an extramarital affair. Even though Balzac's stories of female infidelity allows for a more equal representation of male and female desires, by becoming a (sub)institution whose main function is the stabilization of marriage, the "affair" remains subordinated to an economy of desire framed by the patriarchal family.

tion of a modern, centralized State in the form of Absolute Monarchy, and then experienced the Revolution, or the sociopolitical upheaval that highlighted the nation as a political subject. Later in history, the novel's affiliation with the nation-state project became a text-generating factor whenever a nation-state entered a foundational period or needed to reaffirm its internal cohesion; this textual production was not, of course, a mere reenacting of the form taken by the Balzacian novel as an agent in the consolidation of the French nation-state. To the contrary, depending on specific sociopolitical contexts, the novel's connection with the nation-state helped in generating diverse kinds of territorial novels. Such is the case, for example, of those novels Doris Sommer calls "National Romances": love stories written in Latin America in the second half of the nineteenth century, a few decades after the former colonies' independence from Spain.[12] During that time, the Latin American nation-states were still striving to achieve social, ethnic, and territorial cohesion. In that context, the novel's contribution to the nation-state project consisted in narrating stories of harmony achieved after a struggle, that is to say romantic adventures culminating in marriage.[13] This cohesion occurs, for instance, in Alberto Blest Gana's *Martín Rivas* (1862), in which the hero's marriage with the gorgeous and rich Leonor allegorizes Chile's bid for unity on three levels: social (Martín is poor but marries into one of the wealthiest families of the country), geographical (Martín hails from Valparaíso, a provincial city, while Leonor lives in Santiago, the capital), and political (Martín is a liberal who had rebelled against the conservative government). By treating both the construction of the patriarchal family and, allegorically, the consolidation of the nation-state, the national romance "actually helped to give a cognitive expression and an emotive mooring to the social and political formations it articulates" (Sommer 51). In so doing, once again, the novel could assist in establishing territorial entities such as the nation-state and the family, while asserting its own territoriality in the process.

---

12. As a romance, Sommer intends a cross between "the use of the word as a love story and the nineteenth-century use that distinguished the genre as more boldly allegorical than the novel" (5).

13. Franco Moretti makes a similar argument about Jane Austen's *Pride and Prejudice* by claiming that the association at the end of the novel between local gentry such as the Bennets and the national elite represented by Darcy turns the "strange novelty of the modern state" into "a large, exquisite home" (18).

Balzac lived in a time in which Europeans had just learned to think in historical terms. While philosophers attempted to unveil the law of historical development, novelists turned this historical understanding into a new genre, the historical novel. Balzac, however, also grasped the connection tying historical change to spatial transformation. He understood that, because of historically based developments, certain places were erased or created, while others underwent functional alterations. Life in Balzac's time was different from the prerevolutionary age because of the emergence of economic powers (such as the financial sector) that were changing the world year by year, that is to say, historically. What is more, life was also different because people were occupying space in a new way, dividing their houses according to fresh rules, choosing new areas of the city for their promenades, and establishing completely novel relations between their dwellings and their workplaces. Balzac was able to capture the essence of these transformations because he understood, represented, and ultimately executed the algorithm of territoriality in the capitalist world: first, to turn territories into emptiable spaces delimited by well-guarded boundaries, and then to fill them with the right people. In *Physiologie,* Balzac's spatial consciousness guides the husband when the latter considers the family home as empty space to be filled with his wife and household staff. This is the exact process undertaken by capitalism as it develops its mode of production in workplaces and geographical territories around the world: "The use of territory to create a sense of an emptiable and fillable space and of impersonal social relationships—developed and reinforced the nature of social and work relationships in capitalism" (Sack 196). In *La Comédie Humaine,* Balzac translated his spatial awareness into the obsessive and lengthy descriptions of spaces, domestic interiors, streets, and landscapes that constitute a staple of his narrative.

While utilizing the novel as a tool for representing and conveying territoriality, Balzac did not invent anything new. Jane Austen, to make the most notable example, had already written novels that operated within the territorial project of its country's landed gentry. In this respect, when Franco Moretti claims that Austen's novels became symbolic forms of the nation-state, he overemphasizes their capability to represent territorial entities (17). Austen's nation was England, which was not a nation-state but a constituent of the multinational statal formation known as the Kingdom of Great Britain since 1707 and as the

United Kingdom of Great Britain and Ireland since 1801 (a few years after Austen started writing). The actual territory described in Austen's novels is even smaller than that of England. As the northernmost location in her novels is Pemberley, a fictional country estate that scholars situate in Derbyshire, what Austen narrates is in fact the southern half of England. In this limited portion of her nation, Austen's works act as active agents in the process that establishes the landed gentry's territoriality. While these novels allude to the nation as an entity looming in the background, upon closer view they narrate the systematic striation of its "wealthiest, most populated area" (Moretti 15). In this respect, Moretti's citation from Raymond Williams is to the point: "What she [Jane Austen] sees across the land is a network of propertied houses and families" (12). At the core of the representation of space in Austen's novel there lies a fertile nucleus: the territoriality of countryside estates and land ownership. As the novel concerns itself with fencing properties, counting acres, and signing marriage contracts, its potential as a territorializing tool comes to the fore. If the Balzacian novel demonstrated a unique territorializing capacity, it did so by offering this potential to the service of the most powerful territorial agent in Modernity, the nation-state. In the following decades, this agent would expand its operations first to the entire European continent, in sync with the crumbling of the ancien régime society, and then, as a colonial power, to the whole planet.[14] By now, in Western European countries, the social context that framed the novelistic age ushered in by Austen and Balzac has utterly changed. However, as the imprints of that age are still inscribed in the novel form, we must keep Balzac's handling of space in mind when we situate today's novelistic writing within the context of the nation-state's demise and the ensuing destabilization of the novel's territoriality.

---

14. The modern-state-inspired territorialization essentially consisted in a bureaucratic process. It is no wonder that a narrative genre such as the novel, whose expressive tools were modeled after bureaucratic writing, as Gianni Celati acutely observes, could prove itself to be a valuable asset in the territorializing practices of the nation-state (39). Again, the novel's potential as a bureaucratic tool had already emerged in Jane Austen's works, in which novelistic writing demonstrated its aptitude for measuring estates, appreciating heritages, and registering marriage contracts.

Narrating Displacement, or How to Complicate the Novelistic Canon

My contention in this book, as I will argue at length in chapter 2, is that territoriality constitutes a crucial feature of the novel's form. Since the first half of the nineteenth century, as the discussion of Balzac's work has demonstrated, novels have assisted the nation-state and other sociopolitical formations such as the modern city and the bourgeois family in apprehending, representing, defining, and ultimately possessing their territories. This practice has turned the novel into a territorially based cultural form in which meaning becomes inseparable from territory, be it that of the nation-state, the modern city, or the bourgeois family. In the past few decades, however, as the places that formerly constituted the setting for a novelistic account of the world have been thrust aside by capital-induced deterritorialization, the novel's language—that is to say, its set of formal, territorially shaped traits—has become increasingly unsuitable to express the surrounding sociocultural context. In other words, as a narrative practice of territoriality that finds itself deprived of its environment, the novel, too, is displaced. As a consequence, the novel form can be argued to constitute "a deterritorialized language, suitable to strange, minor uses," like the tongue spoken in Prague by the German community in Kafka's time, according to Deleuze and Guattari (*Kafka* 30). Narrating displacement is the minor use I shall discuss in this study. As Deleuze and Guattari argue, minor is "that literature which a minority writes in a major language" (*Kafka* 29). The major language in which displacement is written is the novel itself, understood as a form defined by a set of historically determined conventions and articulated by each individual writer according to his/her individual pronunciation. Novels of displacement are strangers in their own language. As such, they become the basis for an "intensive" use of the novel form, for a practice that stretches the representational tools of the novel beyond their limits (*Kafka* 35).

The minor, intense novels that narrate displacement complicate the novelistic canon in the age of global capital. This occurs because the narrative tools that in the novelistic tradition were geared toward conveying territoriality reverse their sense in novels of displacement; they no longer convey the ability of a certain subjectivity, be it a single individual or a community, to mark his/her/its place, but rather the crisis of this subjectivity's connection to place: dis-placement.¹⁵ Today, in the global editorial market, novels of displacement are undoubtedly in the minority. They convey an approach to the rendition of our reality that sharply differs from the contemporary novelistic canon. The latter, as I will discuss in depth in chapter 2, pivots around the globalized novel, which mirrors in its content and form the ongoing, capital-driven erosion of cultural and geographical difference. By going against the grain, novels of displacement constitute a minoritarian, innovative body of fiction. Significant novels of displacement are, for example, works such as G. W. Sebald's *Austerlitz* (2001), Simona Vinci's *Strada provinciale tre* (2007), Chimamanda Ngozi Adichie's *Half of a Yellow Sun* (2007) and *Americanah* (2013), Aleksandar Hemon's *The Lazarus Project* (2008), China Miéville's *The City & The City* (2009), Giannina Braschi's *United States of Banana* (2011), Rachel Kushner's *The Flamethrowers* (2013), and Hala Alyan's *Salt Houses* (2017), some of which are mentioned in this study. At the top of this sample of texts, I must, of course, position the four case studies that I analyze in depth in this book: Bernardo Carvalho's *Nove noites* (2002), Daniel Sada's *Porque parece mentira la verdad nunca se sabe* (1999), Zadie Smith's *White Teeth* (2001), and Mathias Énard's *Zone* (2008).¹⁶

Novels of displacement deserve to be investigated for two reasons. First, the spreading of displacement represents a momentous phenomenon in today's sociocultural context. Displacement affects increasingly large segments—indeed the majority—of humankind. Everybody who has to cope with global capital's power to dwarf subjective agency and flatten cultural and geographical specificity experiences displacement. Second, narrating displacement constitutes a key passage in the development of novelistic discourse. As a historically territorial form, today the novel can survive only by taking on the transformations that the relationship between subjectivity and place has undergone in our age. Analyzing this process, as this study intends to do, amounts to measur-

---

15. In the past, innumerable were the cases of novels that narrated stories of people lost or displaced. But they did so in a context of territoriality, in which being displaced represented the exception, however intriguing this exception might be. Today, instead, displacement has become the rule in human moods.

16. From here forward, I will shorten the title of Sada's novel to *Porque parece mentira*.

ing the novel's capability to help all of us understand how the world is faring today. Key to this operation will be verifying if and how one of the novel's key traits, territoriality, can be tweaked to function within our present-day, deterritorialized world.

The four novels that I introduced above as case studies are chronologically situated (in terms of their date of publication) in between (no pun intended) the time of Bhabha's analysis and the 2010s. In other words, they find themselves straddling the gap between Bhabha's interstitial unhomeliness and the ubiquitous displacement now so apparent. From this historical situation, these novels capture the deterritorializing trend that defines the turn of the twenty-first century. As for their languages, these novels were written in Portuguese, Spanish, English, and French, respectively. It is not, however, as representatives of the novelistic traditions in their languages that they become the object of this investigation; they do so because each of them possesses a unique ability to focus on a key situation among the several in which today's displacement can be experienced: intellectual pursuit of truth (*Nove noites*), organized crime involving public officials (*Porque parece mentira*), migration (*White Teeth*), and war (*Zone*). Furthermore, these four novels narrate various kinds of back-and-forthness, or the incessant, bouncing movement that today unfolds on land and sea, both along the planet's south-north axis and west-east axis. Here, I am referring to the bidirectional journeys between Brazil and the United States in *Nove noites*; to the repeated crossing, in both directions, of the border between Mexico and the United States in *Porque parece mentira*; to the whirlwind-like traffic of people, cultural elements, and linguistic signs between Jamaica, the United Kingdom, and Bangladesh in *White Teeth*; and to the waves of military expeditions, deportations, diasporas, and war crimes that have hit the shores of the Mediterranean since the dawn of civilization in *Zone*. Finally, my four case studies epitomize adjustment, as the drastic change of scenario represented by present-day, negative deterritorialization compels their authors, like any novelist involved in narrating contemporary displacement, to refine the novel form. This refinement aims at creating novels capable of transcending the state-informed, bounded territoriality that has shaped the spatiality of the novel since the early nineteenth century. These novels become the ultimate epitome of the situation they narrate, as they must undergo their own displacement in order to convey what it means to be displaced.

Novels of displacement belong to a larger trend comprising a variety of cultural forms, all engaged in the rendition of our troubled relations with place. Indeed, from popular culture to high culture, innumerable are the works that in the last two decades have turned displacement into materials for artistic representation. As for popular culture's ability to thematize displacement, I want to start by mentioning *The Americans,* a spy thriller television series created by Joe Weisberg for FX and aired from 2013 to 2018. It narrates the daily alienation suffered by two KGB agents disguised as a normal, married American couple during the Reagan years. Much like *The Americans,* the highly successful *Breaking Bad* (written by Vince Gilligan and aired on AMC from 2008 to 2013), in which the main characters live two overlapping but incompatible lives, presents displacement as the condition of those who never fully belong to the place in which they live. This is precisely the mood also experienced by Choi Yoo-jin (or Eugene), the hero of another television series, *Mr. Sunshine,* created by Kim Eun-sook and aired on tvN in 2018. A former runaway slave who fled to the United States as a boy and has returned to his native Joseon (today Korea) as a Marine Corps captain, Choi affirms that "Americans call me a Korean and Koreans call me an American" (Episode 15). The displaced characters in *The Americans, Breaking Bad,* and *Mr. Sunshine* find themselves entrapped in a dual allegiance to two conflicting lifestyles and their corresponding values; they are constantly forced to be in a place and, simultaneously, somewhere else, thus experiencing the painful conflict that arises whenever the body is out of sync with the mind.[17] Popular culture's internally divided heroes gesture toward a "playing field" that comprises "two hearts, two generators of reality: the physical world and the virtual world," as in Alessandro Baricco's felicitous metaphor for the coexistence, in our post-digital-revolution life experience, of an analog dimension side by side with its digital counterpart (*Game* 90).

As for high culture, in the visual arts, an already sizable and growing number of installations are engaged in the rendering, discussion,

---

17. The theme of the dual allegiance also pervades Martin Scorsese's film *The Departed* (2006), in which several key characters are torn by conflicting loyalties to law and crime. Ultimately, before the conclusion of the story, they all end up switching sides, that is to say, being displaced.

and recreation of displacement. As an example of this trend, I want briefly to touch upon Do Ho Suh's *Seoul Home/L. A. Home/New York Home/Baltimore Home/London Home/Seattle Home* (1999), a project that, in its author's words, "was about transporting space from one place to the other—a way of dealing with cultural displacement" ("'Seoul Home/L. A. Home'—Korea and Displacement"). Do Ho Suh's installation consists in the fabric replica of a Korean house, in actuality the house of the artist's parents. By repeatedly moving the home from one location to another, Do Ho Suh disconnects it from its original, physical site. His goal was to challenge the notion of site-specificity and, in so doing, cope with his own, culturally based, displacement: "Once you take that piece [the fabric replica] from its own site and display and transport it in a different place, this idea of the site-specific become highly questionable" ("'Seoul Home/L. A. Home'—Korea and Displacement"). *Seoul Home/L. A. Home* shows that it is not so much materiality (that site, that house, that room) that counts in our relationship with place as the structure of our experience, which can be recreated if we engage again in the operation we carried out for the first time when we felt ourselves at home: establishing meaningful relations with a place that matters to us.[18]

In the artistic rendering of displacement, the novel occupies a unique position as the only cultural form that has been utterly territorial throughout the last two centuries. Paraphrasing Bourdieu, in the field of the rendition of displacement, the novel owns the greatest amount of cultural capital. It is a capital that originates in the novel's own territoriality and in the cognitive and narrative tools that several generations of novelists have forged to turn the relationship between subjectivity and place into novelistic material. To this epistemic advantage, one should add the fact that, as a territorial genre in a world in which the very idea of place is endangered, the novel is undergoing a potentially lethal crisis. Novels of displacement represent an answer to

---

18. Other installations involved in the rendition of displacement are: Michael Naimark's *Displacements* (1980–84 and 2005), Ana Torfs's *Displacement* (2009), Tim Head's *Displacement* (2013), Sean Anderson and Arièle Dionne-Krosnick's *Insecurities: Tracing Displacement and Shelter* (2016), and Julia Wachtel's *Displacement* (2017). Manuel Álvarez Diestro's *Displacements* (2013), finally, stands out in the category of short films. Remarkably, and differently from what occurs in novels, feature-length films, and television series, the word "displacement" appears in the title of all these works.

this crisis. To summarize, the novel constitutes the only current cultural form that (1) can arrive at the representation of displacement through a process of self-reflection and for which (2) negotiating displacement is a matter of survival, exactly as it is for people in the real world. For this reason I have decided to focus my argument on novels, with the hope of encouraging further investigations aimed at expanding this inquiry into the other domains of contemporary culture.

Chapter 1 investigates the larger context for the practice of the novel in the present age. It focuses on two phenomena: the current crisis of the nation-state (taken as an archetype for the predicaments of other modern territorialized formations) and the advent of software as the immaterial support for capital's reterritorialization. The globalized society that emerges from the current processes of deterritorialization and reterritorialization is characterized by a deep dualism. This dualism pervades all facets of reality today, from computers, split into a visible user interface and an invisible layer of software, to society, divided into the bulk of humankind on the one hand and on the other a narrow circle of high finance and software corporations in possession of a disproportionate amount of power, knowledge, and wealth.

Chapter 2 discusses how the context analyzed in the previous chapter bears on novelistic writing. It argues that the currently polarized sociocultural environment exercises an adverse effect on the novel, a genre concerned with the middle station in life and committed to telling the truth about ordinary people's daily lives. For novelistic writing, today's unfavorable context compounds the difficulty of having to apply narrative tools informed by territoriality to the rendering of a deterritorialized world. These problems elicit two possible solutions. From the sheer number of copies circulating, the majoritarian answer is the writing of globalized novels à la Dan Brown's *The Da Vinci Code* (2003). In this type of fiction, places are described according to the stereotyped criteria of tourist guidebooks, historical and cultural difference is exoticized, and plot becomes an accumulation of stock narrative tricks. The minoritarian answer is represented by novels of displacement, fiction that upholds the novel's historical commitment to telling the truth about individuals and societies. Today, this means narrating our key mood, displacement. In so doing, novels of displacement keep alive the connection between the novel and territoriality. This time, however, territoriality no longer informs the novel as a practice (marking a place) carried out by sociopolitical actors (the State, the city, the family) that do business with the novel, so to speak, but as a longing for a meaningful albeit impossible relationship with any place whatsoever; it is a negative experience of territoriality, the only experience of this kind that a displaced subjectivity can have.

Chapter 3 builds upon the analysis of displacement that I carry out in chapter 2 by investigating Bernardo Carvalho's *Nove noites* (2002). In this novel, the narrative of anthropologist Buell Quain's unexplained suicide in Amazonia is framed within the story of the search for the records of his life and death. As this quest does not accomplish its goals, the novel's frame story becomes nothing more than an inchoate narrative of the epistemic problems facing novelistic writing in the digital age. At the end of *Nove noites,* as the Pentagon becomes involved in the composition and circulation of fiction, the novel as such ends up being displaced: what occurs to the novel form is no different to what happens to the displaced subjectivities of our time, when powerful, external agents take over their places. In *Nove noites*, the displacement at the formal level of the text adds up to the displacement at both its content level (Quain's life) and its structural level (the disrupted frame story).

Through a meditation on place, chapter 4 brings to completion the theoretical discussion carried out in chapter 2. While the latter deals with the displacement of the novel form, the former analyzes the displacement of contemporary subjectivity. In our age, despite the appearances, displacement does not occur due either to our vastly increased physical mobility or our practice of virtually vacating places through mobile communication technologies. Displacement occurs when subjects who move on the ground and/or communicate through mobile technologies are deprived of their agency. In chapter 4, I apply this hypothesis to the discussion of two experiences of contemporary spatiality: the hyper-places theorized by geographer Michel Lussault and the ride-sharing company Uber.

Chapter 5 further develops the theoretical argument presented in chapter 4 through the analysis of two novels of displacement, Daniel Sada's *Porque parece mentira* (1999) and Zadie Smith's *White Teeth* (2001). My discussion focuses on the narrative rendering of home and on characters' spatial disorientation. Sada sets his novel in a fictional northern Mexican state, located just south of the Texas border. By combining the story lines of ninety characters, Sada creates a labyrinthine novel in which no temporal order can be recognized. Because of the novel's complete achrony, space becomes the only dimension for ordering the representation. What interests me in this novel is its characters' sheer inability to experience place, as Sada manages simultaneously to make home a living hell and resettlement in a different location impossible.

In *White Teeth*, Zadie Smith tells the story of several migrations to London in the second half of the twentieth century. Key in this novel is the fact that the third person, omniscient narrator knows the facts of life much better than the characters themselves. Intellectually dwarfed by this narrator, the novel's characters are deprived of that kind of historical understanding they would need to make sense of the historically determined spaces they inhabit, both at home and in the outside society. As a consequence, these characters are poorly equipped for reading the global metropolis, which makes Smith's novel a showcase for the links between historical ignorance and spatial displacement.

Chapter 6 completes the investigation conducted in chapters 3 through 5 by discussing lack of agency as the symptom that disrupts today's dominant ideology of universal, free mobility. Building on Slavoj Žižek's theory, I argue that novels of displacement aid us in coming to terms with this symptom and the mood stemming from it. Then, I finish my study with a close reading of Mathias Énard's *Zone* (2008), the story of a disturbed veteran of the wars in the former Yugoslavia. *Zone* aptly concludes my book in that its hero suffers from both forms of displacement that concern my investigation: he is epistemically displaced, in that he lacks the instruments for making sense of the historical events he witnesses, and spatially displaced, as a character engaged in a journey to nowhere.

Finally, the postscript enquires into a trait shared by all the novels I discuss in the previous chapters: the presence of textual inconsistencies, either with the historical record or with the data provided by empirical reality. By focusing primarily on *Zone*, I suggest that these inconsistencies foreground contemporary novelists' struggle to maintain the tradition of the novel as a truthful narrative of everyday life. This difficulty stems from a habit that is typical of Internet users who obtain their knowledge from Web searches: basing the cognitive value of a piece of information not on verifiable truth but on the number of its connections to outside networks, no matter how shaky the epistemic soundness of the obtained results appears to be. As this practice infiltrates novelistic writing, contemporary novels host areas of ambiguity in which truth can hardly be separated from opinion. The emergence of these areas bespeaks the end of the epistemic environment in which novels have been written since the inception of modernity.

CHAPTER 1

De- and Reterritorialization in the Age of Global Capital

Software and Global Capital

As I anticipated in the introduction, it was the fashioning of electronic tools for gathering, storing, processing, and conveying information that made possible capital's journey from a national to a global scale. In this respect, Sassen aptly argues that the "digitization of instruments and markets was critical to the sharp growth of the global capital market and thereby enabled the financializing of economic criteria" (*Territory, Authority, Rights* 337). Along the same lines, Andrew Leyshon and Nigel Thrift argue that software has allowed for "the capitalization of almost everything," or the massive widening of the pool of assets that can be mobilized as collateral for financial operations: "What made the mining of these new seams of financial value apparently possible is the development of computer software that enables individuals to be assessed, sorted and aggregated along dimensions of risk and reward" (108). Digitized software allows supranational finance to encode and control the flux of money and wealth set free by the neoliberal policies that have been in place since the early 1980s. As Manovich persuasively argues, "Software is what also drives the process of globalization, allowing companies to distribute management nodes, production facilities, and storage and consumption outputs around the world" (introduction).[1]

As software-enhanced capital rises from the local to the global scale, the power of making the economic and political decisions that affect the general public has shifted from elites situated in a national setting, where leaders were still identifiable and decision processes at least partially understandable to the ordinary citizen, to institutions and corporations operating at a planetary level, where acronyms replace names and choices are motivated by an inner, silent logic that refuses to explain itself by default. In this context, the average inhabitants of our planet are required to make a leap of faith: they must believe that their limited perception of reality fits into the bigger planetary picture, supposedly available only to the remote centers of power in charge of today's world. In so doing, they agree with the principle that lies at the foundation of the current distribution of power/knowledge: what appears limited and partial at the local level can become a coherent whole only when it is seen from the (invisible) summit.

Here the modus operandi of globalization agrees with the logic of computer software, as outlined in Chun's rhetorical question: "Who really knows what lurks behind our smiling interfaces, behind the objects we click and manipulate?" (*Programmed Visions*, introduction, first section). Chun argues that software's combination "of what can be seen and not seen, can be known and not known—its separation of interface from algorithm, of software from hardware—makes it a powerful metaphor for everything we believe is invisible yet generates visible effects" (*Programmed Visions*, introduction, first section). Chun is undoubtedly correct in pointing out separation as the essence of software. However, I would suggest that the software's form, its reliance on an invisible, albeit decisive, core that remains hidden beneath a visible layer, represents something more concrete than a metaphor. For this is also the form that commodities assume. As Marx argues, what makes an object into a commodity is the fact that the social relations between human beings that provide this object with value (aka the relations of production concerning the workers whose work creates value) take on

---

1. See also Chun: "Without them [computers] there would be no government, no corporations, no schools, no global marketplace, or, at the very least, they would be difficult to operate" (*Programmed Visions*, introduction).

"the fantastic form of a relation between things" (the exchange value expressed through money as its general equivalent) (*Capital* 165). This coexistence of two sets of relations, one visible but fantastic and another hidden but decisive, represents what Marx calls "the mysterious character of the commodity form" (164). Thus, software is not a metaphor. To the contrary, it is the commodity form sold on the market, because the use value of software (what we enjoy about software) is its arcane essence, its being made up of a luscious outer layer for our eyes to see and an invisible, commanding core that runs the show.

Tout se tient, and we really do live in a wondrous time. Today, capitalism, the system that presides over the production of goods and services in our society, relies on a principle (the invisible running the visible) that not only pervades every aspect of life by informing the commodity, but is itself sold as a commodity in the form of software; and it is the most important commodity, I should add, as it runs the machines that allow our society to function. In managing the global economy as well as in software-driven computers, what matters is the invisible: it is there that the chain of command begins. At the level of both the planetary financial system and the tools that enable this system to function, "one obeys the law to the extent that it is incomprehensible" (Chun, "On Software" 44). Within the framework provided by the profound imbrication of software and global capital, I shall now discuss a process that plays a crucial part in the deterritorialization characterizing the present age, notably the weakening of the nation-state's monopoly on the exercise of sovereignty. As this monopoly has been a pillar of both external relations among states and internal relations within states for almost four centuries, the discussion of its current overturning must start by briefly introducing the historical event that originated it, the 1648 Peace of Westphalia.

A Post-Westphalian Order

In 1648, in the Westphalian cities of Osnabrück and Münster, plenipotentiaries coming from all over Europe signed the treaties that ended the Thirty Years War. The Peace of Westphalia inaugurated a new era in international politics, based on the uncontested primacy of the State in the realm of sovereignty. No other subject, such as religious or military orders, churches, or guilds, could legitimately challenge the state's sovereign power. As the "fiction of sovereignty," to borrow a term from Wendy Brown, comprises features such as supremacy, absoluteness, perpetuity over time, and territoriality, the Peace of Westphalia ushered in an era of new relations not only among states but also between the State and its subjects (ch. 1). However, in the last four decades, entities initially operating in the economic domain and then in other areas of society have called into question the very principle of the state's unchallenged sovereignty. To understand this process, it becomes imperative to have a discussion of the relations that today intervene between the financial sector of the world economy and the nation-states.

Toward the end of his treatise on capital in the twenty-first century, Thomas Piketty proposes the introduction of a worldwide tax on capital (*Le capital au XXIe siècle* 835–40). This tax would aim not so much at increasing the state's revenues—the rate of the imposition would be a mere 0.1% for every taxpayer, no matter the size of his/her/its wealth—as at reigning in capitalism. By collecting this tax, Piketty argues, fiscal administrations around the world will be able to gather precious data on capital, thus bringing about democratic transparency in the realm of finance (841). In accordance with the Enlightenment-like spirit that pervades Piketty's work, by taxing capital, the fiscal apparatus would function much like the commission for the cadastre in eighteenth-century Lombardy, which garnered information that allowed the Austrian administration to ascertain the true value of private wealth. Even while he proposes this tax, however, Piketty also recognizes that it cannot become operative: in the subtitle of the book section dealing with the taxation of capital, he calls his project "a useful utopia" (836). Piketty's self-acknowledged defeat is due to the fact that financial capital and nation-states today play in different leagues. While international capital moves at unmatched speed to penetrate all corners of the planet, the apparatuses of the nation-states limp behind, encumbered by their parochial dimension: late capitalism's "quantum leap" from the national space to the global space depends on the former's inability "to register the utter permeation of capital into formerly undreamed of places" (Tally 76). The asymmetrical relationship between financial capital and territorial nation-states appears consistent with the very nature of capitalism, which has never been territorial because it targets "not the earth, but 'materialized labor,' the commodity" (Deleuze and Guattari, *Thousand Plateaus* 528).

The material foundation for financial capital's expansion on a global scale is provided by a phenomenon that Deleuze and Guattari noted in 1980, at the very dawn of globalization: the existence of "an enormous, so-called stateless, monetary mass that circulates through foreign exchange and across borders, eluding controls by the states, forming a multinational ecumenical organization, constituting a de facto supranational power untouched by governmental decisions" (*Thousand Plateaus* 527). In the following decades, the nation-states have become increasingly unable to exercise sovereign power over the supranational corporations that manage the flow of this monetary mass. As a consequence, in the years spanning from 1980 to the first decade of the twenty-first century, a paradigm shift emerged in the relation between capital and the nation-state, whereby the state's power has decreased, while that of capital has symmetrically grown. It is a well-known historical fact that other phases of worldwide growth in the history of capital have preceded the present globalization; in this respect, the aggressive push outside the national borders that characterized nineteenth-century capitalism appears particularly interesting, because at that time the nation-state was already a key player in the economic field. In that age, however, the international expansion of capital followed a logic contrary to that of the present day, as that earlier expansion ultimately aimed at building up national capitalism: the result was a fierce competition among countries that led to the outbreak of WWI. In present-day globalization, instead, capital develops in a way that weakens its connections to national institutions, starting from the nation-state.

In order to describe this state of affairs, John Urry utilizes a metaphor that appears remarkably effective: "Especially significant are the flows of people, monies, environmental risks, taxation revenues and information which partially evade control by national states who increasingly function as 'gamekeepers' or regulators rather than 'gardeners'" (186). Indeed, during the European debt crisis that followed the 2008–09 worldwide recession, it was to a new gardener, the IMF, that a few nation-states had to surrender part of their sovereignty. The IMF was able to dictate its agenda to national governments, like those of Portugal, Greece, and Ireland, on a key aspect of the national budget such as taxation. The very imposition of taxes, however, represents the modern state's first raison d'être, since it was a king's ability to collect taxes through a trusted bureaucracy that allowed him to curtail the power of feudal lords (Sassen, *Territory, Authority, Rights* 48–49). Still, during the debt crisis, because of certain national governments' inability to borrow at the high interest rates demanded by financial markets, the norm of the nation-state as the sole possessor of the right to levy taxes was suspended. "Sovereign is he who decides on the exception," as stated in Carl Schmitt's well-known dictum (5). As it required exceptional measures, the economic crisis that framed the IMF's infringement on the fiscal prerogatives of the nation-states was exactly the sort of context in which the true sovereign emerges: in this case, it was not the national government.

What occurs in the financial sector is simply the most egregious example of the nation-state's difficulty in holding on to its former monopoly of power. Over the last thirty years, in fields as diverse as international trade, the protection of the environment, human rights, and the punishment of war crimes (in different manners according to each country's clout in the world arena), nation-states have been surrendering portions of their sovereignty to corporations and/or to other types of private organizations. As Wendy Brown argues, this process appears to be irreversible: "As nation-state sovereignty wanes, states and sovereignty do not simply decline in power or significance, but instead come apart from one another" (ch. 1).[2] In the dramatic tone that is typical of his prose, Franco Berardi argues that after the 1970s "capitalism decided to get rid of the state's mediation: techniques of recombination and the absolute speed of electronic technology allowed capitalism to turn control into an internal operation" (77). Less colorful, but equally cogent, Arjun Appadurai argues that in our time "the nation-state, as a complex modern political form, is on its last legs" (19).

In the three decades that separate us from the 1980s, the world order established with the Peace of Westphalia (1648) has crumbled. We live in a post-Westphalian order in which the nation-state's sovereignty has been eroded by global movements of capital, the politi-

---

2. Dardot and Laval argue that in our age the nation-state underwent not so much a decline as a transformation of its "format" and role. Nowadays, "the State is perceived as a *business serving businesses*" (370, emphasis in the original).

cal rationalities of neoliberalism, and "the activations of power related to, but not reducible to capital—those that traffic under the sign of culture, ideology and religion" (W. Brown, ch. 1). The inception of a "post-Westphalian order" implies not the disappearance of the nation-state, but the notion of its survival as continual crisis. As we all know, since the term "postmodernism" was coined, the prefix "post" refers to a condition in which the past is still with us, as heritage, nightmare, and/or nostalgia, lingering in the background and affecting our current situation (W. Brown, ch. 1). The increasingly common practice of building walls around national borders to protect them from external intrusions represents a conspicuous manifestation of the nation-state's survival in a condition of permanent crisis.[3] These walls do not aim at fending off threats from other states—this would occur in a Westphalian order—but instead show the nation-state's inability to manage the movements of nonstate transnational actors, be they individuals, goods, or organizations (W. Brown, ch. 1). Rather than functioning as demonstrations of the nation-state's might, walls are spectacles of its depleted sovereignty. In Guy Debord's theorization, "The spectacle is not a cluster of images, but a social relation between people, mediated through images" (16). What is spectacularly mediated through the walls built around national borders is the relation between citizens who demand protection and nation-states unable to deliver security, all of which calls into question the state's historical justification. The existence of the State, as Richard Muir notes, is never guaranteed definitively: "In order to survive and flourish, the state must continually justify itself to its inhabitants" (82).

The site of this spectacular mediation is crucial. Modern states are the product of a transition from authority defined as a lord's power over subjects personally linked to their sovereign to authority estab-

---

3. Wendy Brown cites walls on the United States–Mexico border, around the West Bank, and around the Spanish enclave of Melilla; an electrified security barrier on the South Africa-Zimbabwe border, a concrete-post structure on the Saudi Arabia-Yemen border, barriers built by India to "wall out Pakistan, Bangladesh and Burma," as well as fences erected by Uzbekistan on the border with Kyrgyzstan and Afghanistan. Barriers that Thailand, Malaysia, Egypt, Iran, Brunei, China, and North Korea have built on their borders complete the picture (ch. 1). Since the publication of Brown's book in 2010, the building of walls has continued around the world, the most infamous of which being the thirteen-foot fence built by Hungary along its Croatian and Serbian borders during the 2015 European migrant crisis.

lished as exclusive jurisdiction over a bounded territory. At the end of this transition, boundaries became a crucial feature in the territorial State. Boundaries and the modern state's sovereignty go hand in hand: "The adoption of precisely known and clearly demarcated boundaries was related to the acceptance of sovereignty as an important basis of statehood" (Muir 130). Ancient political formations, instead, ignored the modern concept of a border. Superpowers such as the Roman Empire and the Frankish Empire, simply ended at a certain point: from there, the land of the Barbarians stretched out in an undefined void (Sassen, *Territory, Authority, Rights* 39).[4]

When nation-states transform a key site for the establishment of their authority—their own borders—into the locus in which to display their helplessness, as occurs in present-day wall building, they demonstrate the profound peril in which their own sovereignty teeters:

> The new nation-state walls are iconographic of this predicament of state power. Counterintuitively, perhaps, it is the weakening of state sovereignty, and more precisely, the detachment of sovereignty from the nation-state, that is generating much of the frenzy of nation-state wall building today. Rather than resurgent expressions of nation-state sovereignty, the new walls are icons of its erosion. (W. Brown, ch. 1)

Here Franco La Cecla's observation that "the less of a center a settlement has, the more difficult it is to define its borders" is on point (101). In the present environment, what we are witnessing is the blurring of borders along with the symptomatization of this blurring in the form of wall building. This process, unveils not so much the disappearance of the nation-state's centers of command as the demise of a central tenet in the nation-state's political formation: its monopoly on sovereignty. On the nation-state's walled border, deterritorialization and territorialization are projected against one another: on the one hand lies the nation-state, on the other, the deterritorialized, unstoppable masses gathered beyond its border. Citizens experience as trauma the state's inability to stop the outsiders; their fear of being swamped by waves of deterritorialization translates into more barriers, now built within

---

4. See also Sack: "Boundaries [in premodern civilization] were never delimited as accurately as they are now because surveying and mapping techniques were limited, and records of land holdings were not kept uniformly and accurately" (76).

the national borders: gated communities, increasingly higher fences, alarm systems, video cameras, security codes. The repetitive character of these practices reveals their traumatic origins.

Global Capital and Territory

The crumbling of the Westphalian order and the emergence of powerful players autonomous from the nation-state represent just two examples of the unknown fluidity that is pervading the contemporary world. Later in this book, I will discuss two other instantiations of this process: the rise of the digital, networked database as a chief repository for public and private records, and the obsolescence of paper-based technology in the composition of texts (in chapters 3 and 6, respectively).[5] For the time being, it appears commonsensical to observe that in our age the traditional, fixed structures that organized our polities, archives, and texts are losing their consistency. We are again living in a time in which "all that is solid melts into air," as in Marx's metaphor for the revolutionary changes that the rising bourgeoisie brought about in his time (*Communist Manifesto* 76). The deterritorialization that is eroding the nation-state's foundation is both a consequence and an enabling factor of this fluidity. Because of this process, along with the nation-state, the very idea of territoriality finds itself at risk.

Michel Foucault wrote, "First of all, the State has been a principle of intelligibility of the real" (*Sécurité* 294). For more than two centuries, initially in Western Europe and then throughout the world, the nation-state both acted as the territorializing agent *par excellence* in the sociopolitical domain and effectively symbolized the very notion of territorialization: as Marcel Roncayolo notes, "The State is usually considered as the most territorial among human organizations" (198). Between the State and its subjects, geographer Maria Luisa Sturani argues, cartography acted as the mediating discourse: "As a representation that makes it possible to take in at a glance portions of space normally outside the direct experience and to confer graphic evidence to

---

5. In 1990, David Harvey tied the "volatility and ephemerality of fashions, products, production techniques, labour processes, ideas and ideologies, values and established practices" to the shift from Fordism to the flexible accumulation that capitalism had engineered in the two preceding decades (*Postmodernity* 285).

immaterial elements such as borders, cartography is a powerful instrument in giving a territorial form to nations, making them visible and conceivable as bounded spatial unities" (354).[6] Sturani's discussion is built along the line of Marxist geographer David Harvey's argument when he claims that the first publication of the maps of British counties, in 1579, allowed people to grasp visually and conceptually the physical place in which they were living and to adjust their political allegiances to this new understanding (*Postmodernity* 228).

The map of the nation-state answered the problem of how to represent the nation in visual terms and allowed the State, as the most representative extant territorial formation, to become a model for anyone wanting to visualize a portion of space and situate him/herself within its borders. Geographer J. B. Harley convincingly argues that maps impart a sense of place within the world to their readers and shape their mental structures, by acting just as print does in Marshall McLuhan's theory (167). Gifted with the molding power that characterizes mass media, for the past two centuries the nation-state map has structured the human perception of physical space along the line of territoriality. It is what Benedict Anderson calls the map-as-logo—the visual representation of the nation-state on maps hanging on the walls of public offices and schools, or printed in textbooks, on stamps and banknotes—which taught us that we belong to a territory (175). Last but not least, the visual representation of this territory told us that boundaries must exist and unbounded space is an oxymoron, two notions that have remained unchallenged until recently.

Given the nation-state's unrivaled capacity to embody territoriality and to convey powerful symbols of territorialization across the body social, the present predicament of the nation-state destabilizes other forms of bounded territorialization. Indeed, despite the hysteria of building walls to protect private spaces, border porosity has spread from the top down: the bounded entities that in the paper age provided human subjectivity with context and identity but are now coping with the erosion of their borders are innumerable. Universities, factories, libraries, bookstores, shops, television studios, hotels, and casinos, all

---

6. As Wilbur Zelinsky argues, "One ought to consider the map of the United States as a meaningful national icon," since "the outline of the forty-eight states has become a familiar symbol and an emotionally potent one in advertisements, outdoor signs, and various folk media" (162).

typically used to require their patrons to pass through doors or gates before entering their premises, these invariably surrounded by walls or other kinds of barriers. Nowadays, these entities are being attacked by nonconventional, context-free competitors (just as states face the competition presented by NGOs), such as virtual universities, online retailers, gambling websites, and online reservation services, which take advantage of the deterritorialized agility of their Web-based formats. At the same time, these same bounded institutions have been eroding their own borders from within, by launching online operations of delocalization, outsourcing, or subcontracting (following again the example of the State, as occurs when the latter subcontracts some of its long-established functions, such as administering prisons or waging war). As a consequence of these processes, expressions such as "I go to school" or "I go to the library" are now in need of disambiguation, at least in terms of the verb "to go."

As suggested in the introduction to this book, the agent driving present-day deterritorialization is capital: "At the complementary and dominant level of *integrated (or rather integrating) world capitalism*, ... the multinationals fabricate a kind of deterritorialized smooth space in which points of occupation as well as poles of exchange become quite independent of the classic paths to striation" (*Thousand Plateaus* 572, emphasis in the original). Along the lines of Deleuze and Guattari's argument, Hardt and Negri maintain that Empire (the political formation that has replaced the nation-state as the ultimate sovereign in the age of global capital) "is the *non-place* of world production where labor is exploited" (210, my emphasis). Remarkably, since the abstract work force that today constitutes labor's most developed and skillful section carries out "an activity without place, and yet ... very powerful," the present-day, placeless capitalist formation is countered by a labor force likewise free from ties to identifiable locations (Hardt and Negri 209).[7]

The depth and extent of the present capitalist deterritorialization can be best appreciated by moving from the open spaces of the global

---

7. Deleuze and Guattari argue that the State practices its own deterritorialization by making "the earth an *object* of its higher unity, a forced aggregate of coexistence, instead of the free play of territories among themselves and with the lineages" (*Thousand Plateaus* 528, emphasis in the original). As the object of capitalist deterritorialization is not the earth but the commodity, capitalism displays a capacity for deterritorialization far superior to that of the State.

market to spaces internal to our bodies. Here Catherine Malabou's argument concerning the existence of a single modus operandi that governs both the global capitalist enterprise and the functioning of our brain appears particularly insightful:

> Cerebral functions are no longer situated in specific areas of the brain. When the brain must carry out a task a specific network is created. However, it is a temporary network that is mobilized only for that task. The clusters of neurons are characterized by their mobility and poly-functionality. The same occurs in a company. Nowadays, workers must be flexible and ready to change projects. Capitalism wants to replace essentialist ontologies with open spaces where beings are constituted by the relations they entertain with the flows, the transfer, the exchanges, and permutations that are, in this space, the events that matter. (95)

Deterritorialization, in sum, concerns not only entities whose relation to a geographical space is easily recognizable but also our ability to conceptualize reality at the most abstract level (as in switching from a world defined by Being to one defined by Becoming) as well as the biological fabric of our thinking machine.[8]

In today's sociocultural context, despite it permeating all the facets of our material as well as intellectual life, capital-induced deterritorialization is not an uncontested process. Indeed a contrary, almost symmetrical trend appears to be at work in all realms of reality. As occurred in other historical periods in which deterritorialization coexisted with its opposite, today deterritorialization is countered by reterritorializing forces that pull in the opposite direction. Since this reterritorialization originates in changes that took place in the production of goods and services, a new leadership has risen within capitalism. As Manovich writes, "In the beginning of the 1990s, the most famous global brands were the companies that were in the business of producing material or goods, or processing physical matter. Today, however, the lists of

---

8. Harvey ties the switch from Being to Becoming in the conceptualization of the world to the "homogenization of space," a capital-driven process that "poses serious difficulties for the conception of place. If the latter is the site of Being (as many theorists were later to suppose), then Becoming entails a spatial politics that renders place subservient to transformations of space" (*Postmodernity* 257).

best-recognized global brands are topped with names such as Google, Facebook, and Microsoft" (introduction). On January 21, 2008, when Manovich looks at the CNN list of the top ten companies, he discovers that Google and Apple occupy the first two places, while "the companies that deal with physical goods and energy appear in the second part of the list: General Electric, General Motors, Ford" (introduction). The latter are typical cases of corporations that thrived during Fordism, the highly centralized regime of accumulation based on Henry Ford's "explicit recognition that mass production meant mass consumption, a new system of the reproduction of labor power, a new politics of labor control and management, a new aesthetics and psychology, in short, a new kind of rationalized, modernist, and populist democratic society" (Harvey, *Postmodernity* 125). In the Fordist era, spanning approximately from the 1910s to the 1970s, corporations territorialized on factories as sites where goods were produced, products designed, labor controlled, and industrial plans drawn.[9] The factory represents another momentous example of those bounded territories, like the State and the disciplinary institutions of society (asylums, schools, and prisons), which became common in modernity and now are in deep trouble, as Deleuze argues: "Today, we are living through a general crisis of all the centers of internment; jails, hospitals, factories, schools, and families" ("Post-scriptum" 241).

The presence of companies such as Google and Apple at the top of the CNN list signals the shift from an industrial economy to an informational economy, whose "first geographical consequence . . . is a decentralization of production" (Hardt and Negri 294). Google, Apple, and the major Internet companies such as Facebook, Twitter, Amazon, eBay, and Yahoo, whose business is producing software, as Manovich rightly argues, belong to that slim group of corporations that dominate the world economy (introduction). They relate with the nation-state in a manner that differs quite starkly from the relationship that linked the big companies of the industrial economy to the countries in which they operated. In the age of global capital, corporations "directly structure and articulate territories and populations. They tend

---

9. Harvey argues that the "symbolic initiation date of Fordism must, surely, be 1914, when Henry Ford introduced his five-dollar, eight-hour day as recompense for workers manning the automated car-assembly line he had established the year before at Dearborn, Michigan" (*Postmodernity* 125).

to make nation-states merely instruments to record the flows of the commodities, monies, and populations that they set in motion. The transnational corporations directly distribute labor power over various markets, functionally allocate resources, and organize hierarchically the various sectors of world production" (Hardt and Negri 32).

The transition from the industrial economy to the informational economy amounts to a twofold, pendulum-like process, whereby capital deterritorializes in order to achieve a global dimension transcending its old territories (primarily the factory and the nation-state) and immediately reterritorializes on software, the connective tissue of today's world. As Kevin Robins acutely observes, "The decentered and deterritorializing corporation transposes a new and abstract electronic space across earlier physical and social geographies. Globalization is realized through the creation of a new spatial stratum, a network topography, an electronic geography" (28). Because of their very nature as actors engaged at the highest level of the informational economy, software producers appear to be ideal case studies for observing the peculiar form that capital assumes by reterritorializing on software. The Internet and software giants—in particular the so-called GAFA: Google, Amazon, Facebook, and Apple—do not deal solely with their customers' experience as buyers of goods, but with the totality of their lives, much as does biopolitical power, according to Foucault.[10] Through their biopolitical capacity, these companies can shape their customers' lives more intimately and more deeply than any company of the Fordist era could do. It has always been true that a capitalist enterprise conveys a world vision, a manner by which to approach life and relate with others. It is the social nature of production that makes this symbolic surplus necessary. In order to make and sell commodities, an entrepreneur has to put people together and give them a sense of purpose. Here Gramsci's observation that "the entrepreneur himself represents a higher level of social organization, already characterized by a certain managerial and technical (i.e. intellectual) capacity" reveals a notable insight (7). The intellectual's job, in Gramsci's thinking, consists in fashioning, clarifying, and conveying the ideology of the social group with which he/she is associated. The intellectual is a purveyor of

---

10. The use of the acronym GAFA has become quite common today in discussions upon Internet giant companies. I found it in Cardon and Casilli, *Qu'est ce-que le digital labor* (42).

ideology, and good entrepreneurs must sell their own ideology (first and foremost to their employees), while bringing their commodities to the marketplace. Historically, corporations have bent over backward to involve their customers in their particular ideology, hoping to make lifetime recruits of them. During Fordism, however, the customer's identification with the maker of the commodity he/she purchased was limited to brand loyalty. Even if consumers feel bound by their allegiance to a certain company, driving a Ford does not truly differentiate one person from another who drives a Toyota.

All of these aspects would change in the age of global capital, because of the exceedingly relational nature of the digitized commodity. Customers buy or receive tools from Internet corporations that create connections with data, people, and objects. In so doing, customers purchase social relations, skills, and knowledge. Because of their biopolitical character, these tools influence their buyers' capacity to represent themselves as subjects interacting with the world. This influence is much deeper than the one exercised by poorly relational commodities, such as cars or refrigerators in the Fordist era. Facebook informs the way its customers experience friendship; Google affects their ability to access and organize knowledge; Twitter shapes the structure of their communication with the outer world. The various forms of connectivity offered by the Internet giants may initially fail to appear as commodities because they are often provided free of charge to customers who do not pay for their exchange value. This seemingly free service represents only what occurs on the attractive outer shell of the process. In companies such as Twitter, Google, and Facebook, "customer relationship" is a code word for data mining: service gratuity is simply the veil that covers the flow of data through which customers pay for their connectedness.

What is more, on the site where most of the interactions between customers and corporations occur, the Internet, these relations do far more than affect the customer's symbolic sphere: they constitute the customer as subject. Key to this constitution is the collection of metadata on users' activities. As Marquard Smith notes so aptly, "Metadata trawls through our searches, monitors our buying habits, . . . accumulating data and information along the way, for its own sake, for purposes ominous or as yet undetermined or unanticipated. . . . All the while it accumulates, number-crunches, and processes, identifying the discernible patterns of our activities as individual profiles that are then offered back to us as desire. But this is more than life-tracking, it is life-*constituting*" (386, emphasis in the original).

For customers of software products, the big Silicon Valley corporations bespeak immateriality. Indeed, immateriality is a quality that these corporations carefully cultivate through the very language they use for describing themselves and their operations. Their headquarters are campuses rather than offices, while what they deliver are intangible services: information, communication, and connectivity. The manufacturer's immateriality accords with that of the product, with the "vaporiness" of software, as Chun describes it (*Programmed Visions*, ch. 2). Furthermore, the same combination of visible and invisible that represents one of software's defining traits is key to the inner workings of software corporations. The set of signifiers that make the company readable by external observers, be they competitors, customers, or partners, is highly visible: the company's logo, its story (the brilliant idea, the startup in a garage, the venture capitalist), the site of its headquarters (Mountain View, Cupertino, Silicon Valley), the biography of its founders (Steve Jobs, Larry Page and Sergey Brin), and its purpose (changing the world, making information available, helping people to connect). This visible shell, a Lacanian symbolic order of sorts, surrounds an invisible core where the corporation manipulates physical matter: Google's and Facebook's enormous repositories of digitized records, Amazon's warehouses and trucks, and the Chinese factories where iPhones and other electronic tools are manufactured. As a layer of experience that resists symbolization, this aspect of the software company corresponds to Lacan's notion of the Real. Popular culture offers an empirical verification of the existence of a visible Symbolic and an invisible Real in software corporations: places such as Mountain View or Cupertino have meaning for many individuals who do not have professional ties to Google or Apple, while no one, apart from those who work there, can name the Chinese towns where iPads are made. The same phenomenon did not occur in the Fordist era, when names such as Flint, Billancourt, or Mirafiori possessed a symbolic power that was a function of the commodities manufactured in those locations.

Sassen has correctly indicated the "simultaneous interdependence and specificity" of the digital and the nondigital (*Territory, Author-*

ity, Rights 345). The hypermobility associated with new technologies must be produced in an actual, physical location: "Much of what happens in electronic space is deeply inflected by the cultures, the material practices, and the imaginaries that take place outside electronic space. Much of what we think of when it comes to cyberspace would lack any meaning or referents if we were to exclude the world outside cyberspace" (343). Albeit indispensable to the function of the productive machine, the world outside cyberspace, or the nondigital realm, has no place in the symbolic narrative of software corporations. The software company is perched on "the Cloud," a metaphor for its vaporiness and unreachable, Zeus-like power, while its huge physical assets, along with the workers it employs, disappear into the remote mortal world below. On earth, the nondigital activities that inevitably accompany software-based operations are erased from the map of enterprises and locations worthy of representation. The overlap of the relation between the visible and the invisible with that between the symbolic and the real also occurs with computers (user interface vs. software) and finance companies (derivatives vs. assets on the ground); all in all, this overlap appears to be a distinctive trait of the age of global capital. As I noted earlier in this chapter, it is our entire, digitized world that takes the form of the commodity.[11] Indeed, it is global capital as such that has reterritorialized on the Cloud, the cyberspace that today constitutes the nurturing soil of global capitalism. The process that in the software industry has generated two ontological levels—the Cloud where symbols are created and power resides, and the powerless earth, deprived of access to the symbolic—concerns capital in its entirety: "The informatization of production and the increasing importance of immaterial production have tended to free capital from the constraints of territory and bargaining" (Hardt and Negri 297).

Production can be decentralized only if a "corresponding centralization of the control over production" takes place: "The centrifugal movement of production is balanced by the centripetal trend of command" (Hardt and Negri 297). What makes this concentration of management possible is software. As global capital functions in a way that follows the model provided and embodied by software corporations,

---

11. On the relation between immaterial financial products and stable income sources stemming from material assets, see Leyshon and Thrift (98).

the very notions of deterritorialization and reterritorialization achieve a more precise articulation. On earth, while the old territoriality based on the nation-state and the factory crumbles, people experience deterritorialization as a process forced upon them by entities they cannot see, much less control. On the Cloud, the agencies who manage power and symbols, themselves free from any link to the territorial entities of the Fordist age, reterritorialize on software; from this immaterial territory they lead the negative deterritorialization that continues to unfold down below.

CHAPTER 2

The Novel between the Cloud and the Earth

The Novel's Discontent in the Age of Global Capital

Guido Mazzoni defines the novel as a genre that narrates the details of ordinary people's daily lives, focuses on the middle station in life, and approaches individuals as isolated subjects identified by their date and place of birth and their profession (242). This sociologically established midpoint matches the position the novel came to occupy in the literary field at the dawn of modernity, when it was carving out its place among the genres codified by the classical canon. The novel stood midway between high, heroic genres, like the tragedy and the epic, on the one hand, and low, plebeian genres, such as the farce and low comedy, on the other. Situated at the center of society and literature, the novel aims to grasp the whole of reality surrounding it. Indeed, as Georg Lukács argues, "The novel seeks, by giving form, to uncover and construct the concealed totality of life" (*Theory* 60). In other words, despite its low profile as a genre geared toward the representation of prosaic lives, the novel aims at a lofty goal: making sense of life in its entirety.

In the age of global capital, processes of polarization, fragmentation, and deterritorialization affect the social field. As discussed in the previous chapter, there are two motivating factors behind these processes: the concentration of power/knowledge and wealth in the hands of a limited number of global corporations, and the weakening of the territorializing capacity of various, significant entities, such as states, families, factories, and universities, to name just a few. As a consequence of these processes, the social field becomes a forbidding context for the development of the novel's key features, such as its mid-position in society and its ambition to reconstruct the totality of life. Put another way, the present sociocultural environment appears to be one of the least favorable to the novel in the Modern Age. My discussion of the novel's situation in this climate intends to detect a course of action that might allow present-day novels to convey a true and thorough representation of life without losing their formal, technological, and epistemic connections to the tradition of the genre. I want to discover if, and how, novels can narrate an antinovelistic world while still maintaining their original identifying traits.

From an epistemic viewpoint, the novel's definitive feature is its determination to tell the truth, as in Ian Watt's definition of the genre's goal: "The purpose of the novel is the production of what purports to be an authentic account of the actual experiences of individuals" (27).[1] In our time, however, a growing number of the activities comprising the individual's life experience (whose nonexhaustive list includes writing, reading, talking, making calculations, sending and receiving correspondence, learning, looking up records, meeting friends, watching movies and television series, having sexual encounters, executing economic transactions, piloting drones, shooting missiles, killing people, and gambling) may, or can only, take place in software-saturated environments. In this context, Watt's argument must be integrated with a proper understanding of what constitutes experience in a world shaped

---

1. Michael McKeon criticizes Watt's work for failing to explain the complexity of the relationship tying the English novel to the romance on the one hand and to its social context on the other. Despite this criticism, McKeon, too, situates the novel within a discursive field defined by the intent of establishing the criteria for conveying truthful narratives. In particular, McKeon stresses the role of the novel as an epistemic tool for formulating and explaining questions regarding the "kind of authority or evidence [that] is required of narrative to permit it to signify truth to its readers" (20).

by software. If we live in a "software society," as Manovich correctly maintains, and the cooperation between software and hardware generates the discursive sphere where our lives unfold, then the contemporary novel must tackle a key cognitive problem: how to come up with truthful renditions of life within this sphere. Two crucial, convergent features of the novel may contribute to the resolution of this issue: the novel's capacity to represent not reality but the discourse that in a given society makes sense of reality, and its ability to get to the core of what it means to live within a certain discursive sphere (González Echevarría, *Myth and Archive* 8). Here, I am thinking of three examples, separated by almost two centuries of history. The first two are taken from the time in which the novel was coming of age: Goethe's Werther, who understands the struggle between individual freedom and society's stability to be the key conflict in bourgeois society, and Jane Austen's heroines, who perceive the ambiguous nature of marriage in modernity as a business transaction founded on love.[2] In both cases, through the insight of its characters, the novel successfully captured an essential trait of the civilization rising from the ruins of the Ancien Régime. This capacity to grasp the essence of life within a certain discursive sphere has remained one of the novel's distinctive traits throughout the Modern Age. My third example, Chinua Achebe's *Things Fall Apart* (1958) represents a convincing demonstration of the enduring vitality of this novelistic feature. As it narrates the tragic life story of Okonkwo—a powerful member of an Igbo clan in Eastern Nigeria who commits suicide when he realizes that his fellow clansmen lack the mettle to fight the colonizers—Achebe's novel catches the historical moment in which clan culture begins to crumble under the pressure of three discursive practices introduced by the foreign invaders: religion, law, and anthropology. Once again, in a sociocultural context completely different from Goethe's and Austen's, the novel displays its ability to comprehend the gist of a transition, as it does today when it narrates displacement. Indeed, it is in times of historical change that we most need the novel as a cognitive tool.

---

2. On the historical meaning of Goethe's Werther, see Lukács: "Werther's conflict, Werther's tragedy is the tragedy of bourgeois humanism and shows the insoluble conflict between the free and full development of personality and bourgeois society itself" (*Goethe* 45).

As I argue in chapter 1, the key experience (rooted in the software form and gesturing toward the commodity form) of living in our age consists in coping with a dualistic world: on the one hand, the surface, which corresponds to the environment of our daily lives, and on the other hand, somewhere high above this surface, the unreachable locus of the invisible agencies that run the global business. Dualism constitutes the current dominant discourse, in that it draws the hegemonic picture of life in our time. Hence, telling the truth—in forms that can become mimetic, allegorical, metaphorical, oneiric, or whatever may appeal to a novelist's disposition—about the duality that informs life in the age of global capital constitutes the contemporary novel's chief task.[3] In this chapter, I will explore the novel's answer to the epistemic and formal questions related to the execution of this task by analyzing (1) the novel's territoriality, (2) the polarization and fragmentation of today's world, and (3) the globalized novel. I will conclude my discussion with an interrogation as to the type of novel best suited to represent our age, followed by the introduction of the novel of displacement as a viable answer to this query.

The Nation-State, the Bourgeois Family, and the Novel's Territoriality

The particular "cultural artifact" we call nation-ness entered political discourse around the end of the eighteenth century following the French Revolution (Anderson 4). A crucial moment in this process came in 1789 when the Declaration of the Rights of Man and of the Citizen stated that the source of all sovereignty "resides essentially in the nation" (Hobsbawm 59). Initially in France, and then throughout Europe, the Revolution brought an end to the Ancien Régime, the three-century-long social and political formation in which the absolute monarchy ruled, the Church attended to the symbolic realm, and the landed nobility performed military functions. The clergy and the nobles amounted to a tiny minority in Ancien Régime societies:

---

3. The contemporary novel's commitment to deliver truthful narratives about today's hegemonic discourse appears to be consistent with Raffaele Donnarumma's observation on the hypermodern subject as someone who "wants to tell the truth" and entertains with his/her reader a relationship based on trust (210).

together they comprised 1.5% of the total population of France on the eve of the Revolution, for example (Piketty, *Capital et idéologie* 102). They owned or managed large estates but enjoyed substantial fiscal privileges, while the bourgeois worked as merchants or professionals and peasants (80% of the total population in prerevolutionary France) toiled under the burden of surviving feudal laws or, in certain European areas (eastern Europe, southern Italy, and southern Spain), even serfdom (Hobsbawm 57 and 60).[4]

Out of the French Revolution, that same deterritorializing event that had terminated the Ancien Régime, a new social, cultural, and political formation emerged: the nation. As Ernest Renan proudly stated in 1882, "It was France's glory to have proclaimed through the French Revolution that a nation existed in and of itself" (sec. 1). As the symbolic and physical site where people, history, culture, and territory entered into a mutual relationship, the nation constituted both the immaterial and material foundation for what became the most powerful, and until very recently unchallenged, territorializing formation in modernity: the nation-state. Throughout the nineteenth century and most of the twentieth century, in an uneven but unstoppable process that spread around the planet, the nation-state overcame local, decentralized forms of authority so as to establish uniform sovereignty on the entirety of its territory.

At roughly the same time that the nation-state came into being through the breaking of the ancient bonds that had tied people to larger communities of kinship and trade, the bourgeois, patriarchal family emerged in the West as the dominant formation in the private sphere.[5] This type of family became the basic cell of society in the domains of the exchange of affection, the reproduction of the species, as well as the transference of wealth, traditions, and male power across generations. The bourgeois family is a deeply territorial entity. Deleuze and Guattari's definition of territoriality as the establishment of critical distance between members of the same species could fit no entity

---

4. For a synthetic description of land ownership and the relations of production in the Ancien Régime, see Hobsbawm, 14–18.

5. The revolutionary State "directly attacked the power of Ancien Régime communities—the Church, the guilds, the nobility, the village, and the familial clan—and, at the same time, defined a new space for the individual and his/her private rights" (Hunt 29).

better than the bourgeois family: every family of this type cherishes the notion of its own uniqueness and the resulting detachment from other families. Indeed, bourgeois families behave as micronations, each cultivating its own traditions, language (in the form of a peculiar lexicon), and culture. And, of course, a family of this kind controls a territory, as it occupies a domestic space that is absolutely private, internally structured, carefully bounded, and decisively protected by fences, gates and/or doors, as well as alarms, doorkeepers and/or security personnel.

In the nineteenth century, the nation-state yielded the political, cultural, and legal context that allowed the family to thrive. It did so by guaranteeing the safety and the management of the territory where the family established its operations. Oftentimes in concomitance with religious institutions, the nation-state also presided over the system of values (patriotism, order, respect for the authorities) that provided the bourgeois family's code of behavior with its ideological authorization. What is more, and crucially so, from the advent of Napoleon's Code (1804), the nation-state issued laws that provided the bourgeois family with a legal framework by defining the rights and duties of its members and determining their prerogatives in relation to the property of the family's assets.

Around the time in which the idea of the nation entered the political and cultural arena, the novel ended the process of its formalization as an independent discourse. As Mazzoni maintains, it was from 1550 to 1800 that the novel completed its emersion as a genre free from both the classical codification of styles and the moral constraints that had ruled over previous narrative genres (196–205).[6] For the establishment of the novel's autonomous discursive space, the decisive event was the novel's differentiation from the romance, a distinction that was formally outlined in Clara Reeve's *The Progress of Romance* (1785). Since that time, the novel has narrated fictional stories that fit into the framework of everyday, empirical reality, while the writers of romances

---

6. McKeon situates the stabilization of the English novel some fifty years prior to the time proposed by Mazzoni: "By the middle of the eighteenth century, the stabilizing of terminology—the increasing acceptance of 'the novel' as a canonic term, so that contemporaries can speak of it *as such*—signals the stability of the conceptual category and of the class of literary products that it encloses" (19, emphasis in the original).

have been free to allow their imaginations to roam beyond the limits of verisimilitude.

Shortly after the establishment of the novel's discursive space, territoriality complemented the traits that defined the novelistic assemblage. As emerges from my discussion of Balzac's *œuvre*, it was through its relationship with the nation-state and the bourgeois family that the novel became territorial. The novel's capacity to function as a refrain was the decisive factor in this process. A refrain, in Deleuze and Guattari's theory, is "any aggregate of matters of expression that draws a territory and develops into territorial motifs and landscapes" (*Thousand Plateaus* 376). Within the behavior of living beings, a refrain—the repetition of a musical motif, a rhyme, a linguistic pattern, or a painted image—is a primary marker of territorialization: "The territory is not primary in relation to the qualitative mark; it is the mark that makes the territory" (367). National anthems, military airs, gang graffiti, and the chants of soccer fans, to name just a few examples, represent pertinent cases of refrains functioning as markers of human territoriality. In the first half of the nineteenth century, as the nation-state established its monopoly on the exercise of sovereignty, the novel began to function as a refrain for marking the state's cultural space.

As a political project, the nation-state considered the conservation of its vital documents, the writing of its history, as well as the preservation and diffusion of its national language, as crucial operations in the construction of its cultural space which, in turn, was viewed as equally real and vital to a country's interest as its geographical counterpart. Within this framework, in the nineteenth century, from Western Europe to the Americas, the novel contributed to the building of the nation-state by providing narrative representation, and repeating it in a refrain-like manner, to three foundational principles in the nation-state's discourse: the consistency of the nation's culture, the country as a diverse but cohesive linguistic space, as well as the existence of clear-cut boundaries separating the nation's cultural territory from that of its neighbors. As Bakhtin argues, the novel "makes of the internal stratification of language, of its social heteroglossia and the variety of individual voices in it the prerequisite for authentic novelistic prose" (264). In the nineteenth century, by functioning as a showroom for all the particular languages spoken within the nation's borders, the novel supports the nation-state's self-representation as the guardian of a linguistic space that is assumed to be both diverse and, insofar as it is comprised within recognizable boundaries, coherent. The novel not only displays the rich linguistic fabric of the nation, but it also demonstrates how the various particular tongues (divided by class, gender, age, profession, geographical area, etc.) spoken in the country can dialogue with one another so as to build a common linguistic playground crisscrossed by never-ending conversation: "The national literary language of a people with a highly developed art of prose, especially if it is novelistic prose with a rich and tension-filled verbal-ideological history is in fact an organized microcosm. . . . The unity of a literary language is not a unity of a single, closed language system, but is rather a highly specific unity of several 'languages' that have established contact and mutual recognition with each other" (295). The novel's operations in the cultural domain were consistent with the long-term target of the fledgling nation-state's policies: establishing perfect coincidence between the state's cultural, linguistic, and political borders.[7]

Throughout the nineteenth century, the novel has marked territories by assisting the nation-state in bounding and mapping the physical and cultural space of its operations. For a novel, marking a territory means being part of a process similar to that described by Moretti when he notes that nineteenth-century historical novels offer "nineteenth-century Europe a veritable *phenomenology of the border*" (35, emphasis in the original). This offering is a crucial function because in that time, Moretti argues, "the need to represent the territorial divisions on Europe grows suddenly stronger" (35). A novel not only provides narrative representations of a state's borders but also finds peculiar means for drawing divides between cultures. It can, for example, emphasize linguistic difference through specific indicators, such as the italicized words badly pronounced by the German-born Baron Nucingen in Balzac's *César Birotteau*: "*Bartonnez-moi, ma tchaire*" instead of "Pardonnez-moi, ma chère" (231, emphasis in the original). Representing the political border and bringing to the fore the boundaries around

---

7. In the nineteenth century, if a nation-state did not consider its political border as coinciding with its cultural border, this discrepancy occurred because the State claimed territory situated beyond its established boundaries. Such inconsistencies occurred, for example, in France with Alsace and Lorraine, under German rule from 1870 to 1918, as well as in Italy with the Italian speaking provinces of the Austro-Hungarian Empire.

the national language are operations consistent with nineteenth-century novelists' practice of turning fiction into a marker of territoriality.

In the nineteenth century, the nation-state was the agency driving the need to represent the territorial divisions that Moretti theorizes: the novel applied its narrative power to the satisfaction of this need. By expressing nation-ness in the fictional mode, the novel took on, embodied, and conveyed the territorial component of this concept: that is to say, of the nation's ability to turn abstract territoriality into a spatially situated entity. It was by carrying out these operations during the historical time in which the nation-state strove to gain complete control over its territory that the novel built its own territorial paradigm. As a consequence, the kind of bounded territoriality which the State administered became the foundation for the novel's own territoriality. This trait persisted even into the twentieth century, when novels either territorialized on entities different from the nation-state or treated sociopolitical contexts that were markedly dissimilar from both nineteenth-century Europe and nineteenth-century America.

The territorial paradigm inspired by the nation-state has shown a remarkable resiliency in novelistic discourse. Paradoxically, at times one finds the strongest proof of this resiliency in novels that convey minoritarian, nonstate-inspired types of territoriality, often occurring when these novels narrate the historical time in which minoritarian territorialities submit to the nation-state. A transition of this kind, for instance, is narrated toward the end of Gabriel García Márquez's *Cien años de soledad* (1967), when the national Army suppresses a workers' strike and puts an end to the magical territoriality of Macondo. The same narrative development, albeit in a slow motion of sorts, defines the plot in Ngugi wa Thiong'o's *The River Between* (1965). Ngugi's novel is set in the 1920s, in the hilly Kenyan terrain inhabited by the Gikuyu. Around the end of the nineteenth century, when the Gikuyu first meet the Europeans, "they were essentially a fluid, acephalous, culture, organized around sub-clans (*mbari*) and distant memories of a common descent" (Gikandi 15). The novel narrates how the Gikuyu space undergoes the colonial striation that comes with the penetration of religion, Western education, and land alienation.[8] The latter is crucial: in *The*

---

8. In his discussion of the subjugation of the Chippewa—a Native American tribe that at the time of their first contact with European settlers lived in an area bordering the western shores of Lake Superior—Sack gives a detailed description of the

River Between, as Dustin Crowley notes, "colonial transformation of place takes the form primarily of land alienation" (18). For an adequate comprehension of the relation between the novel and State territoriality, not only in *The River Between* but in novelistic discourse at large, what matters is the following: along with the arrival of the colonial State (a nation-state 2.0 of sorts), the novel, the very *The River Between*, arrives as well. The traditional narrative's forms—the epic, the legend, and oral storytelling—cannot narrate the new territoriality that has descended on the Gikuyu land: only the novel can do so.

As for the domestic space, starting from the narration of bourgeois lifestyle in the nineteenth century, the novel approaches it by singing the refrain of the family's territory. In the nineteenth century, the novel actually does something more than simply territorializing on the bourgeois family: it assimilates the grammar of domestic territoriality and saves it for future use. The development of novelistic discourse in the following century proves this point. A novel such as *Things Fall Apart*, for example, deftly territorializes on a polygamous family in an Igbo clan in Eastern Nigeria. In describing the living quarters of Okonkwo's family in Umuofia—the *obi* where the head of the family resides and rules, the three huts for his wives and their children, the barn and the "medicine house," as well as the wall that protects the family's compound—the novel gives a territorial dimension to both the power relations inside the family and those between the family and the outside world (14). In so doing, the novel displays the same talent at territorializing domestic institutions that it applied to narratives of family life set among the English gentry and French bourgeoisie a century and a half earlier. The example of *Things Fall Apart* shows that the novel form seems able to function as a kind of artificial intelligence (perhaps one of the oldest in history): it first learns the algorithm of territoriality in the context of the bourgeois family and then becomes able to apply this knowledge to the narrative of an utterly different sociopolitical environment.

In carrying out its territorial operations, the novel utilizes tools that belong to the quintessential tradition of narrative genres. Narratives, Robert Tally reminds us, produce a "literary cartography" that

---

establishment of European territoriality upon Native Americans' territoriality (6–15). The process described by Sacks proceeds along the line of the colonial striation Ngugi wa Thiong'o narrates in *The River Between*.

"becomes a way for readers to understand and think their own social spaces" (6). Just as maps do, novels can also mark, make readable, and ultimately usher in the social formations that have a vested interest in managing space. Significantly, while the modernist avant-garde successfully challenged certain traits of the nineteenth-century novelistic paradigm, such as the omniscient narrator, the close-knit plot, and the hierarchically organized language, it did not, in general, call into question the novel's territoriality. One has only to consider novels such as Virginia Woolf's *Mrs Dalloway* (1925) or Leopoldo Marechal's *Adán Buenosayres* (1948), who territorialize on London and Buenos Aires, respectively; or Faulkner's stories, which are territorial to the point of creating their own land, Yoknapatawpha County. Even in the second half of the twentieth century, novels written according to the principles of Latin American magical realism still territorialized on spaces created ad hoc, starting with Macondo in *Cien Años de Soledad*. As for the domestic territory, in Richard Yates's *Revolutionary Road* (1961) and Zadie Smith's *On Beauty* (2005), for example, the family home still stands, as solid and bounded as in Balzac's *Le lys dans la vallée* (1836).

Polarization and Fragmentation in the Age of Global Capital

The larger context for the novel's territoriality appears to have changed in the last decades of the twentieth century. In 1982, Benedict Anderson had still defined "nation-ness" as "the most universally legitimate value in the political life" of his time (3). However, only fourteen years later, in 1996, Nicholas Negroponte wrote that "as we interconnect ourselves, many of the values of a nation-state will give way to those of both larger and smaller electronic communities" (7). In this book, I investigate the novel's situation in the age anticipated by Negroponte's statement. The crisis of the nation-state that Negroponte envisioned appears to be of utmost importance for the novel because of the connections between novelistic territorial practices and the establishment of the nation-state. In this respect, this study crucially asks whether or not the novel is still able to embody territoriality in an age in which the nation-state, the territorial entity that has traditionally comprised and protected other local and/or private territorial formations, appears to have entered the epoch of its decline. As I discussed in chapter 1, the deterritorializing phenomena of our time, such as the porosity that affects national borders and the increasing mobility of wealth, persons, records, and symbols, are countered by an oppositional trend pulling toward territorialization. Because of these conflicting tendencies, our life experience stretches between two planes: the territorialized Cloud where power/knowledge resides and the deterritorialized earth where the powerless operate. It is worth recalling that present-day deterritorialization is anything but a liberating process. It is a guided-from-above operation, in which the big corporations of international finance and software exercise agency. As David Golumbia argues, "Today the world is unevenly covered many times over by entities we routinely refer to as multinational corporations, just as much as and in some ways more completely than it is covered by State-based governments" (144). In this context, the Cloud/earth antithesis represents an effective metaphor for the present state of the world, which is characterized by a dualism just as profound as the image of the sky high above the land suggests. One could counter that human societies have always been unequally divided into the powerful and the powerless: the sky has always appeared unreachable to those living on the surface of the planet. However, if Marx could call the Parisian Communards "heaven-stormers," thus implying a chance, albeit remote, for humans to reach the heavens, in postindustrial societies the sky seems to have moved up several notches and dualism to have widened accordingly (*Civil War* 127). Lukács wrote that "the novel is the epic of a world that has been abandoned by God" (*Theory* 88). Today the gods have returned to earth, not to Olympus but to Silicon Valley, Wall Street, and the City of London. What is more, dualism and the digital are one and the same. Dualistic is the mythology of the digital age: Gates vs. Jobs, Microsoft vs. Apple, proprietary software vs. open source software, Android vs. iOS. Dualistic is the binary code of zeros and ones we use for translating analog reality into a language that our computers can understand.[9] Dualistic are the pairs of terms that help us grasp the ontology of the computer: hardware and

---

9. Galloway argues that "late modern anxiety" is characterized by threats that "have now become, like the computer itself, *binary*." This occurs because we now worry about dangers that "promise to arrive not with small pricks of pins and needles but with a total collapse without recourse" (ch. 4, emphasis in the original).

software, ROM and RAM, as well as visible icon and invisible algorithm. Dualistic, above all, is the confrontation between the human user and the machine.

Present-day dualism is so pervasive that even a novel (*The Silent History* by Eli Horowitz, Matthew Derby, and Kevin Moffett) cited by Amy Hungerford as a case of "diffusion of authorial control" becomes an argument *a contrario* for the existence of a dualistic power structure in any software-based media object (111). *The Silent History* is a novel contained in an iPhone application. In addition to guiding readers through the main story line, the app novel gives access to several "field reports" that can be read only in specific places accessible by means of a GPS device built into the application. The novel interacts with its readers by inviting them to produce field reports that "are gathered and selectively added to the novel itself" by the authors (Hungerford 111). While the GPS allows readers to pinpoint the locations where field reports become readable, it also gives the authors the means to follow each reader's movements through the text: "It is possible for Horowitz and Quinn [the app developer] to know how far each reader has read in the story, for instance, and how fast they read it, and on what day" (Hungerford 111). As Hungerford adds, of course, "there is nothing to suggest that Horowitz and Quinn are interested in the creepier forms of surveillance and control that one can easily imagine given these features of the technology built into the novel" (111). Whether or not Horowitz and Quinn intend to carry out unsavory Big Brother tactics, it strikes me that this interactive novel constitutes a perfect case study of the reality described by Chun when she notes that, "for a computer, to read is to write elsewhere" ("On Software" 46). In *The Silent History*, the very application software that enables the readers to read the maps of the novel's locations also transcribes their movement on the ground and their progress through the text. Indeed, this appears to be a distinctive trait of living in the digital age: any time a user's agency seems to grow (by uploading a post on Facebook, writing a review on Amazon, or discovering an Italian restaurant on Google Maps), it does so in the context of accentuated dualisms of power. In this situation, a superior, invisible agency mines data out of the very activity that is supposed to generate empowerment. As Francesco Lapenta observes, this occurs each time users utilize Information Communication Technologies (ICTs):

> The apparent promotion of flexibility and the autonomy enhancing qualities of new ICTs also come in constant tension with an opposite function that may allow us to interpret these communication technologies as new organizational and regulatory systems. . . . In these systems, not only are [sic] information linked back to their local referent (the physical place and the body of the user), but the user (and their surrounding place) is transformed into information, a commodified image, once again embedded in a controlled, and socially and economically structured system regulated by new and old actors, and by new and old agendas. (223)

This peculiar, technologically based dualism compounds the well-known dualistic nature of the commodity, which pervades every corner of the world under global capitalism. In sum, the very antagonism that, as Thomas Harrison persuasively writes, runs deeply through Western philosophy—with its opposite pairings of form and content, soul and body, phenomenon and noumenon, and so on—is also embedded in all the strands of today's public discourse, whether of power, technology, or the economy (70).

The oligarchic structure of both the world economy and the Internet is suggestive of another type of polarization, this time concerning the circulation of capital and information. In this respect, Carlo Formenti has noted that both the financial sector and the Internet have reached an unknown monopolistic concentration: ten great banks and financial companies, the likes of Goldman Sachs, Deutsche Bank, and BNP Paribas, control 90% of the all derivatives that circulate in the world, while the traffic on the Internet is dominated by the four giants known under the acronym GAFA: Google, Amazon, Facebook, and Apple (17). By contrast, the auto industry, which is more than a century old, in 2013 still consisted of twelve different groups whose production accounted for around 80% of all the vehicles made in the world. The concentration of capital in the two sectors of the economy that embody the age of global capital is coeval with the phenomenon that Thomas Piketty calls the explosion of wealth inequality. From its start in 1980, this process has led to the income-polarized society of our time and the dwindling of the middle class in the West (*Le capital au XXIe siècle* 464). In this respect, economist Mariana Mazzucato notes that the share of the national wealth owned by the top 1% in the United States prior to the 2007 financial crisis was "a staggering 22.6%," as compared to 9.4% in 1980 (introduction). If the present trend of income inequality in the United States continues, as Piketty argues, in 2030 the disparity of wealth could reach a level that existed only during the Ancien Régime (*Le capital au XXIe siècle* 415).[10] At the planetary level, recent data present a picture of income inequality that appears consistent with the disparity occurring in the United States. The *Global Wealth Databook 2015*, created by Credit Suisse economists, describes a pyramid of wealth distribution in the world in which adults are divided into four bands. These bands are defined by yearly income on the basis of these numbers: under USD 10,000; between USD 10,000 and USD 100,000; between USD 100,000 and USD one million; and over USD one million. As for the allocation of wealth among these bands, "the base level of the pyramid contains 3.4 billion adults, or 71% of the global population, but accounts for only 3% of global wealth. In contrast, dollar millionaires comprise 0.7% of all adults, but collectively own 45% of all assets" (99).

Be it technologically based, monopoly driven, or income related, the dualistic ontology that informs today's world narrows the space for those human aggregations and practices that the novel has historically narrated. Clearly, in the dualistic reality that characterizes the age of global capital, Mazzoni's very notion of a middle station of life is endangered, let alone the interest in the details of ordinary people's everyday lives. As technology, industry, and finance are developing in a way that erodes the novel's sociocultural foundation, novelistic discourse faces a complex predicament. Society appears to have taken a path that could lead it back where it stood before the blossoming of novelistic discourse (Piketty's return to conditions in line with the Ancien Régime), when the supersized heroes of the tragedy still dwarfed the prosaic characters of the novel. From a sociological point of view, in other words, we are living through an age that should dissuade us from the practice of the novel. The same dissuasion could also come from observing the dualistic nature of spatiality in the age

---

10. Piketty presents the case of the United States (but inequality is on the rise in all wealthy nations), where the wealthiest 10% of taxpayers moved from earning 30–35% of the national income in the 1970s to 45–50% in the first decade of the twenty-first century. If this trend continues, the wealthiest 10% of taxpayers will earn more than 60% of the national income in 2030 (*Le capital au XXIe siècle* 415).

of global capital. On the one hand, our age presents the novel with the smooth space of Earth: here territorial boundaries blur and mobility prevails over stability.[11] On the paradoxically striated space of the Cloud, by contrast, information, wealth, and power territorialize on software. Hence, one of the two dimensions that define the reality narrated by the novel—space—appears divided by an unmendable fissure: the totality of life that the novel should attempt to convey is forever gone, and novelists are to choose between two irreconcilable types of spatial partiality.

Albeit conceived in the 1960s, Debord's theorization of the spectacle as the commodity's supreme form still represents a viable tool for tracing the thread that weaves together the various phenomena I have just described. In Debord's thinking, the spectacle is the ultimate manifestation of the fetishism of the commodity; it is the arcane ability of the commodity to turn human relations into relations between things that manages to project itself onto the consumers' mind. By constructing individuals as spectators who are, by definition, detached from the object of their contemplation, the spectacle produces separation.

> In the spectacle, one part of the world *represents itself* before the world and becomes superior to the world. The spectacle is nothing more than the common language for this separation. What connects spectators is only an irreversible attraction to the very center which keeps them in a state of isolation. The spectacle reunites what is separated, but reunites it as separated. (30, emphasis in the original)

The entities and operations that territorialize on the Cloud, where the monopolies in control of finance and information have settled, correspond to the part of the world that in Debord's theory presents the spectacle of itself to the rest of humankind; by contrast, the deterritorialized earth where goods and services are produced becomes the site that hosts the spectators. A single narrative gaze cannot embrace the distance between these worlds. The gap yawning between the Cloud and the earth creates obvious problems in regard to the novelist's synthetic scrutiny. What is more, at the very level of the earth, a unify-

---

11. What we actually have on earth is one planet-wide, formatted space in which digital systems of control and data mining have replaced the old striations created by the nation-state and the other territorial formations of the paper age.

ing approach to reality appears equally difficult: down on the surface of the planet, each spectator, as such, lives in isolation and can deal only with his/her own spectacular fragment. Separation, polarization, and fragmentation all contribute to create an incoherent world that resists novelistic representation. While everyday reality crumbles, symbols coalesce into remote aggregates of power/knowledge that appear unreachable from the novel's position in the middle station of life.

The Globalized Novel

The success reached in the worldwide editorial market by "the globalized novel" (or as Vittorio Coletti terms it, "*il romanzo mondo*"), that is to say fiction that follows in the footsteps of Umberto Eco's *Il nome della rosa* (1980), constitutes the best proof of the novel's current predicament. Dan Brown's *The Da Vinci Code* (2003), a work that immediately stands out for the sheer magnitude of its success as a commodity, constitutes a quintessential example of the globalized novel. With eighty million copies sold in six years, immediate translations into forty-four languages, and a cinematographic version (Columbia Pictures, 2006) that grossed 224 million dollars worldwide in its opening week alone, Brown's novel was born and bred global. As Stephen J. Mexal maintains, *The Da Vinci Code* "is a global spectacle in a way that no novel has been previously" (1090). The defining trait of the globalized novel, Coletti holds, is its disconnection from the cultural context of its creation:

> Great traditional novels ... are always visibly marked by a linguistic or national culture, or, in other words, by a cultural homeland that more or less corresponds to their authors' country and its history. Books like Eco's and Brown's instead belong to the land of their readers (who are everywhere) rather than their authors'; they are to be associated with a literary culture and a cultural ideology rather than a particular nation or society. (79)

I would argue that a novel like *The Da Vinci Code* does much more than simply belong to the land of its readers: it is actually constitutive of a new, ideologically uniform landscape, superimposed over the territories that had once been the readers' homelands. What is more, *The Da Vinci Code* assists in establishing the position from which this homogeneous landscape is to be observed. Indeed, in Brown's novel, the surface of our planet appears as if seen from above and at a distance by an observer who can make out only the details accessible to his/her ideologized lens. The sites where the novel's plot unfolds—a few well-known places such as the Louvre Museum, the Church of Saint-Sulpice, and Westminster Abbey, in the global cities of Paris and London—are described according to the stereotyped criteria of a tourist guidebook: "Sighing, she raised her eyes and gazed out at Paris's dazzling landscape. On her left, across the Seine, the illuminated Eiffel Tower. Straight ahead, the Arc de Triomphe. And to the right, high atop the sloping rise of Montmartre, the graceful arabesque dome of Sacré-Cœur, its polished stone glowing white like a resplendent sanctuary" (84).[12] The description of London follows the same pattern: "In the distance, now, the skyline of London began to materialize through the dawn drizzle. Once dominated by Big Ben and Tower Bridge, the horizon now bowed to the Millennium Eye—a colossal, ultramodern Ferris wheel that climbed five hundred feet and afforded breathtaking views of the city" (368). As Coletti argues in his discussion of Brown's fiction, "There is nothing less local than a place presented by a tour guide, as proved by the fact that those who are familiar with that place find it difficult to recognize it" (76). In both of the above descriptions, the city skyline functions as the formal device to ensure that readers, accustomed to having seen hundreds of analogous panoramas in movies, on postcards, and in photographs, find themselves in familiar territory: as the foreignness of the location recedes from view, the globalized reader can enjoy a text that does its best to erase all sense of difference.

It is this removal of difference, and not the mere disengagement from the context provided by its author's cultural homeland, that transforms a novel into a globalized commodity. In the high tradition of the genre, a novel is expected to provide readers with a fresh knowledge about reality, as the etymological root of the term in the Italian *novella*,

---

12. This is the traditional narrative device of the novel as a travel book. In 1967, Giacomo Debenedetti noted the use of this technique in Pirandello's rendition of Monte Carlo's casinos in his 1904 novel *Il fu Mattia Pascal* (323–32). In an age of low-cost flights, it comes as a surprise that novels can still appeal to readers by carrying them off to faraway places at the incomparably cheap price of the cost of a book.

recent information about something or somebody, demonstrates. Writing a novel should mean to go out into the world and return with meaningful facts arranged in such a way as to allow for their apprehension under an original perspective. Globalized novels, instead, return bearing carbon copies of the knowledge we already possess about the world. Hence, the reader's net gain is zero: what he or she experiences within the reading is simply a separation from the places whose identity the novel chooses to gloss over.

The strength of *The Da Vinci Code* as a commodity consists in its being an ideological product to the power of two: not only does it convey the core of a key contemporary ideology, that of separation (be it the Cloud from earth, the interface from hardware, spectacle from spectator, or spectators from one another), but it does so in an ideological way, by disguising ideological consumption as an aesthetic experience. This two-fold function nicely fits Žižek's definition of the ideological habitat as "a social reality whose very existence implies the non-knowledge of its participants as to its essence" (21). In Debord's terms, *The Da Vinci Code* mimics the relation linking the spectacle (the Cloud) and the spectator (the earth) within a world fashioned by the big corporations that administer software and manage global capital. As the text encourages its readers to identify themselves with the spectacle/Cloud, thus presenting them with an imaginary escape from their condition as spectators, this exercise in mimicry turns into a quintessentially ideological obfuscation. After presenting its readers with a collection of postcards, *The Da Vinci Code* then relegates them to the role of spectators who know next to nothing of Paris and London. Similarly, big software corporations convey to us an image of themselves that conceals the earthly component of their daily operations.

Novels of Displacement

At first glance, globalized novels may appear to repeat the operation Balzac carried out in the 1830s, when he territorialized his fiction on the nation-state, the key agent in the stabilization of French society after the Revolution. By territorializing on the Cloud, as *The Da Vinci Code* does when it narrates a world structured along the lines of global capital's dualistic ontology, the global novel might seem to mirror Balzac's move. After all, Balzac operated in accordance with the political project carried out by the socioeconomic elites of his time: to rally around the nation-state as a bulwark against a looming social insurgence that threatened to become even more radical than the 1789–93 Revolution. However, the parallel between Balzac and the globalized novels of our age obtains only on a superficial level. Globalized novels lack the epistemic drive, the urge to know that innervates Balzac's *œuvre*. It is this cognitive longing that inspires a key step in Balzac's narrative project: identifying the crucial mood of the society he had set out to narrate. Grasping this mood and narrating the ways in which it percolated into the lives of his contemporaries constitutes the Balzacian version of Lukács's discovery and construction of the "secret totality of life"; it also represents a fundamental aspect of Balzac's program to deliver a truthful representation of French society by way of fictional prose.

In *La Comédie humaine*, this key mood is one of lust, as Baron Nucingen's foolish love for Esther Gobseck proves. It is a bipolar kind of lust, in which the longing for erotic pleasure and the greed for money are stirred by the same urgency. Both passions are driven by an overarching need to transform the object of desire into a possession. In the gendered universe narrated by Balzac, male heroes crave money with the same urgency with which they desire a woman, while they possess the latter with the same rapacity they apply to hoarding the former. Lust spurs the actions of human beings and multiplies their will and ability to act, while requiring society to build structures for its management and providing novelists with intriguing subject matter. By recognizing lust as the key mood in postrevolutionary France, Balzac apprehends what otherwise would have remained hidden beneath the glossy surface of social convention, and thus helps his fiction to gain decisive cognitive ground. This surplus of knowledge with respect to his contemporaries—including the big names of his day—allows Balzac to narrate capital's reterritorialization on the nation-state without partaking in the self-celebratory, ideological narrative of bankers and speculators. In other words, he refuses to be duped by the spectacle that beguiles his contemporaries: he knows better because he understands the truth of those who mastermind the spectacle according to the mood that shapes their very existence.

In Balzac's novelistic project, what can still be helpful today is the method used. From a novelist's point of view, identifying the crucial mood prevailing upon his/her contemporaries represents a key epistemic move now as it did in 1830; this identification allows the writer to comprehend society from within, so to speak, thus escaping the trap of its ideological envelope. Due to its insightfulness, this move appears just as sensible now as it was two centuries ago. By contrast, what is lacking in contemporary globalized novels à la Dan Brown is exactly this impetus to investigate the key moods of our age, which explains their shallow characters and their lifeless landscapes. If this is the case, however, what mood should become the focus of novels epistemically committed to digging down to our society's core? I believe that the answer is displacement, the mood of those who live in an age of a profound dualism of power/knowledge and see their lives being defined by overpowering, unreachable agents.

As a narrative of displacement, consider, for example, a novel such as China Miéville's *The City & The City* (2009). It narrates the story of two fictional city-states, Besźel and Ul Qoma, which share the same territory as if one city were mapped onto the other.[13] As they must respect the intangible, virtual border that separates Besźel from Ul Qoma in every corner of their shared territory, the citizens of both cities become skilled in the practice of "unseeing" and "unhearing" the objects and the persons that belong to the other city. Encounters between individuals that are simultaneously foreigners and neighbors occur continuously in the busy streets of Besźel and Ul Qoma, thus forcing people to live in a state of permanent high alert: in each of the states, failure to "unsee" is a breach of the foundational Law. Rebecca Walkowitz notes that in the book's logic, "where you are legally . . . depends on how you walk, what you wear, how you speak, what you acknowledge, and what passport you hold" (6). Legal residency, in other words, is cultural and bureaucratic, but not territorial. This detachment of residency from place, that is to say this extreme form of deterritorialization, occurs

---

13. Miéville's novel gives novelistic representation to the same concept—dual allegiance—that structures two television series I have already mentioned, *The Americans* and *Breaking Bad*. However, while in these series the hero's subjectivity splits in order to comply with two conflicting loyalties, in *The City & The City* it is place that virtually comes apart while hosting two incompatible sets of inhabitants.

at a terrible price, as cyclical uprisings aimed at the unification of the two cities are heartlessly quashed by the "Breach." The latter consists of a mix of secret police and the invisible ruling elite, with vague allusions to the Guardians in Plato's *Republic*. As such, it exercises ultimate authority over the recognizable political leaders of Besźel and Ul Qoma (perhaps a reference to the current state of affairs in world politics and international finance) and strictly enforces the separation between the two cities. In so doing, the Breach forces displacement onto its subjects. Indeed, the unification of the two cities would be the only way for their citizens to inhabit a livable, unsupervised place. It is only in this place, unreachable due to the Breach's methodical counterinsurgency, that the inhabitants of the two cities could escape their displacement and establish productive relations with the human and natural landscape that surrounds them.

A novel like *The City & The City* is a symptom of the radical type of displacement that defines our time, of the mood that lies at the foundation of Miéville's dystopia. As Jonathan Crary argues, present-day, radical displacement is rooted in the way we organize the production of goods and services, or in the 24/7 environment in which we live. In a 24/7 world, as all of us are completely integrated into an unceasing cycle of production and consumption, we lose all of our temporal and spatial references: "24/7 steadily undermines distinctions between day and night, between light and dark, and between action and repose. It is a zone of insensibility, of amnesia, of what defeats the possibility of experience. To paraphrase Maurice Blanchot, it is both of and after the disaster, characterized by the empty sky, in which no star or sign is visible, in which one's bearings are lost and orientation is impossible" (17). If displacement is the mood that epitomizes life in our 24/7 world, then this mood must be the focal point of novels committed to rendering the truth. Being dis-placed, however, implies entertaining a problematic relationship with one's own territory, be it home, a city, or a country. Therefore, the novelistic representation of displacement appears to be at odds with that kind of territoriality we have considered as a key feature of the novel since the early nineteenth century. Indeed, displacement as the defining trait of life in our time hints at a problematic scenario for the practice of the novel as we historically know it. Even during the two centuries of modern novelistic writing that preceded the novel's territorialization, in which novels were written within a nomadic paradigm, at the end of the day the novelistic hero inevitably finds a place he/she can call home. This is what occurs for Don Quijote, Moll Flanders, Tom Jones, Candide, and Jacques le fataliste, to name just a few examples of wandering, but not deterritorialized, characters. It goes without saying that going home (or making a place home) at the end of a journey becomes an even stricter requirement in novels written after the establishment of territoriality as a defining trait in novelistic discourse. After all, Sal Paradise, the protagonist of Jack Kerouac's *On the Road* and the novelistic hero who epitomizes rootlessness in the years that follow WWII in the United States, would not have been able to conceive his plan of living on the road without relying on his aunt's house as the shelter from which he could start each time his feet felt the itch to travel, and to which he could return to when they became tired of the journey.

There is nothing new, of course, in the above considerations: Ithaca, we all know, is the definitive place in the Odyssey, the only one that Ulysses could have never bypassed. What I would like to point out, instead, is the change of climate taking place in the contemporary novel; a change that appears even more remarkable given the significance of the tradition it breaches. Let us take, for example, Simona Vinci's *Strada provinciale tre* (2007). It tells the story of a woman who runs along the side of a highway and becomes entangled in various incidents along the way. This woman is known only by her first name, Vera ("true" in Italian). She is not identifiable by her birthplace, date of birth, or occupation, as novelistic characters should be according to Mazzoni's theory discussed at the beginning of this chapter; nor can she be identified by the way she talks, as she speaks in standard Italian deprived of the regional inflections that usually mark the speech of native Italian speakers. The novel catches up with Vera when she is already on the road; she neither comes from an identifiable place, nor is she heading toward a particular destination. She certainly cannot rely on an aunt's house as a providential cocoon. Vera's story is not about a journey but about displacement in its sheer etymological sense: displacement as the conceptual and practical negation of having a place, just as disbelief means not having faith. *Strada provinciale tre* represents a noteworthy work of fiction because of its straightforward approach to the key epistemic problem facing contemporary, truth-seeking novels: how to handle territoriality in an age in which the surface of the planet is swamped by deterritorialization. Vinci's work suggests a way for the novel to escape this predicament: by narrating territoriality as the experience not of a presence but of a lack of presence. Instead of participating in the marking of a place, as territorial novels do, the novel of displacement signifies the absence of this very place.

As a chain of linguistic signs, however, how can a novel rely on absence as one of its foundational elements? Were the novel to be based on this absence, its signs would originate in a void, in a kind of foundational gap. Albeit counterintuitive, this hypothesis works when we throw desire into the mix. To experience desire means to be affected by somebody or something that is missing: the wanted object could be within our grasp, but if we want it, then we do not have it.[14] Desire becomes the source of the linguistic signs that express our longing; while the absence of a territory alone cannot successfully anchor a narrative, the desire stemming from this absence can do so. As the target of desire, the absent territory relates to the novel in a way that parallels the relation tying *das Ding* to the subject in Lacan's theory. As the missing object that captures the entirety of the subject's drives, *das Ding* represents "the primary exteriority that orients the whole development of the subject" (*Le Séminaire* 65). It is the interrogation about *das Ding* that molds the subject by structuring the latter's unconscious as language. In the course of this study, I will argue that a relation of this type also informs narratives of displacement, since it is the longing for a lost territory that sets fiction in motion and gives it structure.

In chapters 3 through 6, I will discuss the two components of the novel of displacement that I deem essential: first, its epistemic tools for discerning truth from falsehood within the documentation of events, and second, the form of its representation of space and place. As I have outlined in the introduction of this study, these sections of my discussion will comprise the close reading of four novels. These novels are worth investigating because they foreground the resilience of a tenet in novelistic discourse that I consider vital for the survival of the novel as a

---

14. See the Oxford English Dictionary's definition n.3 for "want," noun: "The fact that a person or [occasionally] a thing is not present: absence."

viable cognitive tool: telling the truth about the dominant sociopolitical formation in a certain age without embracing its system of values. By adopting this nonconformist stance on reality, novels of displacement can deliver valuable knowledge on the current human condition, thus justifying their selection as an object of study. In the following chapters, I will further elucidate the value of these works as tools to decipher the dominant forces at play in our time.

CHAPTER 3

Epistemic Displacement in Bernardo Carvalho's *Nove noites*

Displacement and Its Narrative

Bernardo Carvalho's *Nove noites* narrates the story of a historical character, Buell Quain (1912–39). An anthropologist from Columbia University, Quain committed suicide while doing fieldwork with the Krahô, an indigenous tribe in Northern Brazil. His life represents a case study of displacement. After growing up in the Midwest, Quain receives his doctorate, travels around the world, and eventually leaves for Brazil in 1938. Once there, he lives mainly in the Amazon rainforest, first with the Trumai and then with the Krahô. In early August 1939, on his way back to the city of Carolina, Quain hangs himself. After his death, the thread of Quain's life dangles in the void: the reasons for his suicide remain utterly unknown, as does the location of his grave (Carvalho 102, 76).[1] Six decades after these events, Bernardo Carvalho sets out to

---

1. By tying Quain's tragedy to the schizophrenia inherent in anthropology, Pedro Erber has offered a persuasive scholarly explanation of the anthropologist's suicide. Erber argues that Quain took his life because he was unable to carry the burden of its split subjectivity as an anthropologist: while he interacted with the Other in the real, present time, he simultaneously had to isolate the Other in a different, premodern temporal dimension (31).

write a story that might explain the anthropologist's suicide and finally give him a place, in the sense not of a tangible site, but of a life story provided with a beginning, middle, and end.

In *Nove noites,* the investigation into the causes of Quain's suicide is carried out by an anonymous, autodiegetic narrator who shares key features with Carvalho: both are males, from São Paulo, journalists, and born in 1960. Consistent with this narrator's profession and the journalistic investigation he performs throughout the novel, I will call him "the Journalist," thus following in Cid Ottoni Bylaardt's footsteps (6).[2] In the narrative structure of *Nove noites,* it might seem that the Journalist shares his storytelling task with another narrator, Manoel Perna, a Carolina resident who befriended Quain in 1939. Perna's contribution to the story, however, consists in a letter/testament that is actually a figment of the Journalist's imagination. It is the Journalist, in other words, who acts as the novel's primary narrator, as the ultimate source of the materials assembled in the text. As the story progresses, the Journalist becomes the fulcrum of his own narrative, and the novel's focus turns to a discussion of the methods he applies to his investigation rather than a narration of the facts he discovers. In *Nove noites,* solving the mystery of Quain's death matters less than assessing the tools utilized to find this solution. Among these tools, the very narrative of the investigation, or its *"mise en intrigue,"* to borrow from Paul Ricœur's theory on time and narrative, assumes the greatest importance (*L'intrigue* 66). Choosing the form that this narrative ultimately will take, as either a journalistic report or a fictional story, indeed represents the Journalist's (and the novel's) key concern. Because of the relevance that this and other methodological issues—all concerning the possibility of proving, configuring, and conveying truth—assume in the text, epistemic preoccupations hold a crucial position in *Nove noites,* which, in turn, makes Carvalho's work a particularly apt example of the epistemic situation of novels of displacement as truth-finding texts in our time.

---

2. In Gérard Genette's theory, a narrator is autodiegetic when he/she is the hero of the narrative he/she recounts (245). Even though the Journalist in *Nove noites* attempts to recount Buell Quain's life story, the end result is a narration of his own investigation into the American anthropologist's death: undoubtedly, the hero of this narrative is the Journalist himself.

From its first lines, *Nove noites* presents the reader with a quintessentially epistemic issue: the mutable, contextual status of truth and falsehood. In the text's opening paragraph, Manoel Perna warns the hypothetical receiver of the letter/testament he is writing: "You are going to enter a land where truth and lies no longer have the same meaning that brought you here" (6).[3] Albeit from his subordinate position as the novel's secondary narrator, Perna provides a crucial contribution to *Nove noites*: eight sections of his letter/testament alternate with the story told by the Journalist. Perna and the Journalist, however, cover different textual areas: while the former writes about events in Quain's life, the latter tells the story of his own investigation into Quain's suicide. In both these sections of the text, as it narrates an inquiry into a violent, unexplained death, *Nove noites* adopts the literary model of the detective story. As known, this genre is built on the assumption that a rational examination of the available evidence regarding an unsolved crime may reasonably lead to the ascertainment of truth. Within this conceptual framework, *Nove noites* assembles three discourses—journalism, anthropology, and the bureaucratic archive—all sharing a common faith in the Western notion of "reason" as purveyor of truth. In these discourses, the search for truth concerns, respectively, contemporary life, non-Western cultures, and the prior acts of public and private bureaucracies. Journalism employs the resources of enlightened reason from a horizontal perspective, by investigating societies leveled by the "now" of contemporaneity. Anthropology instead adopts a vertical approach. It is from their own "elevated" point of view that Western anthropologists consider the objects of their inquiry, the non-Western communities they situate in a stage of history that precedes the onset of Modernity (seen as the project of the Enlightenment).[4] As for the archive, it provides the inves-

---

3. Manoel Perna reiterates his skepticism on the possibility of arriving at stable forms of truth. After his initial statement on truth and lies, he states that "truth is lost among contradictions and absurdities," (6) and then suggests that "truth depends solely on the listener's trust" (21). Finally, Manoel Perna repeats his initial warning at the beginning of the novel almost word for word towards the end of his testament: "truth and lies do not hold the same meanings that brought you here" (117).

4. Sophia Beal introduces the idea of a vertical gaze in her analysis of Quain's stance vis-à-vis the indigenous people he was studying. Quain "longed for an unobtainable distance from others, an impossible vertical gaze from above" (145). This longing contrasted starkly with Quain's desire to be fully incorporated into the world of the Krahô (146).

tigative mind with both a proven method for safekeeping the products of its labor and the storage location from which the results of past investigations can be retrieved. The search for truth constitutes the key concern of this discursive assemblage even if the unfolding of the plot contradicts the initial investigative thrust of *Nove noites* (Bylaardt 232). There is no doubt that the novel unveils a world in which there is no place for either the truth of journalism or that of the detective story. What is more, the archive is of little help, to say the least. This development, however, does not counter the fact that the text's preoccupation is the question of truth, be it that of journalism or of the detective story. In the end, the novel reveals that truth rewards neither discourse, but in so doing it confirms that its chief goal consists in assessing the achievements and the instruments of the inquiring mind.

Regarding the overall preoccupation with truth that emerges from the discursive fabric of *Nove noites*, the novel's initial paragraph achieves its full meaning only if one considers the actual receiver of Manoel Perna's letter/testament. This addressee is not the individual (a supposed American friend of Quain) to whom Perna alludes without explicitly naming him, for the simple reason that Perna never wrote any such letter: it was the Journalist who did so, as he admits later in the novel (121). Perna's letter is utterly fictional; in particular, the relation between the letter's addressee and Quain is a product of the Journalist's imagination. As a consequence, the novel's reader is the letter's ultimate addressee, as Marília Rocha Ribeiro correctly observes (312). Hence, the land in which the reader is expected—the territory where truth establishes a relationship with falsehood that diverges from everyday reality—is not the Amazon rainforest described by Perna, but the novel itself. At the beginning of this crucial conversation between the text and the reader, Perna's statement makes clear what is at stake in *Nove noites*: both the literary text's ability to tell the truth and the form that this presumed truth may take.

Archives, Journalism, and Fiction

To discuss the potential of *Nove noites* as a truth-finding narrative, I will first situate Carvalho's work within the ongoing crisis of the partnership between the archive and the novel, and then discuss how this crisis bears on both the text's narrative structure and the author's strategy for legitimating his work as a reliable truth-finding tool. In *Nove noites*, the archival scene is characterized by the overabundance of available documentation. From this oversized repository, the Journalist chooses to base his investigation almost entirely on evidence collected from letters. The epistolary archive in the text comprises seven letters sent by Buell Quain; mail written by Ruth Benedict (Quain's mentor at Columbia University), Heloísa Alberto Torres (the director of the National Museum in Rio de Janeiro), and other anthropologists, mostly from Columbia University; letters written by Brazilian authorities in charge of the government's relationship with the indigenous tribes; and letters written by Quain's mother and Quain's sister. The entire repository of documents that the Journalist gathers is much larger and diverse than this collection of letters. We can infer this fact from sources the Journalist mentions throughout his investigation: newspaper articles, Quain's report on his work with the Krahô, the journal of the Swiss anthropologist Bernard Métraux, Quain's birth certificate, the transcripts from two interviews carried out by the Journalist, and a report on the attempt by Quain's father to have the State Department investigate his son's death. Two mug shots (frontal and in profile) of Buell Quain and a photograph portraying seven anthropologists (Charles Wagley, Raimundo Lopes, Edson Carneiro, Heloísa Torres, Claude Lévi-Strauss, Ruth Landes, and Luiz de Castro Faria) in the Brazilian National Museum in 1939 are documents of a completely different type (23, 27). In addition to being produced through a nontextual medium, these pictures are the only documents that the reader can assess by him/herself, without having to pass through the Journalist's narrative mediation. Essential biographical data on Quain's relatives (his father, mother, sister, and sister's children) complete the dossier. At any rate, the Journalist possesses enough information to write a detailed biography of Quain, outline the story of the anthropologist's family before and after his death, discuss the state of anthropological research in Brazil in the late 1930s under Getúlio Vargas's dictatorship (1937–45), and describe the relationship between Brazilian institutions, Columbia University, and the American academe at large. The Journalist also narrates the massacre in Cabeceira Grossa, a Krahô village in which white ranchers killed twenty-six natives a year after Quain's death, and outlines the changes this tragic event brought about in the Brazilian Government's policy towards the Krahô. From the acknowledgements page, we learn that, in the real world, this textual archive is the product of Carvalho's research within a macrostorage collection that comprises several libraries and repositories scattered throughout Brazil and North America: from the National Museum in Rio de Janeiro to Concordia University in Montreal as well as from the University of São Paulo to the North Dakota Historical Society, all duly mentioned at the end of novel (151).

Manoel Perna's letter/testament, obviously a document of an entirely different nature, completes this collection of records. Written in the form of a testimony and endowed with the status of a legal document, Perna's testament mentions an eighth letter, which Quain would have sent to the same unknown and fictional American friend to whom Perna is addressing his own letter. By spelling out the reasons for Quain's suicide, as Perna presumes, the anthropologist's eighth letter should convey the information missing from the documentation gathered by the Journalist. However, this letter is pure fiction: the Journalist/Carvalho reveals this fact when he breaks the fourth wall and admits to having fabricated Perna's letter/testament. Since the latter represents the textual evidence for the existence of Quain's eighth letter, the admitted fictitiousness of Perna's testament obviously encompasses the nonexistence of Quain's eighth letter in the real world (121).

By admitting to having fabricated Perna's letter, the Journalist eliminates one of the possible solutions to the lack of a credible explanation for Quain's suicide: the creation of a document that, despite being fake, receives authenticity through a fictional procedure. Historically, from Defoe to DeLillo, this ploy has functioned as a magic bullet of sorts for novelists struggling with a shortage of records: the discovery of a "hidden manuscript" being the classic example of this authorial technique. Besides filling a crucial lacuna in the archive, a document like Perna's testament would have "realized the fiction, making the fictional appear real, authenticating the present meaning through a proposed resemblance to the past," as fictionalized records do in Lilly Koltun's clever analysis of a digitized archival clip inserted into Oliver Stone's *Natural Born Killers* (128). By discarding this option through the revelation of his own invention, the Journalist acknowledges that his archive will forever remain incomplete. His awareness will have a decisive impact on his choice of genre for the text he is writing.

The incompleteness that mars the documentation on Quain's death might seem inconsistent with the Journalist's success at retrieving and arranging records. Indeed, in just eight months and without ever leaving Brazil, he manages to build a remarkable archive on Quain's life, despite the fact that most of the records he retrieves are stored outside the country.[5] He can accomplish this feat only because he benefits from the communication networks of the digital age, which allow people to connect on the fly, via email, and quickly access digital databases through websites and online search engines (12, 138). The Journalist operates in the world of "electronic communication, a world of textual overabundance in which the written texts that are offered go far beyond the reader's ability to take advantage of them" (Chartier 139). It is by working within this technological environment that the Journalist is able to amass an impressive amount of records in a short time. The sheer quantity of information he collects, however, by no means guarantees that he will reach his goal of writing a persuasive narrative of Quain's life and deeds. Indeed, just the opposite occurs, as we can infer from the Journalist's statements about the literary genre of the text that he intends to create. Early in the novel, the Journalist makes this comment about a Brazilian anthropologist he interviewed on the subject of Quain's death: "She [the anthropologist] supposed that I wanted to write a novel, that I had a literary interest, and I did not contradict her" (12). The text is clearly ambiguous, as it leaves the reader in the dark about the Journalist's true interests. Later in the story, the Journalist twice repeats his intention to write a novel, but his statements appear to be simple pretexts for explaining his fixation on Buell Quain to individuals (two anthropologists and a member of the Krahô tribe) he meets during his inquiry (66, 85). As Bylaardt argues, until the final pages, "the novel genre comes up now and then only to justify the Journalist's actions and to ensure that his investigation will not lead people to believe he was fooling around with a serious subject" (234). It is solely toward the end of *Nove noites* that the Journalist finally makes a crystal clear comment on the genre he has in mind for his project. Frustrated by his inability to retrieve helpful information on the reasons for Quain's suicide, the Journalist comes to terms with his investi-

---

5. The Journalist's investigation begins on May 12, 2001, when he reads a newspaper article mentioning Quain's suicide (11). It ends on February 19, 2002, when he takes a flight to New York, where the last episode of the novel will take place (142).

gation's failure: "At that point, I was disposed to turn it into a real work of fiction. Lacking alternatives, I was left with that choice" (141). In sum, fiction becomes a viable option only as a way out of the investigative impasse in which the Journalist is mired. For the epistemic status of the text that the Journalist has created, crucial is the fact that, through the Journalist's two metanarrative comments (the admission of the fictional nature of Manoel Perna's testament and the acceptance of the fictional nature of his own writing), he alters the arrangement of his own archive. In so doing he makes a post-Newtonian move; he fashions a repository that replicates Tacita Dean's *Girl Stowaway*, an archive that, as Hal Foster states, "implicates the artist-as-archivist within it" and represents "an artistic equivalent of the uncertainty principle in scientific experiment" (12).

From the above description of the Journalist's archival quandary, the lack of records concerning the reasons for Quain's suicide clearly emerges as a decisive blow to the integrity of his archive. Had these records existed, they would have constituted the proven truth on which the Journalist would have anchored both the record series on Quain's biography and all of his comments on the anthropologist's death. The lack of these papers prompts a wild game of conflicting interpretations and, inevitably, the dissemination of errors: as Carlo Sini writes, after the event that founds truth, the erring of truth from one interpretation to another takes over (38). In the case of Quain's suicide, as the event that interests the Journalist evades documentation, the interpretative game suffers from a foundational gap right from the start. As a consequence of this void, the Journalist must recognize that his own interpretation will never achieve the status of a truthful reconstruction of the events that interest him.

When the Journalist discovers that an overabundance of documentation does not mean completeness, he comes across an epistemic problem typical to the digital age. This complication can be understood by considering Google's modus operandi, which makes sense in a context of an overabundance of data. As known, Google Search answers a query by presenting the inquirer with a list of web pages that are related to the string of words entered in a search box. In this list, connectivity is the discriminating factor: pages that have more links to and from other pages are placed at the top of the list. This method relies on sheer quantity, because the greater the number of pages inventoried in

Google, the higher the probability that the system functions. Furthermore, incompleteness is accepted by default, because inventorying all the pages on the Web is an impossible enterprise. However, the very reason for this incompleteness—the fact that new web pages are created at unfathomable speed—enhances the method's chances of success. The greater the number of existing pages ensures a greater number of pages inventoried by Google, thus proportionally increasing the number of contacts and the likelihood that this quantitative method functions. Thus, the overabundance that would seriously hinder a paper repository, such as a bureaucratic archive, a library, or a book, is the sine qua non condition for the storage and dissemination of information in the digital age. As a novelist limited by the material dimensions of the object he creates, however, Carvalho cannot manage overabundance in the same manner as Google. Above all, he cannot ignore the other side of overabundance: incompleteness. He must strive for a careful selection of records and a completeness of information within the limits of the documentation he is able to collect and organize.

Clearly, even in the digital age, a novel still remains a physically limited entity. Despite partaking in the boundless immateriality of the digital document during the phase of its composition, a novel is constrained by the physical limits of the paper book (these limits are immanent, so to speak, even in electronic formats such as Kindle), the material object that contains its text in its final stage of production. On the one hand, a contemporary novelist must possess thorough knowledge of the materials he/she is utilizing to compose a novel, while on the other hand, he/she must fight the tendency toward overabundance that is inherent in contemporary archival practices. The very notion of completeness, however, is historical. In nineteenth-century novels, retrieving an original document is usually represented as a feasible achievement, even if it requires time and effort: Colonel Chabert is buried in a mass grave, but after climbing back into the world of the living he has his identity certified by a notary. Thus, the record series of Chabert once again has an origin. In our post-metaphysical time, however, it is increasingly difficult to find fiction that narrates the retrieval of original records. It seems that our mistrust in any primary, metaphysical entity has undermined the very idea of the origin not only in terms of the universe, history, and language, but also in the case of novels and archives. The missing archival record regarding

Quain's death would have represented "the center of his desperation," as the Journalist describes the anthropologist's imagined eighth letter (140). This center is lacking in *Nove noites,* just as the idea of the center has become a mere historical illusion in contemporary philosophy and epistemology (Bylaardt 232). In *Nove noites,* as the spatial metaphor of the missing center suggests, this incompleteness equates to displacement, in the literal sense of the loss of a place: first as Quain's missing grave, and then as the empty shelf space that the records of his suicide should have occupied.

In *Nove noites,* incomplete documentation leads to a narrative conundrum. The solution to this problem is the explicit identification of the text's genre as fiction. As I discussed above, this occurs when the Journalist realizes that he will never complete the archive whose gaps he has temporarily filled with Manoel Perna's fabricated testament: it is then that he decides to adopt fiction as a way out of his predicament. Acknowledgement of structural problems affecting the documentation available in the text, as well as the demonstrated fictionality of the solution to these problems, are related to the key authorial decision to turn the epistemic problems of the digital age into a major theme in *Nove noites.* The epistemic displacement fictionalized in Carvalho's novel does not mechanically depend on the fact that he is writing in the digital age. To the contrary, this type of displacement originates in the author's choice of elaborating original, minor narrative answers to crucial questions, such as the status of truth in our time, the reliability of digital databases, and the cognitive uncertainty that the overabundance of records brings about. Within this context, albeit made necessary by the structural incompleteness of the novel's archive, the Journalist's decision to write fiction remains ambiguous. It signals, in fact, a move not from nonfiction to fiction, but from one type of fiction (Perna's fictional testament) to another. What the Journalist abandons is the kind of fiction that belongs to the established tradition of the novelistic genre: a savvy mix of truth and imagination that functions as a credible explanation for facts otherwise shrouded in mystery. This type of fiction hegemonized the discourse of the novel for almost two centuries, until postmodern writers took open pleasure in its unveiling. What of the other sort of fiction, the one to which the Journalist resorts as his only option for the story he is attempting to write? What kind of fiction is this? How, and why, does this fiction differ from the more traditional sort that the Journalist rejected? What occurs in the novel's final episode provides an answer to these questions.

Shortly after coming to terms with the fictional character of his narrative, the Journalist leaves for New York where he hopes to meet the son of Andrew Parsons, an American photographer who might have had connections to Buell Quain. The Journalist had identified Andrew Parsons through a second thread of investigation, prompted by the memory of a distant but fortuitous encounter. In the hospital room where the Journalist's father spent the last months of his life, a delirious old American patient had called the Journalist by the name "Bill Cohen" and treated him as a long-lost friend. Twelve years later, when the Journalist comes across the article mentioning Buell Quain's suicide, the memory of that spoken name, "Bill Cohen," comes to mind. Along with the memory, a conjecture emerges: "Bill Cohen" might have actually been a mispronunciation of Buell Quain. From the Journalist's recollection, two parallel lines of investigation follow: one aiming to clarify the reasons for Quain's death and the other directed at gathering information on the dying American. Upon his identification as Andrew Parsons through a lucky inquiry in several Brazilian hospitals, this American patient becomes the imaginary addressee of Manoel Perna's letter/testament. In short, the dying American represents the very lynchpin of the Journalist's entire fictional composition, which he first created according to the classic tradition of the novel and then dismantled in postmodern fashion through his admission of having fabricated Manoel Perna's testament.

In New York, truth appears in a delusional form, when the Journalist sees the fleeting likeness of Buell Quain's features in the face of Schlomo Parsons (Andrew's son): "He looked like Buell Quain in one of the photographs that his mother had sent to dona Heloísa" (145). The whiff of a connection to Quain's tragedy also seems to emanate from Schlomo Parson's life story. Abandoned by his father less than a year after his birth, at age seventeen Schlomo learned that his true father was not Andrew Parsons, as he had always believed, but an unknown man "who had died in the heart of Brazil" while attempting to return home to meet his son (147).[6]

---

6. The truthfulness of Schlomo Parsons's story is dubious, as the man appears to entertain an uncertain relation with the truth. At the beginning of his conversation with the Journalist, he pretends to be fifty-seven, only to contradict himself a

By fashioning such a conclusion for *Nove noites,* Carvalho appears to embrace fiction as a mix of canonical literary devices and record-free imagination. In the Journalist's meeting with Schlomo Parsons, truth manifests itself through a well-tested literary tool, the anagnorisis, as a discovery of a hidden paternity. It is this discovery that makes the novel's plot intelligible. In her analysis of *Nove noites,* Yara Frateschi Vieira correctly identifies the presence in Carvalho's novel of a subterranean, feuilleton-like narrative complete with all the ingredients of the genre: mistaken identity and final recognition (however incomplete and uncertain) of paternity (214). To these clichés noted by Vieira, I want to add the obvious reference to problematic paternity signaled by the choice of Sigmund Freud's middle name, Schlomo, for a man abandoned by both his presumed and his real father. In addition to this excess of literariness, the ending of *Nove noites* is also marred by factual inconsistencies. As the Journalist is well aware that Schlomo Parsons has no interest in talking to him, he can enter Schlomo's apartment in New York only by impersonating a deliveryman for a private mail carrier who comes to pick up a package. It is only through this exchange of identities (yet another literary ruse) that the Journalist is able to gain Schlomo's confidence and hear his story. Even in the possible worlds of fiction, however, private delivery employees wear uniforms and have customers sign an appropriate form when they pick up a package; it is practically impossible that a veteran New Yorker such as Schlomo Parsons would ever let an unknown individual in street clothes impersonating a mail carrier into his house. The success of this ruse appears to contravene not only our contemporary semiotic Encyclopedia, as Eco would have called it, but also the conventions of the novel itself. The representation of possible worlds, consistent with the reality we experience in our daily lives, indeed represents one of the most steadfast conventions of the novelistic genre. Carvalho's contravention may appear trivial, but it is this very infraction that makes possible the novel's sole, alleged epiphany of truth—Quain's traits appearing in Schlomo's countenance. It is worth adding that this feeble form of truth is

---

few minutes later by saying that he was less than a year old, before the outbreak of WWII (September 1939), when his father went to Brazil. As stated, this conversation takes place in May 2002, thus proving that Schlomo is sixty-three years of age when he meets the Journalist.

the only real epistemic gain achieved through the Journalist's demanding investigation.

At the end of his visit, after finding no pictures of Quain among those Schlomo still keeps as a legacy of Andrew Parsons (thus exemplifying how the hard evidence of the archive works against record-free fiction), the Journalist concedes that "there was nothing that could prove a connection between Quain and the photographer [Andrew Parsons]" (149). In sum, the world of the archive (where evidence-based truth prevails) and that of fiction (where truth is a construction) never coalesce at the end of *Nove noites*. This disconnection takes the form of a narrative blockage, as the evidence found in the archive cannot become the foundation for a story, while the narrative told in the novel cannot function as a stop-gap for fixing an incomplete record series. The archive remains silent, as the only narrative to come from its shelves is that of archival research, while fiction survives only by clinging to its stock traditions and, at the same time, stretching its own conventions beyond their limits. As for both journalism and anthropology, they generate mere self-reflexive narratives. The journalistic investigation into Quain's suicide does not manage to record the reasons for the anthropologist's death but instead what occurs during the inquiry into these very reasons. The same mirroring effect characterizes anthropology: the Journalist's sojourn with the Krahô results in his narrated reactions to the experience of living with the tribe, but this narration provides no new knowledge about the Krahô culture. At the end of the day, all the discourses assembled in *Nove noites*—journalism, anthropology, and the archive—are displaced: they are out of sync with the reality they are meant to decipher. Hence, as an assemblage of discourses that remain substantially mute, what is displaced above all is the novel itself. One symptom of this displacement is the ending of *Nove noites*, in which the narrative achieves completion only through an uneasy compromise between complying with traditional novelistic practices, such as the recognition of a hidden identity as the plot's climax, and transgressing the genre-based conventions that frame those same practices. By inserting instability into the narrative and overextending the field to which the novel's representational tools are applied, Carvalho turns *Nove noites* into an example of minor literature, at the level of both its form and its content: it is a destabilized novel that tells the story of a displaced individual. Indeed, narrating displacement constitutes the novel's main concern, as it appears from the fact that the main actors in the narrative (Buell Quain, Manoel Perna, Andrew Parsons, Schlomo Parsons, the Krahô, and all the indigenous tribes mentioned in the novel) are all displaced subjectivities. No one is more displaced than the Journalist himself, a character who begins a journalistic investigation, accomplishes nothing with it, goes to New York in a last-ditch attempt to rescue his work by interviewing a supposed key witness, plays a trick on an old man, retrieves no useful information, and is left with the task of writing the story of his failure. Through his inquiry, the Journalist hopes to rescue Buell Quain from the particular displacement he suffered as an individual who committed suicide for unknown reasons. His investigation aims to discover these reasons; his ultimate purpose is to create a place for Quain within the larger human community by presenting Quain's life experience in an understandable and sympathetic manner. As this investigation turns into a failure, the character's displacement only multiplies that of the narrator: displacement becomes a condition shared by both Buell Quain and the Journalist.

The Journalist's failure to turn Quain's life into a narratable story stems from the particular status of fiction in our age, an issue that becomes critical in the novel's final episode, when the Journalist has already settled for narrating Quain's life as a fictional tale. It is at this point that another type of fiction (the third mentioned thus far in the novel) infiltrates the text: "Fiction began on the day I set foot in the United States. The February 19, 2002 edition of the *New York Times* that was distributed on the plane announced the Pentagon's new strategy: disseminating news—including false news, if necessary—through international media; affecting 'foreign audiences' by all possible means" (142). With the Pentagon's entrance into the field of literary creation, the practice of fiction in *Nove noites* can be assessed from a new vantage point. Fiction, as it appears in the novel, can be:

1. A credible invention that fills a gap in the archive: Manoel Perna's testament.
2. A spectacle created and managed by a powerful political agency: the Pentagon's false news.
3. The novel as an invention completely disconnected from the archive: the story of the Journalist's meeting with Schlomo Par-

sons. As the Journalist is an alter ego of Carvalho, the novel's author, this type of fiction can be defined as (contemporary) novelist's fiction.

As the novel discards the first type of fiction as an impracticable exercise, only the Pentagon's fiction and the novelist's fiction remain at play. This fact gives rise to the question: which of the two fictions has the greater chance of succeeding as a communicative tool, that of the Pentagon or of the novelist? The answer is disheartening: because of the sheer disproportion between the instruments possessed by the likes of the Pentagon and those handled by a novelist, the latter's fiction is dwarfed by that of the former. In our time, Carvalho suggests, fiction is created in the Cloud. In this context, fiction composed on earth fights an uphill, perhaps unwinnable battle to assert itself in a discursive field dominated by threatening giants.

At this point in the novel, the Journalist's displacement can be fully appreciated: it takes on three forms, all of which originate in his loss of agency. To begin with, it is as a rational, independent investigator, the likes of which we may encounter in detective stories, that the Journalist is displaced.[7] Had he operated in the epistemic field to which this investigation belongs, that is to say a field characterized by a paucity of documentation and correspondence between records and facts, he would have acted as a powerful agent in that context and would have succeeded. Instead, as he carries out his investigation within a field defined by the presence of the digital, networked database, he finds his agency diluted by the necessity of having to operate within an unbounded repository. Second, as highly powerful actors such as Google or other big companies of the Internet dominate the business of managing and retrieving data, the Journalist's agency as a researcher in the global repository of records is dwarfed by the competition. He strives to do his job, but he fails: surrounded by the mighty agents that have overflowed his working space with data, he is displaced at home. Here, as the Journalist's condition does not differ from that of any

---

7. The Journalist's failure as an investigator guided by his own rational mind partakes in the overall demise of Western rational thought in *Nove noites*. As discussed earlier, the three discourses embedded in the novel—journalism, anthropology, and the archive—all fail to achieve appreciable goals and are reduced to self-mirroring narratives.

Internet user who strives to find information on the Web, his displacement is emblematic of our own widespread mood. Finally, by introducing the Pentagon into the literary field as a creator of fiction, Carvalho calls his reader's attention to the kind of players who are currently participating in the game of producing and circulating narratives. The agency of these players now overwhelms that of any writer. The Journalist's plight, whose name, again, is displacement, is the contemporary novelist's plight.

To summarize, displacement in *Nove noites* is arranged on three levels, corresponding to the novel's content, structure, and form. On the first level, displacement concerns the events the novel narrates: the story of Buell Quain, his wanderings throughout the world, and, above all, his incapacity to settle down in life and even in death. Quain's missing grave, the absence of a final physical place for his body, represents the epitome of his spatial and existential displacement. The structural displacement, instead, concerns the narrative of the investigation into Quain's life. This tale should function as a frame story within which the extant information on Quain could develop into its own narrative. As the Journalist's investigation goes nowhere, the frame story does not come together, thus displacing the novel's structure. Finally, on the formal level, displacement affects the novel form as such. This instance of displacement becomes evident at the conclusion of the Journalist's inquiry into Buell Quain's life. It is at this point that the novel finds itself displaced by the intrusion of an external, superior agency (the Pentagon) into its field of operation, as occurs with all the displaced subjectivities that operate in the age of global capital. This intrusion is crucial: it constitutes an invasion of the novel's discursive space as well as an encroachment upon the novel's capability to perform its historical function in society. Here, I am referring to González Echevarría's argument that the novel's task is to reveal the conventionality and ultimate literariness of the discourse that in a certain epoch embodies authority. To do so, the novel assumes the form "of a given kind of document endowed with truth-bearing power by society at specific moments in time" (*Myth and Archive* 8). If this is the case, then, in its final episode, *Nove noites* stages an extraordinary turnaround of positions involving the novel on the one hand and the powers that be on the other. For, at the end of the day, it is not the novel that assumes the form of an authoritative document but the latter, in the form of a Pentagon report, that cloaks itself in literary fiction. After this reversal of roles, what practice is left for the novel? Becoming minor fiction. When documents endowed with truth-bearing power, like a Pentagon report, assume the form of literary fiction, then the novel cannot help but embrace fiction as an intensive, strange, and minor practice. In *Nove noites*, the text achieves the status of minor fiction through a process of self-disclosure. Indeed, minor fiction demeans itself as the last option for writers unable to complete a truthful work. Minor fiction exhibits the banality of its traditional tools and its own carelessness in handling the factual details of the world it describes.

CHAPTER 4

On Places, Hyper-places, and Agency

A Relational Theory of Place

Place enables our being in the world: as Joshua Meyrowitz forcefully argues, "We are always in place, and place is always with us" (22). In the experience of place, a fundamental truth obtains: place "always represents a human product" (Pred 279). Our operations become crucial here, since place is intrinsically linked to our engagement with the world. Place results from our practices, in particular from their "reiteration . . . on a regular basis" (Cresswell 2). As we carry out these reiterated practices, we produce place by establishing differences among the entities that we meet in the space that surrounds us:

> Space becomes place . . . when we differentiate—emotionally, physically, and experientially—between the objects space contains. Space becomes place when we transform or shape these objects according to our meanings, hence producing place, or when we socially negotiate these meanings and transform them into shared "values" or social norms and conditions to interact among and with the objects place contains. (Lapenta 213)

Since the objects involved in these transformations and the subjects interested in the social negotiations of their meanings are not contained within preestablished boundaries, place is defined by its openness. Jeff Malpas, to whom my discussion here is largely indebted, persuasively argues that "a central feature of the idea of place (even though it may not carry across to all the senses of the term) would seem to be that of a certain open, if bounded, space or region" (*Place and Experience* 22). It is in this open territory that subjectivity emerges and grows: "Place is . . . that within and with respect to which subjectivity is itself established—place is not founded on subjectivity, but is rather that on which subjectivity is founded" (35). For example, characters such as those described by Bernardo Carvalho in *Nove noites* are doomed to displacement in that they are unable to found their subjectivity on the places they attend. Crucially, the foundation of subjectivity on place is an inclusive process: no subjectivity may claim an exclusive relation with a certain place, while the latter can become the foundation of innumerable subjectivities. What is more, it is the interaction involving subjectivity and place that makes agency possible: "The language of place, of self and other, of subject and object, describes the world in a way that is tied to the possibility of agency and attitude, and not in terms of physical process alone" (*Place and Experience* 37).

The physical features of a region as well as its historical heritage participate in bringing about the emersion of place, without becoming its dominant factors.[1] By its own definition, place needs geography and history. Since it is our practices, however, that cause a certain region to coalesce into a place, the latter end up transcending those same landscapes and traditions. Boundaries play a crucial role in this process. Although they belong to the geographical and historical heritage of a place, they do not function as insurmountable fences around it. This porosity occurs because the very existence of place is predicated upon a constant traffic tying its inside to its outside: "Place's inflow and outflow are such that to be fully *in* a place is never to be confined to a punctuate position; it is to be already on the way out" (Casey, *Getting*

---

1. On the never-ending process that brings about place, see also Gibson, Luckman, and Brennan-Horley: "It is the jostling and interactions of a multitude of 'things' that make 'place' what it is. Rather than assume that it ever was 'stable' or 'proper,' place comes to be understood as 'becoming,' a continually unfurling phenomenological mix" (124).

Back 29, emphasis in the original). To better understand this process, we should conceptualize the boundaries of place as horizons rather than borders. As Malpas argues, in a place, the horizon "delimits what is given within and holds open the possibility of connection to that which is without" ("Place of Mobility" 33). As the ultimate perimeter of place, the horizon represents a condition of possibility: there would be no place to which to move unless any given place existed in relation to an encompassing horizon (Casey, *Getting Back* 62).

The appreciation of this openness becomes instrumental in separating displacement as approached in this study—or the mood emerging from the awareness that remote but commanding agencies are taking control of our places—from a feeling that today is becoming increasingly popular in the public opinion of various countries: the nostalgia for the lost place—be it the village, the region, and/or the country—of the past. This feeling is rooted in the conception of place as the geographical locale that represents the main source of identity for a culturally homogeneous community. A key corollary of this notion consists in viewing the identification with a certain locale as an exclusionary process. When we uphold this view no other community except our own, and no individual except those who belong to our community, may claim roots in our place. Appropriately, Massey calls this conception a "'reactionary' notion of place" (152). In the last decade, this exclusionary, identity-focused approach to place has been gaining enormous traction among the natives and long-standing residents in several countries, such as Italy, Hungary, the United Kingdom, India, and the United States, to name just a few. Viewing place as an instrument for exclusion, like a fortress keeping invaders outside, oftentimes goes hand in hand with a nostalgic view of the past, seen as an age in which migrants did not call into question political and cultural borders by means of their perennial movements. I consider this conflation of place with identity as a politically toxic and philosophically flawed idea. By discussing this issue from a postcolonial perspective, Stuart Hall argues that when a culture makes a symbolic investment in a particular place, that investment inevitably excludes all outsiders. He defines "this very strong, well-bounded version of cultural identity" as "ethnicity" ("New Cultures for Old" 181). Cultural identity as ethnicity "is often experienced as if it were a part of our biological nature because it is tied up with the sharing of the culture between members with a long and unbroken common genealogy, kinship, residence and descent" ("New Cultures for Old" 181). This emphasis on the long-term links between a closed community and the bounded territory where it resides leads to a metaphysical approach to place, "Thinking about the world in terms of deeply rooted, fixed places with clear boundaries and stable associated identities can be characterized as a sedentarist metaphysics" (Cresswell 8).

In this study, I shun metaphysics and support a notion of place based on a relational approach. Thinkers belonging to different schools of thought substantially agree on this methodology and its result. A feminist scholar like Massey, for example, argues that "place is really a *meeting* place, a moment in networks of social relations and understandings; these relations are constructed on a far larger scale than what we happen to define for that moment as the place itself, be it a street, a region, or even a continent" (155, emphasis in the original). Similarly, a philosopher such as Malpas, who is influenced by phenomenology, maintains that "places are nevertheless *relational*, arising in the interrelation of things, even while they also support such interrelatedness; moreover, places themselves constitute *networks of relations*" ("Place of Mobility" 33, emphasis in the original).[2] Under a Marxist perspective, finally, in his discussion of relational space (space comprised of objects that contain within themselves their relationships with other objects), Harvey argues that "an event or a thing at a point in space cannot be understood by appeal to what exists only at that point. It depends upon *everything else* going on around it (much as all those who enter a room to discuss bring with them a vast array of experiential data accumulated from the world)" ("Space as a Key Word" 124, my emphasis). Once situated in a network of relations, each of which contributes to its construction, place cannot clearly function as the sole purveyor of fixed, exclusionary identity.

---

2. Edward S. Casey does not emphasize the relational character of place but its ability to refer back to origin and home, both meant as unique entities that have value in and of themselves rather than through their being connected with other entities. "Place is first and foremost the site of the origin, while the home territory embodies the plenitude that being placeless so painfully lacks" (*Getting Back* xii). To lack a primal place is to be "homeless," not only in the literal sense but also in the sense of being without any effective means of orientation in a complex and confusing world.

In the age of global capital, the sheer number of relations that can be established from a place has grown exponentially. This occurs because our places now host so many communication tools of an unfathomable capacity, each of which multiplies immensely our own capability to connect with the outside world. As they allow for the two-way traffic of messages from a wide array of other locations, the digital devices created in the last four decades provide today's places with a connectivity incomparable to that offered by the analog devices (television sets, typewriters, telephones) of the paper age. Our software-driven age has exponentially magnified Harvey's "everything else" that surrounds an event situated at a single point in space. If this point happens to be the place where we live and operate, we discover that the relation between this site and our virtual territory (or the ratio between the size of the place where we reside and that of all the other places we can reach from this point) has taken on a dimension that would have been inconceivable during the paper age. The place we inhabit now is a minimal fraction of all the places with which we potentially interact. As Meyrowitz persuasively observes, "Although we always sense the world in a local place, the people and things that we sense are not exclusively local: media of all kinds extend our perceptual field. And while all physical experience is local, we do not always make sense of local experience from a purely local perspective" (22).[3]

Richard Ek has noted that in our time, "traditional notions of space and place as equal to physical distance and physical locality no longer apply or at least have to be complemented or nuanced to a significant extent" (39). This erosion of the physical component of the spaces we inhabit has led some scholars to envision a possible liberation from place. Already in 2001, still one year ahead of the launch of the Blackberry, the first true smartphone, Barry Wellman argues that "mobile phones afford a fundamental liberation from place, and they soon will be joined by wireless computers and personalized software" (7). Seven

---

3. On the mixed character of contemporary space, see also Eric Gordon and Adriana de Souza e Silva: "It is increasingly common for people to inhabit a hybrid of physical and digital spaces, mediated by the use of mobile and location-aware technologies" (89). Casey, instead, maintains that place and digital technology are separated by an irremediable contradiction: "When I use wireless technologies that take me out of place, no matter how convenient or practically valuable that move can be, I move into a disembodied experience that deprives me of the very basis of my identity and my autonomy" ("Going Wireless" 177).

years later, Rickie Sanders focuses instead on the effects that communication and transportation technologies induce in our relations with geographical space. By taking us "out of fixed spaces," these technologies, he maintains, brought "the promise of dramatic social, economic and political changes that seemed to herald the absolute freedom from the confines of location" (181). However, even though the digital connectivity provided by mobile phones, tablets, and computers enables us to virtually vacate our places at will, we remain emplaced beings. And this emplacement occurs for the simple reason that we are embodied subjectivities: "The structure of embodied 'being in place' is [thus] the basic *ontological* structure within which the *empirical* circumstances of human lives are worked out" (Malpas, "Place of Mobility" 29, emphasis in the original). In the present context, then, it makes more sense to speak of a "renegotiation or construction of place, rather than an impossible liberation or emancipation from place" (Lapenta 214). Because of this renegotiation, in the digital age, our emplacement assumes a new character, based on the fact that our connection to place, rather than being enabled by our body alone (however enhanced by various kinds of equipment) is mediated through a body-technology relation. Fascinated by this relation, those who speak of a liberation from place make a fallacious substitution. For, what achieves liberation from place is not our embodied being, but our tools: while the equipment of the paper age was solidly emplaced—the landline telephone being the perfect example—the present, mobile technology is not. Thus, we ask, "Where are you?" when we call somebody on a mobile phone. Our interlocutor, however, is still emplaced somewhere in the world, even if he/she connects with us through a tool that we cannot pinpoint on a geographical location. In this context, our technologically augmented bodies transform our places by inflating the latter's capability to entertain relations with the outside world. Even though we often lack the instruments for situating in space the other end of these relations, our inability to place something or somebody in the world does not necessarily make place disappear. To the contrary, place becomes even more visible as one of its foundational features, relationality, grows significantly in importance. As place remains there, our virtual vacating of places by way of technologically based connectivity cannot lead us to a liberation from place. Nor can it represent the reason for the alienation from place that amounts to modern day displacement.

As for physical mobility, the other defining feature of the age of global capital, scholarly debate must still reach a consensus whether or not it is a source for contemporary displacement. As Tim Cresswell observes: "The relationship between place and mobility is also marked by disagreements between those who see mobility and process as antagonistic to place and those who think of place as created by both internal and external mobilities and processes" (9). In this study, consistent with the dynamic approach to place that I have outlined so far, it is the latter position that functions as the interpretive tool for today's mobility. Indeed, in and of itself, mobility means "more" rather than "less" place. As it occurs with mobile communication, even physical mobility enhances our capability to establish relations between our places and the outside world, thus amplifying one of the key elements in the experience of place: its relationality.

Even though mobility as such does not prevent human beings from entertaining a constructive relation with place, nevertheless physical moving can lead, under certain circumstances, to displacement. Massey grasps these circumstances in her analysis of the time-space compression in the age of global capital:

> In a sense at the end of all the spectra are those who are both doing the moving and the communicating and who are in some way in a position of control in relation to it—the jet-setters, the ones sending and receiving the faxes and the e-mail, holding the international conference calls, the ones distributing the films, controlling the news, organizing the investments and the international currency transactions. These are the groups who are really in a sense in charge of time-space compression (149).

But there are also groups who are doing a lot of physical moving, but who are not "in charge" of the process in the same way at all: the refugees from El Salvador or Guatemala, and the undocumented migrant workers from Michoacán in Mexico, crowding into Tijuana to make a perhaps fatal dash across the border into the US to grab a chance of a new life (149).

In the above citations, by analyzing mobility in the context of the social structure of our global polity, Massey carries out her discussion on a political ground. Within this framework, she makes a crucial distinction between those who move and those who are moved around the world; or, between those who exercise agency through their mobility and those who experience mobility as a form of submission to somebody else's agency. I want to argue that the latter suffer from displacement, while the former do not. Hence, my point is that it is not physical mobility per se, but the sociopolitical context in which this mobility occurs, that brings about displacement. When this context prevents those who move on the ground from exercising their agency, displacement occurs. The lack of agency as the decisive factor in experiences of displacement represents the working hypothesis structuring this book: "disagency" brings about displacement.

Let us now verify this hypothesis in two specific instances.

Hyper-places in the Age of Global Capital

To define the new form taken by space in our time, geographer Michel Lussault has coined a neologism, "hyper-spatiality." It signifies "the unknown and crucial role of connectivity, or the systematic possibility of connecting: as we can freely move from one space to another, and then to yet another through hyperlinks, we can also tie any space to another and then to another again. One can do so through mobility networks and, above all, hyper-linked communication" (ch. 1). In this new context, however, places do not disappear. To the contrary, as a common drive toward cohabitation leads humans to come together on the surface of the planet, places survive in a new form, as hyper-places (*hyper-lieux*). Since the mid-1990s, the emblematic hyper-place is Times Square, in which eight-story-high screens bound the area and, at the same time, open it toward an unbounded outside world that is made of digital images and digital data.[4] Hyper-places are points of over-accumulation of people, objects, flows, data, capital, and sur-

---

4. In Lussault's analysis, Times Square bounced back to glory from the troubles of the 1970s because of the establishment of a Business Improvement District in the area (1992), Disney's investments in and around Broadway (1993–99), and Mayor Rudolph Giuliani's security policy (1994–2001) (ch. 1).

plus value. A hyper-place is the site where we can experience a type of media-based ubiquity that consists in "being perfectly and integrally present here and now, while, from this very place, we decentralize ourselves through our simultaneous connection with other spaces" (ch. 1). In a hyper-place, we are free to join other individuals in temporary clusters based on mere "spatial affinity." Our identification with these aggregations remains weak, as "we do not transform our momentary connection into ineradicable roots able to define our identity" (ch. 1). As Lussault argues, the hyper-places physically present on the planet—malls, airports, train stations—find their digital counterparts in the hyper-places built on the social networks and in the virtual spaces of the Internet. Consistent with the fleeting nature of the links humans establish with hyper-places, Lussault continues, the experience of hyper-spatiality develops along the lines of an older practice, the *flânerie* discovered by Baudelaire and theorized by Benjamin; and this is true for both real and virtual hyper-places. Within this approach, those who crisscross the hyper-places of today's *mondialisation* would be considered *flâneurs*, emulators of their nineteenth- and twentieth-century predecessors. As such, they would represent "the ideal type of our age" (ch. 2).[5]

Baudelaire's *flâneurs*, however, are "independent spirits" whose concealment in the urban crowd results from a conscious decision: it is indeed their pleasure "to call the crowd home" (*élire domicile dans le nombre*) (22). It is worth bearing in mind Baudelaire's original notion of *flânerie* when one considers the context in which today's *flâneurs* would live. "Geopower" (*géopouvoir*), Lussault's term for defining the ability of certain social actors to manage our globalized space, can be extremely helpful for comprehending this particular context. Geopower consists in the ability "to build material spaces of life that end up being more or less prescriptive instruments." Furthermore, it "tends to deny individuals their essential condition of co-habitants so as to

---

5. Lussault distinguishes *mondialisation* from globalization. The former represents a revolution in the way we inhabit the planet. It creates a new World (*Monde*, capitalized in the original), characterized by the predominance of urbanized spaces throughout the planet: today, urbanization is the main force for instituting and imagining the World (ch. 1). Globalization instead consists primarily in an economic process: it shatters the boundaries that protect the national economies and creates a single, world-wide market (ch. 1).

downgrade them to 'customers' moved by technology and assigned to certain spatial operations, to certain emplacements" (ch. 4). Although extremely precise in his definition of geopower's features, Lussault fails to describe how geopower functions in shaping and ruling hyper-places, the territories that inevitably represent the choice areas for the exercise of its authority. Indeed, where else would geopower apply itself, if not on the points of over-accumulation of people, data, and capital?

In his analysis, Lussault is moved by the noteworthy goal of conveying a nonparanoid representation of globalization and by the equally remarkable intent to show how humans, stirred by their urge to cohabitate, can leave their imprint on any space they happen to populate, no matter how unfamiliar it may initially appear. Nevertheless, the absence of an analysis of geopower's operations in today's hyper-places weakens his powerful depiction of how the energy of global capitalism concentrates on the glittering hotspots where customers and commodities mirror one another. In particular, Lussault does not discuss the relation between the two prefixes that characterize his two neologisms: he does not explain how control over the "geo" can bring about the "hyper." A hint in this direction, however, surfaces in Lussault's definition of hyper-places as spatial embodiment of *mondialisation*. As they augment reality by making everything visible, hyper-places "hide the conditions of their economic, technological, and political possibilities." In their incommensurable growth, contemporary metropoles seem to look for semiotic solutions that can prevent any real "challenge to that growth and to the use of resources for its generation and maintenance" (ch. 2).

Therefore, on the structural level, hyper-places abide by the same principle of the invisible running the visible, which inspires the commodity form and informs both software and supranational high finance: welcome to the club, *Monsieur* Lussault! Based on this structural uniformity, we cannot simply infer the existence of a single, all-encompassing center of power: an inference of this sort would amount to an exercise in negative political theology beyond the interests of this study. Instead, what appears evident here is the widespread functioning of a common practice inspired by the dualistic ontology that shapes the contemporary world. We can witness this very dualism informing the current cycle of deterritorialization and reterritorialization, as well as the repartition of knowledge and the allocation of wealth among classes: in all of these contexts, as I discussed in chapter 1, the gulf in terms of power/knowledge yawning between the two poles of present-day dualistic society is one of the largest (if not the largest) in all of modernity.

Returning to the notion of *flânerie*, what matters is the fact that hyper-places, too, operate within a discursive frame inspired by the dualism mentioned above. How then, in the presence of such disproportion in the exercise of power, can a practice of subjective independence like *flânerie* come to pass? Today, who can truly claim to enjoy the modern metropolis from the perspective of an "independent spirit," as a *flâneur* should do, according to Baudelaire? Baudelaire's *flâneur* is an artist (inspired by the Dutch painter and illustrator Constantin Guys) who can aimlessly wander through the modern city due to his mastery of both the urban landscape and the routes negotiated by its inhabitants. Indeed, it is *flâneurs'* superior knowledge of the metropolis that separates them from those who move about the city for work or business. This kind of knowledge is not readily available in the context of the hyper-place, which by definition hides the economic, technological, and political conditions that make its emergence possible. Practices inspired by geopower lie at the root of these conditions. For a deeper perspective on these practices, I would like to examine one particular figure who makes a living by moving in and around contemporary hyper-places: the Uber driver. Present in the urban landscape since 2009, this figure can be considered as the final product of the revolution in the relationship between capital and labor that started in the early 1980s with the crisis of Fordism and the ensuing decentralization of industrial production.

On Place and Agency in Our Time

Uber, the well-known ride-sharing company, claims to be a software provider. The company does not call its drivers employees or even contractors, but rather "partners," "users," or "customers." This semiotic game tallies well with the company's advertisements, which are aimed at prospective drivers, lured in with the promise of total control over their own performances as far as working hours and locations are concerned. Despite the self-image it promotes, Uber still must manage the time and space of its workforce, as any entrepreneur must do: in particular, it must find ways to both entice drivers to work longer shifts and direct them to areas where the demand for rides is higher. Uber has resolved these issues by means of the dynamic pricing model that it has elaborated for its fares. In compliance with this model, the same route may fetch a different fare depending on the supply of, and demand for, Uber drivers at the time a ride is requested. Thus, in a certain area, when the demand for rides is high and there are not enough drivers, Uber fares increase to attract more drivers there and satisfy the demand for rides. Within this system, the company and its drivers pursue conflicting goals: while Uber is interested in keeping the supply of drivers high in order to lower fares and attract more customers, drivers are interested in keeping the supply low, so as to raise fares and make more money.

Uber implements what Alex Rosenblat and Luke Stark define as "a regime of automated and algorithmic management" (3759). In the working environment shaped by this regime, "the combination of blind passenger acceptance with low minimum fares and the algorithmic determination of surge pricing" reveals "how little control Uber drivers have over critical aspects of their work and how much control Uber has over the labor of its users (drivers)" (3762). Key to the relationship between capital and labor within the company itself are the "information asymmetries" that "emerge via Uber's software-based platform through algorithmic labor logistics shaping driver behavior, electronic surveillance, and policies for performance targets" (3777). There is nothing surprising in this imbalance. Indeed, it has been in place since the early application of software to policies of control. In this respect, Adriana de Souza e Silva argues that "once one creates computers that are invisible and extensive, it becomes hard to know who is controlling what and who is observing what" (21). De Souza e Silva supports her argument by quoting from N. Katherine Hayles, who in a 1996 article "observes that in the beginning of the 1990s 'employees at the PARC are provided with interactive badges that communicate with sensors in the ceilings, which in turn signal confirmation about the employees' locations to a computer network'" (22). As software-empowered tools have always had the potential to become controlling devices, what happens with the Uber platform is only one occurrence in a pattern of events, which is typical of the age of software-enhanced capital.

By relying not only on the information asymmetries built into the Uber platform but also on a vast array of psychological tricks and behavioral techniques borrowed from video game design, Uber successfully pressures drivers to work longer shifts and/or move to the areas the company determines to be more profitable. Uber drivers receive "push notifications" such as, "Are you sure you want to go offline? Demand is very high in your area. Make more money, don't stop now!" (Rosenblat and Stark 3768). Or, when drivers try to leave the platform before completing the twenty-five rides that would earn them a signing bonus, the application sends them encouragements like "You're almost halfway there, congratulations!" (Scheiber). In other cases, the platform sets arbitrary goals for its drivers and sends them messages like "You're $10 away from making $330 in net earnings. Are you sure you want to go offline?" (Scheiber). In the words of Ed Frantzen, an Uber driver interviewed by Noam Scheiber for the *New York Times*, "It [the Uber application on Frantzen's smartphone] was always, constantly, trying to get you into a certain direction." In the same article, other drivers testify to Uber's success in having them stay online for a longer time than they had initially foreseen, move to zones chosen by the company, or change the time of their shifts according to the management's input. As in Lussault's theorization of geopower, Uber has built a space for human cohabitation that functions as a prescriptive instrument. The drivers who inhabit this space are denied their essential condition of co-habitant and downgraded to "'customers' moved by technology and assigned to certain spatial operations, to certain emplacements" (ch. 4).[6]

As they operate under the constraints of geopower, Uber drivers inhabit the same kind of split reality that characterizes Lussault's hyper-

---

6. Harvey argues that "working class movements are . . . generally better at organizing in and dominating *place* than they are at commanding *space*" (*Postmodernity* 236, emphasis in the original). Uber's exercise of geopower, then, represents a case in which capital succeeds in taking control of the very place where commodities are produced. Crucially, this takeover is made possible not by the instruments of the disciplinary society theorized by Foucault, but by the techniques of the society of control that Deleuze discusses in his "Post-scriptum sur les sociétés de contrôle."

spatiality. They are at the same time *in* a physical place—the urban area where they perform their services—and *on* the Uber platform—the online site whose gates (the login credentials and passwords needed for operating the application) filter the visitors coming from the outside. Indeed, the Uber platform is nothing other than a digitally constructed hyper-place. I would argue that the experience of space through a double-sided, *in*-and-*on* relation represents the distinctive trait of spatiality in the age of global capital. In the Uber driver's understanding of space, what matters is that the driver's agency dwindles in both aspects of his/her *in/on* experience (being *in* a place and operating *on* a platform). In Malpas's theory of space, by contrast, the structure of subjectivity coalesces in and through the structure of place; crucially, it is agency that becomes a key factor in this process, as it represents the catalyst around which the elements constitutive of subjectivity organize themselves: "Subjectivity . . . is to be understood as constituted in terms of an interplay of elements, organized specifically in relation to the concept of agency" (*Place and Experience* 175). What weakens Uber drivers' agency is the sheer lack of intentionality that characterizes their actions. Donald Davidson, who views intentionality as inseparable from agency, gives the example of a navy officer who falls against a button because a wave hits his battleship and upsets his balance; if this button sends a torpedo that in turn sinks the *Bismarck,* then "we will not count him as an agent" (54). If applied to Uber drivers, Davidson's example reveals that they, too, cannot be counted as agents. They indeed push the gas pedal and turn the steering wheel of their car, but the wave jostling them around by means of the asymmetric control of information and calibrated use of technology is the Uber software itself, the true agent in charge of the whole ride-"sharing" operation right from the start.

The depleted agency that defines the Uber driver's working experience also informs the hyper-spatiality that Lussault associates with the digitized environment of social networks. As digital communication represents an embodied experience, Lussault argues, the individual him/herself might become "a connected, and perfectly ubiquitous, hyper-place" (coda). Lussault supports his hypothesis through a reference to the adolescent practice of "networked publics," as theorized by social media scholar danah boyd. Boyd's research demonstrates how American teens are able to turn the Internet to their advantage by creating virtual places for their social interactions with their friends. One could counter boyd's argument by maintaining that "if one accepts that a meaningful notion of everyday life is inseparable from its fugitive anonymity, then it would be difficult to grasp what it might have in common with time spent in which one's gestures are all recorded, permanently archived, and processed with the aim of predetermining one's future choices and actions" (Crary 76). In spite of the wisdom of Crary's argument, the more uncomfortable aspect of boyd's narrative of present-day online socialization is that American youths are hanging out on the Internet due to their complete inability to meet in physical places.[7] Authorities, be they parents, police, or city administrators, have successfully managed, boyd argues, to exclude American teenagers from the places—malls and drive-ins—that used to be the hangouts of previous generations (20). Social networks "are the only 'public' places in which teens can easily congregate with large groups of their peers" (21).[8] There is no doubt that "humans can not only appropriate, but also cohabit the digital space," as Lussault maintains (coda). At the same time, the evidence provided by Lussault and boyd tells us that the young women and men who create new digital sanctuaries are in fact escaping from forces much stronger than themselves: "Today's teenagers have less freedom to wander than any previous generation" (boyd 86).[9]

As boyd summarizes, "By imagining teens as balls of uncontrollable hormones, society has systematically taken agency away from youth over the past century" (94). It seems that we are once again dealing with Davidson's navy officer and his sinking of the *Bismarck,* with the additional qualification that the spaces offered by the likes of Facebook or Instagram are panoptica to the nth power, in which users cohabit a

---

7. Some of the teens interviewed by boyd are well aware of their condition. Tara, a sixteen-year-old from Michigan, recognizes that "she would much prefer to hang out with her friends face to face but finds it impossible" (84). Boyd herself acknowledges that the teens she met "repeatedly indicated that they would much rather get together with friends in person" (85).

8. Boyd seems to underestimate the role played by interstitial places such as parks (especially those for skateboarding) as hangouts for youths.

9. "In 1969, 48 percent of children from kindergarten through eighth grade walked or biked to school compared to 12 percent who were driven by a family member. By 2009, those numbers had reversed; 13 percent walked or bicycled while 45 percent were driven" (boyd 87).

prestructured area crisscrossed by data mining tools—not exactly the conditions for the full exercise of one's own agency. It is the very technological environment in which social media carry out their operations that appears to generate the surplus of power and knowledge that they enjoy over their users. As Urry argues, the "miniaturized machines" that enable our digital transactions have a peculiar meaning: "Such machines means [sic] that inhabiting them is to be connected to, or to be at home with, 'sites' across the world—while simultaneously such sites can monitor, observe and trace each inhabited machines [sic]" (180).

In this environment, the Uber drivers' condition is, of course, particular: their specific relation with their employer in terms of workers' rights, ownership of the means of production, and legal status determines their spatial situation. What matters here is that their condition appears to be increasingly common among all workers employed by companies such as Lyft, Postmates, Amazon Mechanical Turk, Instacart, and Deliveroo, all of which operate in the growing sector of the on-demand, or gig, economy. What is more, as Scheiber argues, "using big data and algorithms to manage workers will not simply be a niche phenomenon. It may become one of the most common ways of managing the American labor force." Key to the current discussion is the idea that the Uber driver's weakened agency epitomizes a broader, present-day human condition.[10] In our time, as J. Nicholas Entrikin has written, "our technological control of nature emphasizes the global, the universal and the objective. . . . Such a view is unable to capture the importance of the moral uniqueness of the individual agent and the source of agency in the local, the particular and the subjective" (26). It is in the very nature of the hyper-place, aka the form that place assumes in the age of global capital, that this depletion of agency is rooted. The asymmetry of power framing the experience of hyper-places undermines the agency of their inhabitants, precisely as it does in the smartphone applications of the on-demand economy. In other words, in the last two decades, we have been all headed down the same slippery slope on which Uber drivers find themselves now.

---

10. Berardi approaches this condition from the point of view of a worker's juridical status in the age of global, digitized capital: "The worker's person is juridically free, but his time is enslaved. Rather than belonging to the worker, time is ready to use by the productive, recombinant cyberspace" (103).

Hyper-places bespeak the present asymmetry of power, starting from the fact that the messages they convey, whether written on eight-story screens, the display of smartphone applications, or directories and timetables, invariably travels in a single direction: from the management to the customer. In a hyper-place, the asymmetry of power is visible in the management's ability to police the borders of the site and direct the flow of information circulating within that site. Hyper-places are sanitized areas where entries from the outside are filtered at the gates. Among the hyper-places Lussault mentions, the strictest control clearly concerns airports. However, the "commercial urbanity" of all hyper-places relies on the premise that the undesirable population can/must be controlled. In Times Square, for instance, as Lussault notes, authorities manage to marginalize the marginals by confining them to the outskirts of the square (ch. 2). Secondly, hyper-places are panoptica. While discreetly hidden video-cameras dot the landscape of commercial districts, malls, airports, and train stations all over the world, in the virtual hyper-places of the Internet, web cookies and similar devices of digital surveillance transform essentially everything that users do into data to be recorded and stored. Strictly controlled borders and panoptical scrutiny make hyper-places radically different from places. There is no doubt that places can become hostile fortresses, as occurs with the homes, gated communities, and countries that contain their inhabitants within walls built to lock out the outsiders. However, places need not be so by default. Openness lies at the foundation of place, and walled versions of place are to be viewed as its degenerations. Counterintuitively, instead, in terms of filters, control, and surveillance, closedness becomes an inextricable component of the experience of the hyper-place.

In Times Square, selected clips from the footage recorded by surveillance cameras are displayed on the screen at regular intervals for the visitors' enjoyment: the latter can see themselves and delight in being seen by others. This mix of self-exhibition and voyeurism is a key ingredient in today's spectacle, as the widespread popularity of social networks demonstrates. In hyper-places and social networks alike, this combination also nurtures the illusion that the digitized traffic of information is equally divided into data moving away from customers and data arriving to them. In reality, however, it is clear that the management of hyper-places, social networks, and websites collects and stores the vast majority of all the data mined, usually with little or no knowledge on the part of the unwitting provider of information. In our time, data collection represents a vital operation for digitized capital. The ability to store and analyze enormous amounts of data is the most important asset in corporations such as Facebook, Google, or Uber. Nick Srnicek persuasively writes that "in the twenty-first century advanced capitalism came to be centred upon extracting and using a particular kind of raw material: data" (38).[11] From airports and malls to social networks and blogs, physical and digital hyper-places become ideal sites for the mining of data, while their users are transformed into nothing more than unpaid providers of the raw material.

The Crisis of Place in Our Time and the Novel of Displacement

While hyper-places are on the rise across the planet, places, understood in Malpas's definition as both the context framing and the ground sustaining subjectivity, appear to be an endangered species. As the impact of globalization and digitalization on our societies intensifies, establishing the interconnection between a place and its inhabitants, as Malpas theorized only two decades ago (*Place and Experience* came out in 1999), seems increasingly difficult, if not altogether impossible. The places that Malpas envisioned are today destabilized by the negative deterritorialization induced by the rise of global, software-enhanced capital. It is in the context of this deterritorialization that mobile communication and geographical mobility take a form that prevents all of us who have not settled on the Cloud from exercising agency; in other environments, mobility (in its various forms) could have led to different results, more favorable to the development of human subjectivity. In this respect, it is sufficient to remind us that in a world of mobile communication "our behavior is increasingly shaped and directed by bureaucratic management systems both corporate and governmental; . . . we are increasingly imprisoned within a network of often electroni-

---

11. On data mining in the context of Geographic Information Systems, Lapenta makes insightful observations: "Geomedia and virtual maps can be considered as the instruments enabling the capitalization, or control, of the new immaterial commodities, and digital identities that dominate these new social environments" (224).

cally mediated consumption and commodification" (Malpas, "Place of Mobility" 35). As for physical mobility, for millions, it does not result from a free choice, but of sheer necessity, as circumstances lying outside the control of the majority of those who move around the world (aka migrants) determine their decision to leave their homes. As John Urry observes, when "mobility is engendered by the instability of economic, social and environmental structures and especially the weakness of local states" what migrants experience is "forced migration" (36).[12] Being the emplaced species that we are, however, we still seem to have a need for place. In this respect, Lussault's discussion of hyper-places has the irrefutable merit of demonstrating how place remains crucial even in the new existential and technological conditions that frame the experience of being a human in our time.

In his introduction to *Place and Experience,* Malpas mentions the relation of Aboriginal Australians to place as epitomizing the ties connecting individuals to their land. For an Aboriginal person, "to be removed from that country to which he or she belongs is for them to be deprived of their very substance, and in past times such removal ... frequently led to sickness and death" (3).[13] Since the industrial revolution and the subsequent waves of mass migration, human communities have developed in a manner that moves inexorably away from the situation that Malpas describes. The advent of global capital has brought about a remarkable leap in this development. This leap can be represented synthetically as a move from place—the open region where agency and subjectivity grow together in and through their unequivocal relation to an individualized space—to hyper-place—the fenced area where subjectivity is partially diluted, space is shared by thou-

---

12. On migrants' agency in our time, Sandro Mezzadra provides a different argument: "Present-day migrations are increasingly characterized by their *autonomy,* not in the sense that one should debunk the importance of the structural reasons for migration, but because of the growing awareness and obstinacy demonstrated by the women and men who are migrating" (emphasis in the original).

13. Australian Aboriginals were not alone in experiencing separation from their place as a cause for disease. In this respect, the origin of the word "nostalgia" is illuminating. This term was coined in 1678 by J. Hofer in his doctoral dissertation at the University of Bâle. Hofer was the first scholar to consider homesickness as a disease (McCann 165). In Hofer's time, nostalgia struck in particular Swiss mercenary soldiers who missed the sight of their mountains while fighting abroad. In allusion to this fact, the malady was frequently called *Schweizerkrankheit* (Swiss disease) during the seventeenth and eighteenth centuries (169).

sands or even millions of individuals, and agency is depleted. Novels of displacement narrate *il sottile dispiacere*, the subtle regret that stems from this paradigm shift; they convey the sadness that our precarious habitation traces upon our lives, despite the glittering lights of Times Square and our digitally augmented faculties.[14] It may appear paradoxical that a genre such as the modern novel, marked by a two-century-long practice of territoriality, can shift so agilely to the representation of displacement, the mood caused by the weakening of that particular territory we call place. However, it is exactly because for centuries novelists have stubbornly situated their works within a place that the novel is provided with the necessary tools for tackling all phenomena related to place, including its crisis. As the genre that began in *un lugar de la Mancha* and has since linked its development to an incredibly diverse array of fictional and real places (from Austen's Bath and Eliot's Middlemarch to Bolaño's Santa Teresa, via Achebe's Umuofia and Garcia Marquez's Macondo), the modern novel is the fittest cultural form for representing the changes in the conception and practice of place that we have experienced in these last four decades. As an emplaced literary practice, the novel is clearly affected by the shifting nature of place in our time. After all, narrating the imbrication of characters and places has been a staple of novelistic writing since Cervantes. If the counterpart of this imbrication in the real world—that is to say the relation between subjectivity and place—is undergoing a change as radical as that occurring in the age of global capital, then the novel cannot help but be displaced. Novels of displacement are self-reflecting narratives geared toward the rendering of the widespread displacement in which they themselves participate.

From a historical perspective, the novel of displacement is intrinsically entwined with developments in the novelistic representation of space within the last two centuries. In the age of realism, novelists described space with the precision of cartographers. They provided readers with viable directions for creating visual images of city and country landscapes as well as domestic interiors. In the age of modernism, instead, writers such as Joyce and Woolf deliberately disoriented their readers. They did so by allowing readers to access spatial features

---

14. I borrow *"il sottile dispiacere"* from the lyrics of "Emozioni," a song written in 1970 by Mogol (Giulio Rapetti) and Lucio Battisti.

through the minds and eyes of *flâneurs* like Leopold Bloom or Clarissa Dalloway, who embodied both distracted observers and, at the same time, well-rooted inhabitants of their environment (Bulson 13–14). Neither the realist nor the modernist strategy for rendering space function successfully in novels of displacement, in which displaced subjectivity supplants both the accurate cartographer of the age of realism, and the distracted but still emplaced *flâneur* of modernism. The existential difference between the latter and the hero of the novel of displacement cannot be stressed firmly enough. While the Blooms and the Dalloways of the modernist novels inevitably return home at the end of the day, no safe haven awaits the roaming protagonists of the novels of displacement. This very placelessness, however, can become a favorable condition for grasping the spatial relations that function in our age. In this respect, Tally argues that "the displaced person is understandably more attuned to matters of place" (13). In the same passage, Tally also quotes a letter in which J. R. R. Tolkien writes that "a fish out of water is the only fish that has an inkling of water" (13).[15] Heroes of the novels of displacement are, in fact, fish out of water. Either by groping blindly through space or by sketching virtual maps in dialogues, monologues, or inner thoughts, they strive to reconnoiter the territories where their adventures unfold. Readers can metaphorically relate the fictional adventures of these characters to their own experiences in the real world, with displacement functioning as the common term shared by both the fictional story and the actual experience. Here the gain is pragmatic: by following along with the fictional characters as they attempt to handle displacement, readers can obtain helpful hints on how (or how not) to orient themselves in real life, when place disappears entirely and space becomes an opaque morass.

In the next chapter, I will discuss the treatment of space and place in Daniel Sada's *Porque parece mentira* and Zadie Smith's *White Teeth*. My discussion will focus on two elements: (1) the fictional representations of home along with its associated practices—staying, leaving, return-

---

15. A similar argument is made by Eric Bulson in his comment on Benjamin's "A Berlin Chronicle": "When we are too familiar with a place, we stop seeing it, but when we lose direction the 'signboards and street names, passersby, roofs, kiosks, or bars' become present in the landscape" (109).

ing, and/or losing one's home—and (2) the characters' attempts at orienting themselves in space. As an embodiment of the territoriality of the domestic space, home is key to the process whereby subjectivity situates itself within the world. In traditional societies, as John Berger writes, "without a home at the center of the real, one was not only shelterless, but also lost in non-being, in unreality. Without a home everything was fragmentation" (51). From a phenomenological point of view, Gaston Bachelard also maintains that home lies at the center of our attempts to construct ourselves as stable beings. Differently from Berger's anthropological approach, Bachelard theorizes a type of centrality that transcends history and is not related to a particular stage in the development of human societies: "Home consists in a body of images that give the human being the reason for, or an illusion of, stability" (34). In our time, we are well aware that simply viewing home as the keystone in the process of our self-orientation leaves aside most of what actually occurs within the domestic space. First and foremost, home constitutes the stage where power conflicts between genders and/or generations break forth. Home can function as such because of its boundedness, according to Sack's theorization: as a bounded place, home can be turned into a territory by "asserting control" over it (16). Rather than a site dominated by male, dictatorial control, as it was in Balzac's narrations, today's home is the arena for the unfolding of a contested type of territoriality; this evolution also explains why the novel is undergoing a process of domestic deterritorialization. No longer the "peaceful" center of our lives, home has become the site where we first experience conflict; despite (or because) of this, home is still a crucial component of our being. As the first plot of land we learn to survey, home remains the focus of our geographies.

As Miguel de Beistegui argues, orientation represents a crucial factor in our experience of the world, since directionality defines the spatiality of our existence: "Existence is always directed at something, intrinsically directional: right, left, up, down, above, beneath, behind, in front are all according to something encountered there, and it is that very thing, in its relation to an embodied existence as proto-place, that provides Dasein with its sense of direction" (147). Similarly, in Kant's thought, the way human beings orient themselves spatially lies at the foundation of all their subsequent exercises of orientation, in particular that logical orientation required for the process of thinking (4–6).[16] Novels of displacement narrate their characters' efforts to make sense of spaces increasingly deprived of places (in Malpas's sense of the term). By assessing their fictional heroes' dislocation and documenting their attempts to find a way out, novels of displacement decode territories that are the fictional counterparts of the deterritorialized spaces created by global capital and software in the real world.

---

16. See also Casey: "The purpose of navigating and getting oriented is to transform an apparently vacuous expanse, a Barren Ground of unmarked space, into a set of what can only properly be called *places* (even if these places still lack proper names)" (*Getting Back* 28, emphasis in the original).

CHAPTER 5

Lost in Space

Daniel Sada's *Porque parece mentira la verdad nunca se sabe* and Zadie Smith's *White Teeth*

The two novels I discuss in this chapter narrate stories set in different sociopolitical contexts. Daniel Sada's *Porque parece mentira* unfolds in Northern Mexico, a territory ruled by opaque, mafia-like powers. Smith's *White Teeth,* instead, takes place in North London, in urban areas where immigrant communities are torn by conflicting political and cultural allegiances. The spatial contexts in which the two narratives occur also appear to be different in nature: primarily public in Sada's novel, and chiefly domestic in Smith's work. Despite their structural differences, these two novels share a common narrative motif: their characters' lack of agency, which becomes the source of their displacement. The very fact that characters in these novels share a common condition, even while living in distinct sociopolitical contexts and in differently organized spaces, motivates and guides my discussion. The emergence of the same frame of mind in such distinct political and spatial situations will strengthen my argument for considering displacement as both a crucial component in contemporary novels and a key mood in our time.

Absolute Power in Daniel Sada's
Porque parece mentira

Porque parece mentira is set in the fictional state of Capila, a vast territory of deserts and mountains south of the Texas border. Capila is part of Mágico, a country whose currency has abruptly devalued, as we are told toward the end of the novel: the allusion to the recurrent crises the Mexican peso has undergone since 1982 is clear. The geographical position and monetary predicament allow us to identify Mágico with Mexico (the names of the two countries also rhyme and in Spanish carry an accent on the third-to-last syllable), while Capila echoes Coahuila, a northern Mexican state bordering on Texas (Zavala 29). It is worth noting that while the names of all the geographical locations in Capila are fictional, those on the northern side of the border are real: San Antonio, Dallas, Brownsville, Austin, Orlando, as well as the states of Texas and Florida.

Porque parece mentira constitutes a complex, rhizomatic assemblage: ninety characters participate in the narrative, each of them contributing to the text with his/her own storyline and the idiosyncrasies of his/her language.[1] By narrating these characters' stories, Sada carries out his project of "creating a farcical mix of geographically, stylistically, and structurally heterogeneous elements" (Espinoza 67). Within this assemblage, four storylines stand out. The initial thread, which represents the narrative backbone of the novel, begins with the event that puts the plot in motion: a robbery of ballot boxes in Remadrín on Election Day (165).[2] Subsequently, the Army opens fire on a march on the state capital to protest the robbery and kills an unknown number of demonstrators. After the massacre, the bodies of the dead are loaded onto a truck and carried around the state to be delivered to their relatives. Later in the novel, while the truck continues its journey, the names of the authorities responsible for the robbery (General Torreblanca) and for the massacre (Governor Bermúdez) are revealed (241, 442).

---

1. In an interview with José Manuel Prieto, Sada claims to have decided to narrate the adventures of ninety characters out of his sheer amazement at the ability of the nineteenth-century novel to incorporate entire galleries of characters (58).

2. In an interview with Raúl Silva, Sada recounts that the first time he went to vote, the ballot boxes were stolen right in front of him.

Among the characters involved in this storyline, Papías and Salomón González play a crucial role. They link the robbery of the ballot boxes to another storyline, this time concerning their parents, Trinidad and Cecilia, and their grandfather, Juan Filoteo. Within the González family, the children's rebellion against their fathers represents a recurring event. While the greedy Trinidad clashes with Filoteo on money-related issues, Papías and Salomón despise their father's conservatism and join the progressive Party of *Dignidad*. In so doing, they engage in the struggle against "a tremendous, irremediable poverty and the fate of receiving handout-like wages for centuries and centuries" (20). It is as political activists that Papías and Salomón join the rally against electoral fraud and disappear when the Army disperses the march. A third storyline concerns Egrencito, a bellhop in Remadrín's sole telephone office. Furious at being passed over for the position of office director after his boss's death, Egrencito escapes being murdered by a city clerk (the city's mayor, Don Romeo Pomar, commissioned the hit) and then heads north. However, rather than crossing the border into the United States, he returns to Remadrín along with another drifter, Conrado Lúa. This time, Egrencito plans to murder Don Romeo Pomar. Finally, the fourth storyline focuses on this same Romeo Pomar, a politician who embodies the worst elements of *caciquismo*. Corrupt, violent, and authoritarian, Romeo Pomar puts his political clout to the service of his private business. Toward the end of the novel, Governor Pío Bermúdez instructs his thugs to kill both Romeo Pomar and his wife. It remains unknown, however, whether or not this order was executed (557).

These four storylines amount to a scant sample of the innumerable threads of events that intertwine with one another in the novel. Alejandro Espinoza finds a fitting spatial metaphor for the novel's structure when he argues that *Porque parece mentira* goes around in circles: the story of the bodies carried around in the truck represents the primary, largest circle, while the other stories inscribe smaller circles attached to the first. Other minor circumferences, in turn, link to these smaller circles (67). In addition to helping us to picture the characters' movements within the novel, the image of the circle effectively visualizes a motif that runs deeply throughout all the narrated storylines: the impossibility of reaching a conclusion. Not a single story in Sada's novel arrives at an actual end point. As the narrative leaves its characters either stranded in the middle of nowhere or back where they began, what readers experience is an uncomfortable sense of helplessness. The spirals traced by the lives of Sada's characters are the narrative counterparts of a feature Espinoza discovers in the novel's linguistic fabric: its *barroquismo*. However, it is not only the language that consists in "ornamental flights that rise up into the air and get lost in the process" but also the narrative itself (Espinoza 69). A mutual sense of inconclusiveness runs through the sentences (language), the characters' lives (content), and the stories (narrative), stitching together every level of the novel into a coherent assemblage marked by impotence and disorientation.

This widespread helplessness is congruous with the context that frames each character's storyline in Sada's novel: a society utterly dominated by an almighty, unchecked power. The circle of "Los de arriba," or the decision makers in Capila (in a reverse citation of Mariano Azuela's foundational 1916 novel, *Los de abajo*), indeed represents the prime mover of all the events narrated in *Porque parece mentira*. In the novel, power is so unreachable that the face(s) and aims of it remain unknown to everyone, including the novel's various narrators.[3] The novel recounts how bureaucracy, the Army, the police, and paramilitary groups behave as tools of power, but never describes how this power truly functions. Readers learn nothing about its internal structure, nor are they privy to the decisional bodies that elaborate long-term strategies and instigate movements on the ground. All in all, in Sada's novel, readers meet just three representatives of power, all made visible by their public role: the already mentioned Don Romeo Pomar; his rival, the businessman Abel Lupicinio Rosas; and Pío Bermúdez, Capila's governor. Holder of the highest political office in the state, Pío Bermúdez is a *cacique* to the power of two. In addition to treating elected mayors as pawns to be moved at his will, he shows complete disrespect for the electoral process, plans assassinations, and orders mass murders. Despite his authoritarian image, however, he also appears to be a puppet in the hands of his wife, Purísima de la Selva. It

---

3. Oswaldo Zavala notes that each of the fifteen periods (each period comprises a variable number of chapters) that divide the novel is narrated by at least one distinct narrator. As the novel proceeds, the differences between these narrators grow so as to "radically modify the context for the narrative" (28).

is Purísima who has the governor kneel before the bishop of Brinquillo to confess his crimes, in a literary reproduction of Michael Corleone's confession to Cardinal Lamberto in Francis Ford Coppola's *The Godfather Part III* (1990).

In *Porque parece mentira*, every discernible symbol of power must conform to an even more formidable authority, as Governor Bermúdez's mix of public strength and domestic weakness demonstrates. The fact is that power is faceless by default, which prevents the text from characterizing any one individual as the possessor of unchecked authority. It is this very facelessness that differentiates power in Sada's novel from its appearance in Latin American literature before the 1980s. In those years, the dictator, "a paternal figure who in turn embodies yet another figure, the *macho*," personified power (González Echevarría, *The Voice of the Masters* 66). And this personification occurred even in postmodern novels still requiring the totemic figure of the dictator, if only to perform on him "the cancellation of a central authority" (82). The anonymous power we encounter in *Porque parece mentira* signals that we have moved to a new era, our own age of financial capital, in which the network becomes the metaphor for power's inner structure, its way of relating to society, and its ability to envelop the body social. In Sada's novel, what matters is not the person who happens to exercise power, but the invisible, round-the-clock presence of power networks in every corner of society. This type of power resists identification with any particular individual who happens momentarily to possess it. In this context, being surrounded by an aura of mystery represents power's principle feature (as well as its most remarkable asset), the second being the utter contempt it shows toward its subjects. In the novel, the political machine running Remadrín, "whose strong point was to despise what was going on in the streets and the central square," embodies this attitude (169, 304). Fittingly, the man who sits atop this machine, Mayor Romeo Pomar, asks himself: "What was the use of killing those poor losers [the demonstrators who protested electoral fraud] other than to show to others like them, in the future, that massive and paranoid rallies of that kind have no reason to take place?" (220). "Nothing can break the cynicism that is inherent in power," aptly comments the narrator of the fourth section of Sada's novel, after narrating the robbery of the ballot boxes

(169). The unmeasurable distance that separates political authorities from their subjects in the state of Capila fictionalizes the increasingly large gap that has been dividing the powerful from the powerless in societies all over the world after the 1980s. It is this gap—itself a consequence of the accumulation of wealth, knowledge, and authority in the hands of a few corporations dealing with software and global finance—that generates displacement in both the fictional landscape of Sada's novel and the real world.

In *Porque parece mentira,* the gulf yawning between power and its subjects appears to grow even larger if one considers the supranational character of the former. In a fictional northern Mexican state, this quality obviously calls into question the relation tying local authorities to the United States. In Sada's novel, this connection appears to be solidly in place. Powerless characters who plan to emigrate to the United States experience all the difficulties of crossing the border illegally, while Governor Bermúdez seems to encounter no problem whatsoever in fetching prostitutes from Brownsville to his ranch or moving Romeo Pomar to Dallas (153, 132). The existence of solid ties between the powerful elite in Capila and their counterparts on the northern side of the border is confirmed when four men from Texas show up in Governor Bermúdez's ranch and are entrusted with the delicate mission of bringing Mayor Pomar back to Remadrín (482). All in all, however, the novel demonstrates but never emphasizes the existence of a link between the authorities in Capila and occult centers of power in the United States. Even in dealing with this issue, *Porque parece mentira* reveals itself to be a product of the age of global capital. In other words, the novel is not set in the era of imperialism but of Empire. As Hardt and Negri maintain, "The imperial expansion has nothing to do with imperialism, nor with those state organisms designated for conquest, pillage, genocide, colonization, and slavery" (166). In Latin America, imperialism corresponds to the age of dictators—tyrants within their domestic borders, but puppets in the hands of neocolonial power on the international stage. Nowadays, imperialism belongs to the past, as "Empire extends and consolidates the model of network power" (167). This kind of networked power, able to transcend national borders and to resist being arranged in a geographically structured hierarchy, is at play in Sada's novel.

Achronic Time and Cartesian Space in
Porque parece mentira

In a text whose narrative structure consists in a cluster of neverending, independent narrative spirals, it comes as no surprise that readers of *Porque parece mentira* would experience fictional time as sheer chaos. This jumbled apprehension of time becomes part of an authorial strategy: destabilizing the novel's temporal fabric in order to engender the reader's displacement. What Sada does in *Porque parece mentira* is the intentional sabotage of the very gist of any narrative that is intended as a story that develops in time. This operation targets the reader, as the one who ultimately is displaced in a novel whose time cannot be decoded. As I will discuss later in this chapter, the characters' displacement, instead, takes on an utterly different course, originating in the abstract, geometrical representation of space in the novel. In order to unpack the temporal disorder that unsettles Sada's novel, I want to bring in Gérard Genette's analysis of temporal order in fictional texts. At the foundation of Genette's discussion lies a view of fiction as a signifying system articulated on two levels: the *story* and the *narrative*. While the former stands for "the signified or narrative content," the latter expresses the signifier (27). The temporal order of the story corresponds to the chronological succession that events represented in the text would follow in our own empirical reality (in which watches and calendars measure time), while the narrative order corresponds to the sequence that those same events create when arranged for expressive purposes. By comparing the two orders, one can discover the fictional text's *anachronies,* or violations of the chronological order (in a Newtonian sense) that characterize a narrative: flashbacks or *analepses,* flashforwards or *prolepses.* Comparing story time and narrative time can make sense only "to the extent that the story order is explicitly indicated by the narrative itself or inferable from one or another indirect clue" (35). This type of inference, Genette argues, "becomes useless for certain extreme cases . . . , where temporal reference is deliberately sabotaged" (35). Sada's novel represents one of these unusual instances: it renders time through such a complex mix of flashbacks and flashforwards that readers cannot count on any narrative order whatsoever to infer the chronological succession of the events arranged within the plot.

Porque parece mentira presents an incredibly rich array of narrative sequences aimed at sabotaging temporal reference. The novel's third period provides an eloquent sample of this disruption. At Genette's narrative level, a simplified sequence of the temporal segments comprising the period is as follows:

1. Election Day in Remadrín
2. In the wake of the elections, Romeo Pomar orders Dora Ríos, the manager of the telephone office in Remadrín, to block all calls coming from outside the city
3. Trinidad and Cecilia's twenty-fifth wedding anniversary
4. Election Day in Remadrín
5. Romeo Pomar's political career
6. Election Day in Remadrín
7. Death of Dora Ríos, three months after the Election Day fraud
8. Egrencito quits the telephone office and goes to City Hall to file a complaint against his former colleague, Enguerrando, now his boss
    a. Meanwhile Sanjuana, Romeo Pomar's secretary, exchanges a kiss with her boyfriend, a government clerk
9. Romeo Pomar orders Crisóstomo, a city clerk, to take Egrencito in his car, drive him to the desert, and kill him
10. In the aftermath of the massacre that followed the robbery of the ballot boxes, Romeo Pomar refuses to step down
11. Sanjuana's boyfriend dumps her and then spreads gossip about their relationship
    a. Egrencito is one of his confidants
12. Romeo Pomar orders Crisóstomo to take Sanjuana's former boyfriend outside the city and kill him
    a. Crisóstomo returns alone
13. Don Romeo comes under pressure to clarify what happened to the demonstrators who are now *desaparecidos*
14. Trinidad and Cecilia's twenty-fifth wedding anniversary
15. In a car on the way to the desert, Egrencito shoots Crisóstomo and then flees to the mountains.

Before analyzing this sequence, a premise is necessary: with the exception of segment 7, in which a reference is made to the three months that have passed after Election Day, the text does not provide temporal markers—such as "after," "before," or "meanwhile"—to assist the reader in deciphering the temporal relations between the various narrative segments. These relations are to be inferred only from the internal logic of the events. The first of these inferences concerns segments 1, 4, and 6: the facts narrated in these segments take place in the conventional present of the novel, as the robbery of the ballot boxes is the incident that puts the entire plot in motion. Segments 3 and 5 are logically situated in the novel's conventional past, even though the text does not provide hints for defining their reciprocal positions. With respect to the novel's conventional present, segments 7–13, plus 15, occur past it, while 3, 5, and 14 are *analepses*, or jumps to the past. As the almost complete lack of temporal markers prevents readers from reconstructing the temporal order of the novel's *story* (in Genette's sense), the time of the *narrative* stands on its own, as a fictional construction disconnected from that of our worldly experience. In Sada's novel, what occurs in the rendering of time corresponds to the act of constructing its language: while narrative time achieves independence from chronological time, literary language liberates itself from the task of representing empirical reality. As Oswaldo Zavala notes, "An unusual view of the universe that cannot be found in the direct experience of reality" is what Sada seeks in the words he combines in his literary prose (28).

The disconnection of the time of the narrative from that of our worldly experience, however, does not represent the most egregious sabotage of temporal reference in this section of Sada's novel; a far more serious violation consists in a chronological inconsistency hidden in the segments 8–13, plus 15. In 8, when Egrencito meets Romeo Pomar, Sanjuana's boyfriend is still dating her. Thus, 11 must take place after 8 in order to give the boyfriend time to dump the secretary and chat about it with Egrencito. However, this cannot be, because Egrencito leaves the city for good immediately after the meeting with Romeo Pomar (segment 9): there is no time for him to be the recipient of the boyfriend's gossip. We arrive at the same inconsistency if we consider that Egrencito kills Crisóstomo at the end of a trip to the desert, which began at City Hall on the mayor's order. Then, how could Crisóstomo have killed Sanjuana's boyfriend, who is kissing her when Egrencito comes to Romeo Pomar's office shortly before leaving with Crisóstomo for a journey from which this same Crisóstomo would never return? The plot of this portion of Sada's novel would makes sense only if the reader could postulate the existence of parallel words in the style of Philip K. Dick's *The Man in the High Castle* (1962): one world in which Egrencito leaves Remadrín, and another in which he remains in the city; a world in which Crisóstomo is killed by Egrencito, and another in which he survives to kill Sanjuana's boyfriend. This assumption would make no sense in the case of *Porque parece mentira,* since the text never implements a deliberate strategy aimed at fostering the reader's apprehension of alternate timelines, as occurs in Dick's novel. Nor can the presence of two conflicting narrative times in *Porque parece mentira* be explained in terms of magical realism, as the latter's cultural and aesthetic tenets are completely absent from the text. What occurs in Sada's novel is the fact that temporal inconsistencies, a lack of time markers, and uncontrollable anachronies prevent even the most sophisticated reader from interpreting the narrative as a chronologically arranged story. *Porque parece mentira* disengages "its arrangement from all the dependence, even inverse dependence, on the chronological sequence of the story it tells" (Genette 84). Because of this disengagement, in Sada's novel, narrative time can be defined legitimately as *achrony,* Genette's term for events, or sequences of events, which appear to be "dateless and ageless" (84).

In Sada's novel, since the various timelines that interweave themselves into the text's temporal fabric comprise events that are often simultaneous, the space where these events occur emerges as a stratified coalescence of different temporalities. What occurs in *Porque parece mentira* follows a recurrent pattern in the cultural products of modernity, whereby the demise of temporal sequence leads to the emphasis on space. This pattern is present in works as diverse as John Snow's map of London and Marcel Proust's *À la récherche du temps perdu.* As for the former, in 1854 John Snow identified the source of a cholera outbreak in London by drawing a map in which he represented "the number and the locations of victims . . . on what is called a dot map." In so doing, he "de-emphasize[d] sequence, or time, and instead emphasize[d] location" (Turchi 84). The same demotion of time occurs in Proust's *Récherche,* toward the end of "Combray" (the first section of *Du côté de chez Swann*), when spatial elements dominate the representation as narrative time moves toward *achrony*. Rather than being temporally arranged, "the narrative order is governed by the opposition Méséglise way/Guermantes way, and by the increasing distance of the sites from the family home in the course of an atemporal and synthetic walk" (Genette 84). Joseph Frank succinctly captures Proust's spatiotemporal arrangement when he writes that "in the case of Proust . . . his use of spatial form arose from an attempt to communicate the extratemporal quality of these revelatory moments" (58). Differently from what occurs in Proust's *Récherche*, in Sada's novel, *achrony* does not originate in the seesawing between past, present, and future, as occurs in the first person narrator's consciousness, but rather in the very nature of time, ontologically characterized by multiplicity, as in Egrencito's and Crisóstomo's two incompatible storylines. It is not time as experienced, but time as it is that turns out to be achronic in *Porque parece mentira*.

In the presence of ontological *achrony* within *Porque parece mentira*, spatiality emerges as the novel's key structuring force. The novel's emphasis on space becomes plainly evident if one considers that a narrative so reluctant to provide temporal markers appears instead quite prodigal of spatial indicators, be they the directions guiding the readers through the novel's barren spaces; the utilization of the truck carrying the bodies of the murdered demonstrators as a circular, unifying motif in the narrative; the diligent naming of all the locations through which the novel unfolds; or the representation of the characters' developments in terms of mappable journeys. The geographical arrangement of the truck's journey constitutes an excellent example of the narrative's ability to function as a map. As this arrangement is delineated early in the narrative, it provides readers with crucial information for the visualization of the novel's space. Later in the novel, the narrator disguises another endeavor to detail the novel's geography within the account of the Army's operations in the aftermath of the massacre, which functions as a sketchy but effective map of the territory where the events unfold: "The traffic was diverted several kilometers before the fork where the road to Fierrorey splits off from the one headed to Brinquillo." The Army also established a blockade outside Brinquillo, before Villa Dunas, to stop traffic heading north. Thus, drivers who wanted to go north had to make a long detour to reach Fierrorey and then continue through Misas, Pompocha, and Múnriz (87).

The novel thematizes its own mapping project through a minor character, Hermenegildo Buenrostro, a cartographer who makes a living by selling maps. He enters the narrative in the novel's eleventh period, when he sells a map to Conrado Lúa on his way back to Remadrín. Hermenegildo's map is accompanied by a written document comprising statistical data on all the animals living in the state, a detailed description of all the roads, and a table of the distances between towns and villages. This addendum translates the indecipherable landscape of Capila into a barely readable text. Rather than building knowledge, Hermenegildo's document represents another case of *barroquismo*, the practice of convoluted, self-referential writing that bears on the written word in Sada's novel. The creation of this document does not seem to justify the name of "messiah," which a disoriented Conrado Lúa confers on Hermenegildo Buenrostro (462). What makes the map seller deserving of this title, instead, is a gesture of radical cartography that he performs by drawing a line across his map from east to west so as to connect six towns ("Metedores-Pulemania-La Caricia-Remadrín-Piélagos-El Nopal Solo") and to divide the state into "two perfect halves" (439). By way of this drastic simplification, Hermenegildo manifests a cartographic principle succinctly stated by Peter Turchi: "Maps are defined by what they include but are often more revealing in what they exclude" (29).

The east-west line created by Hermenegildo Buenrostro intersects at a right angle with the other straight line present in the text, this time going from south to north, from Brinquillo to Múnriz. This line connects the locations mentioned in the description of the Army's operations after the massacre of the demonstrators. The geometrical figure of the cross, generated by the intersection of these two perpendiculars, represents the spatial archetype of the novel, the *ur-map* presiding over the organization of space in *Porque parece mentira*. As I discussed in chapter 1, we owe to Harley the recognition of mapping as a practice of power, based on the capacity of maps to affect users with their inner logic. Maps are to be considered for their "effects of abstraction, uniformity, repeatability, and visuality in shaping mental structures and in imparting a sense of the places in the world" (166). This being the case, what kind of spatial understanding does Sada's *ur-map* convey to the readers of his novel? And how does this spatial comprehension combine with the novel's temporality, given the inexorable interdependence of space and time in the late twentieth-century conceptualization of our worldly experience?

Spacetime and Displacement

A novel whose spatiality is informed by two perpendicular intersecting lines leads to a Cartesian understanding of space. It is a type of space that appears to be "fundamentally grid-like" and approachable through "geometrical coordinates" indicating "the part of that space that is a given body or bodies" (Tally 27).[4] By presenting readers with a universe in which Cartesian, geometrically readable space coexists with labyrinthine time, the novel fosters an understanding of its characters as entities moving in space rather than developing in time: *achrony* precludes the possibility of interpreting the characters' adventures as temporal sequences, while Cartesian coordinates, instead, allow the readers to pinpoint their positions in space and trace their movements.[5] Readers of Sada's novel can hardly venture a guess as to when an event occurs but can always determine where it takes place. Temporal *barroquismo* coexists with geometric space, just as, in the seventeenth century, the spirals in baroque visual arts lived alongside the grid of Cartesian coordinates. In the novel, the baroque spiral physically overlaps Cartesian perpendiculars as the truck carrying the demonstrators' bodies contin-

---

4. In the experience of space, the grid points toward both the past and the present. As Aldo-José Altamirano notes, grid-like spatiality defined the urban space in colonial times, when Philip II's "*Leyes de Indias*" established a uniform model for urban planning throughout Latin America: "From the sixteenth century to the nineteenth century, Hispanic colonial urbanism turns the chessboard into a universal urban model for the entire continent: everything must conform to the same model, as the *Leyes de Indias* clearly dictates" (20). At the same time, grid-like spatiality defines space in the age of GPS. This space is characterized by what Jeff Malpas defines as quantitative relationality. This type of relationality does not concern places but positions. It operates as a purely spatialized idea of the sort exemplified in systems of coordinate geometry: it "does not work through the heterogeneous, horizontal structure of place, but rather through the essentially homogeneous, leveled-out structure of position and so of extended spatiality" ("Place of Mobility" 34).

5. The grid-like spatiality that characterizes Sada's novel corresponds to Harvey's "absolute space": it is the space of Newton and Descartes, that of Euclid and of all manners of cadastral mapping. Socially, it is the space of private property and other bounded designations ("Space as a Key Word" 121).

ues to inscribe circles on Capila's geometrically divided space. A similar coexistence of opposing configurations also defines the characters' and the readers' distinct responses to the contradictory spacetime of the novel. Readers are lost in the novel's time, but can easily orient themselves in its space. Characters, instead, while obviously untouched by how their own timeline is edited and pieced together at the narrative level, find themselves irremediably lost in the novel's geometric space, a disorientation that occurs because there is no room for place (in Malpas's sense) within the Cartesian grid. When Hermenegildo Buenrostro effaces the human presence in Capila by cleaving his map in half, he translates into a spatial language the absolute displacement of the novel's characters.

There is not a single character in Sada's novel who can relate to space in the manner described by Malpas. No character manages to project him/herself onto a portion of space of his/her choosing in order to turn it into a place, where he/she could make room for belongings and live as a being among other beings. Put bluntly, nobody dwells in *Porque parece mentira*. In his discussion of the geographical turn of the human sciences after 1989, Edward W. Soja upholds "an explicitly situated ontology in which existence and spatiality are combined through intentional and creative acts inherent to being-in-the-world, entering into relations, involvement. This existential spatiality gives to being a place, a positioning within the 'life world' (Edmund Husserl's *Lebenswelt*)." Existence means "*emplacement*" (emphasis in the original), "a passionate process that links subject and object, Human Being and Nature, the individual and the environment, human geography and human history" (134). There is no room for Soja's *emplacement* in *Porque parece mentira*. In Sada's novel, sooner or later all of the key characters are forced to leave the locality where their existence is situated; in other words, the novel programmatically dismantles place, thus carrying out by narrative means the same operation that Cartesian spatiality executes at a conceptual level.

In *Porque parece mentira*, the most efficient of the narrative tools for disrupting place is the systematic deconstruction of home: home becomes the site where people commit suicide, relatives fight with each other over money, and children spit in the face of their fathers. Above all, home, in the dual sense of the family's house and hometown, is a place to be abandoned, as the people of Remadrín do during the mass exodus that follows the military occupation of the town (507). However, what makes the displacement of Sada's characters absolute is not their forced expulsion from their homes, but their inability to settle down somewhere else. It is not the eviction from but the obliteration of home that allows for absolute placelessness in Sada's novel.

To better understand the connection linking the deconstruction of home to absolute displacement, I want to briefly touch upon Cormac McCarthy's *No Country for Old Men* (2005), another story set in the region neighboring the US–Mexico border, albeit this time on the Texan side. Four of the novel's five main characters either lose their home for good or eschew the very experience of living at home. They are "young" characters who do not belong to the generation of "Old Men" mentioned in the novel's title. Their irreversible homelessness originates in events and practices somewhat related to narco-trafficking. Despite the sweeping deterritorialization that narco-trafficking and drug addiction bring to the country, the novel still pivots around its physical as well as ethical center: Ed Tom Bell, the Sheriff of Terrell County (the fifth main character). Sheriff Bell is the only relevant character in the story whose life hooks to a solid anchor, in the form of a patriarchal home: "When he (Sheriff Bell) pulled up in the driveway behind the house his wife was looking out from the kitchen window. She smiled at him" (136). The existence of a character like Sheriff Bell, firmly situated in a place he can call home, prevents displacement from assuming an absolute dimension in *No Country for Old Men*. It is only in the novel's last episode, when the Sheriff retires, that absolute displacement begins to loom over Terrell County. As the deterritorialized country becomes a forbidding environment for "Old Men" like Sheriff Bell, his generation surrenders to younger, intrinsically homeless individuals. An epitome of the latter is Anton Chigurh, the placeless and amoral killer who emerges as the ultimate winner in the struggle between law and crime in Terrell County.

Contrary to what occurs in *No Country for Old Men*, no character can count on a solid and enduring relation to home in *Porque parece mentira*. In the latter, since the narrative systematically dismantles the very idea of home, displacement promptly acquires an absolute character. As examples of this process, let us consider four stories whose protagonists are key characters in the novel: Cecilia, Egrencito, Conrado Lúa, and Don Romeo Pomar. Cecilia leaves her native Arras as a young woman to settle down in Remadrín, where she marries Trinidad González. After more than twenty-five years in Remadrín, she leaves the town along with her husband to head back to Arras. They are seen one last time at a bus stop in Torción. Egrencito moves back and forth between Remadrín and the Mágico–US border. Once in Remadrín, he is seen for the last time as he leaves his colleague Enguerrando's house. Conrado Lúa shuttles between Pulemania and Remadrín before heading to the US border. He then turns south and stops in Pompocha. Nothing further is known of his movements. Don Romeo Pomar is kidnapped by the governor's hitmen who have been ordered to kill him somewhere between Remadrín and the Mágico–US border. Readers will never learn his fate. Emblematic of the lack of finality that mars the characters' movements is the unfinished journey of the truck that carries the bodies of the fallen demonstrators. The arrival of the truck in Remadrín triggers the entire narrative, since the very appearance of the bodies reveals a mass crime that touches the lives of everyone in town. After naming, with its usual precision, the locations where the truck stops, the novel leaves the truck to circle around and then disappear from the narrative. All the actors in the novel seem to submit to a centrifugal movement, as if their being-in-the-world were characterized not by emplacement but by a compulsive drive toward an undefined and unreachable exterior. The centrifugal movement of the characters matches the novel's intimate constitution. As Espinoza persuasively argues, the structure of the novel "expands from inside to outside, as the author starts leading readers towards the margins, each chapter visiting the curve of this circle over and over again" (67). The *barroquismo* intrinsic to the endless circular movement of both characters and plot refers once again to the seventeenth century, a culturally displaced age in which the spirals drawn by painters, sculptors, and architects conveyed their culture's disorientation in the presence of a universe that geographic discoveries and Galilean science had deprived of its long-established reference points.

Figures of Displacement

In Sada's novel, the absolute displacement that informs the narrative is figuratively embodied by two narrative motifs: the ghost and the *desa-*

parecido. As for the former, the text is continuously haunted by ghostly, restless figures that now and then come to disturb the living. These ghosts' appearances are often connected to events that upset characters' lives. For example, a big-nosed woman who looks like a "threat from the afterworld" knocks on Cecilia's doors when the latter is fretting over the fate of Papías and Solomón, her children who have been missing since the day of the massacre. The big-nosed woman shows up again during the crucial night when Trinidad and Cecilia decide to leave Remadrín for good. Another ghost, the long-dead Olga Judith, materializes at the silver wedding anniversary of Trinidad and Cecilia; then, after the massacre, Olga goes around knocking on doors in the streets of Remadrín. In the meantime, Dora Ríos, the dead manager of the telephone office, also knocks on doors.[6] By now, however, the souls of the missing demonstrators have taken over Remadrín, a ghost city abandoned by its inhabitants.[7]

Ghosts are figures of displacement to the power of two, in that they do not even belong to a universe of their own. Ghosts have no place to stay: the world of the dead becomes unbearable to them, while that of the living shuts its doors against them. In Sada's novel, ghosts share their placelessness with the *desaparecidos,* individuals erased from the society of the living without being admitted to that of the dead, a condition symbolized by their missing graves. Strictly speaking, the *desaparecidos* are the demonstrators whose bodies were not found after the massacre. In a narrative sense, however, *desaparecidos* are all the characters whose storylines vanish in the middle of nowhere. Above all, Trinidad's and Cecilia's children, Papías and Solomón, are *desaparecidos,* as they never return from the march to Brinquillo. Their absence haunts their parents throughout the novel, from the moment Trinidad and Cecilia first hear of the massacre to their decision to leave Remadrín forever. As a synecdoche of the constitutive loss upon which the novel is constructed, this absence besets the entire narrative. What *Porque parece mentira* narrates are cases of politically motivated disap-

---

6. Espinoza sees ghost-like features even in Cecilia, "a postmodern *Llorona* [in Mexican folktales, a legendary woman who goes around looking for the bodies of her dead children] who possesses a careful maternal instinct" (66).

7. Abandoned by the living and populated by ghosts, Remadrín becomes another Comala, the village where Juan Rulfo set his *Pedro Páramo* (1955), a crucial novel in the Mexican literary canon of the twentieth century. For Sada's acknowledged debts to Rulfo, see Sada, "Daniel Sada" (59).

pearances of the kind that have plagued Mexico since the 1960s. Historically, this type of disappearance represents the most annihilating form of displacement, in that it erases the very possibility of place from a being's existential horizon, even place in the form of a graveyard. As a narrative motif in the novel, the *desaparecido* illustrates the causal relation linking absolute power to total displacement.

At the end of the novel, Trinidad and Cecilia write down their new address in Arras, the town where they plan to live, on a piece of cardboard nailed to the front door of the house they are leaving for good. They hope that their children may return one day and see their note. Carried away by the wind, the message flies over mountains, deserts, and "an ominous river of speaking waters" (601), finally coming to rest on top of a cactus. It remains stuck there forever, its letters slowly fading away. By narrating the effacement of its language, the novel represents its own displacement.[8]

Historical Displacement in Zadie Smith's *White Teeth*

In Zadie Smith's *White Teeth*, characters fail to grasp the historical processes that have caused their migrations to the global metropolis. Their poor historical understanding, in turn, becomes the cause of their own displacement. Smith's characters do not have a choice: they do not fashion their own tools for making sense of history. To the contrary, their historical comprehension is determined a priori by two textual elements: (1) the novel's approach to the narration of history and (2) their relation with the novel's omniscient narrator.

White Teeth narrates the story of three families living in the northwestern London suburb of Willesden Green during the last quarter of the twentieth century: the Joneses, who are British on the paternal side, but whose maternal branch, the Bowdens, hail from Jamaica; the Iqbals, from Bangladesh; and the Chalfens, "third generation by way of

---

8. Zavala notes that "the ending of the novel is eroded by time, as if even its very language had arrived at a point of exhaustion" (37).

Germany and Poland, née Chalfenovsky" (328). In the novel, the individual stories of these fictional characters are framed by a sequence of historical events, spanning from the Indian Mutiny in 1857 to the Fall of the Berlin Wall in 1989, via the Kingston earthquake in 1907 and the assassination of Indira Gandhi in 1984. In spite of these historical references, history does not yield significant knowledge in *White Teeth*. This occurs because the novel ignores the dictates of the historical record so as to subordinate the account of the past to the needs of fiction. The novel's narrator hints at this approach to the rendition of historical events in a comment regarding the teaching of history in school. While the average school today, she affirms, "is aware of the complex forces, movements and deep currents that motivate wars and spark revolutions," in the days (the 1940s) when Archie Jones (a key character in the novel) was attending school, "history was a different business . . . : taught with one eye on narrative, the other on drama, no matter how unlikely or chronologically inaccurate" (254). It is this notion of historiography that informs the narration of the historical past in *White Teeth*.

Turning history into a drama largely free from the constraints of the historical record is what the narrator performs with her account of the friendship between Archie Jones and Samad Iqbal (another key character in the novel). Their story begins on April 1, 1945, when Archie (17 years old) and Samad (19 years old), both volunteers in the British Army during WWII, are on their way from Athens to Thessaloniki, as driver and wireless operator, respectively, of a Churchill tank. Their task is to "make sure the roads of communication stretching from one end of hell to the other were fully communicable" (87). Two weeks later (that is to say on April 15), while the tank is heading to Sofia, Bulgaria, Samad vents his bitterness for being left out of the final battle against Germany. It used to be different, he says, when he was fighting in Italy with the Bengal Corps. On his second day of fighting, Samad claims, he "shot from the air the enemy as he approached the Gothic Line, breaking the Argenta Gap and pushing the Allies through the Po Valley" (89). Eventually, he was accidentally shot by a fellow soldier, lost the use of a hand, and ended up being assigned to the bridge-laying division of "losers" where he now serves. Apart from the incongruity of an incapacitated soldier deployed to a combat zone, Samad's story does not stand the test of the historical record. The battle of the Argenta Gap (a two-mile corridor of flat land stretching between the Reno River [on the west] and Comacchio Lake [on the east] in northern Italy) was fought from April 10 to April 19, 1945. It was only toward the end of the battle that the Allies were able to break through the German defense, thus opening up the road to the north, toward Ferrara and the Po River.[9] Hence, on April 15, Samad is claiming not only to have fought in a battle that is still underway roughly 600 miles west from the area in which he is located, but also to have determined an outcome, the Allies' invasion of the Po Valley, that is yet to come. Even taking into account that Samad, as a wireless operator, could have learnt of the fighting in Italy, it appears nonsensical for him to fabricate such an outlandish lie, and to embark on prophecy, to boot. Hence, it is not the character who is responsible for such a cavalier handling of the historical record, but the narrator, and ultimately the writer, of course. Indeed, the fictional veil appears to be extremely thin here, because the creation of a narrator who happens to be a lousy historian occurs in real life, in the author's workshop, and is dependent on an authorial decision.

Other historical mishaps blemish the narrative of Samad and Archie's war adventures after April 15. Their journey on the tank comes to an abrupt end on May 6, 1945, when a broken track forces the crew to make an emergency stop in a Bulgarian village "west of Tokat" (106).[10] Unfortunately for the narrator's credibility, Bulgaria's entire territory was occupied by the Red Army on September 8, 1944 (Crampton 183). It remained under Soviet rule until 1947, when the Peace Treaty between Bulgaria and the Winners of WWII was signed. Just as it would have been impossible, in mid-April 1945, for Samad to be in northern Greece and, at the same time, in Italy, it appears unthinkable that the Red Army would have allowed a British tank to roam freely in a territory under its control. In that period, both the Soviet Union and the Western Democracies were consolidating their geopolitical positions in Europe and Asia, in a climate characterized by increasing tensions between the Allies in the fight against the Axis Powers. That

---

9. See Jackson and Gleave: "As daylight faded on 18th [of] April it seemed reasonably certain to the 8th Army that the German hold on the Argenta Gap had been broken" (284).

10. Tokat is a city in Anatolia, Turkey, more than 200 miles east of Ankara and 800 miles east of Sofia (106). Utilizing Tokat as the geographical reference for a Bulgarian village appears to represent another bizarre handling of the established truth, this time presented in the form of the cartographic record.

antagonism would grow after the surrender of Germany and Japan, and lead in a few years to the conflict that would be known as the Cold War. Be that as it may, after spending two weeks stranded in this Bulgarian village, Samad and Archie meet a platoon of no less than eight English-speaking Russian soldiers. These soldiers are, allegedly, "on their way to Poland to liberate the work-camps" (106). All of the camps situated on Polish land, however, were liberated by the Red Army in the second half of January 1945, during the Vistula-Oder offensive (January 12–February 24, 1945) that pushed the German lines to the river Oder, deep behind the original 1939 Germany–Poland border (Liddell Hart, 662–69). In late May 1945, when Germany had already been defeated and the war in Europe had ended a couple of weeks earlier, the Soviet Union had absolutely no need to send troops to free the camps, and in any case not via Bulgaria, one thousand miles south of Poland (Poland bordered the Soviet Union).

White Teeth belongs to the significant tradition of novels that reveal factual inconsistencies in the events they narrate as soon as the latter are submitted to fact-checking. In the twentieth century, for example, a case in point is represented by James Joyce's *Ulysses* (1922), a novel that appears to be punctuated by errors. They go from mentioning a theory on Irish myth years before it was published, to fashioning two alternative beginnings for the love story between Leopold Bloom and Molly Tweedy.[11] In the words of Luca Crispi, the problematic inception of this romance "is one of the many instances in *Ulysses* when "the 'facts' in the fiction—as well as some of the seemingly analogous facts outside the novel—do not cohere" (105). Another instance of the troubled relationship that certain novels entertain with historical precision comes from Maria Corti's historical novel *L'ora di tutti* (1962). Despite setting her work in 1480, Corti narrates of a character, Nachira, a fisherman from Otranto, who remembers his encounter with a swordfish weighing around "eighty kilograms" (281). In order to know, however, that a kilogram (the mass of a cubic decimeter of water) existed, human-

---

11. In *Ulysses*, Haines, an Englishman interested in Irish folklore, mentions a certain "Professor Pokorny of Vienna" who "can find no trace of hell in ancient Irish myth" (239). The problem, as noticed by Fritz Senn, is that Julius P. Pokorny was seventeen in 1904, the year in which *Ulysses* takes place ("James Joyce's *Ulysses*" 324). Senn maintains that Pokorny published his views on Irish myth only in 1917 ("James Joyce's *Ulysses*" 327). Joyce should have come across Pokorny's essay in

kind would have to wait three centuries, until "the day of 2 *nivôse* of year IV of the Republic (22 December 1795)," when the metric system came into law in revolutionary France (Kula 263).[12] This anachronism is not alone in *L'ora di tutti*, as characters happily grow and eat tomatoes twelve years before Columbus's first voyage to the New World.[13] What is most remarkable in this case of inaccuracy is the intellectual profile of Maria Corti, one of the most eminent Italian philologists of her time, a scholar, in other words, devout to the principle that the meaning of a word is firmly rooted in its historical context. Given the blatant character of the author's factual errors in *L'ora di tutti*, one could think that Corti embraces fiction as a way to escape from the strict rules of her everyday trade and take a vacation from the tyranny of exactitude.

In the light of such examples, Zadie Smith's indifference to historical accuracy in *White Teeth* might appear to be simply one more case of a novelist too absorbed in her art to think that her readers might busy themselves with fact-checking her story. In this study, however, the point is not the historical inconsistencies in *White Teeth*, per se, but how Smith relates them to her peculiar view of novelistic writing and how this approach translates into her narrative strategy. In this respect, when the narrator was praising the fact-free manner of teaching history in Archie's school days, she was actually spelling out her own method for narrating historical events.[14] This method squarely matches the author's view on the relation between fiction and historical events, as described in a 2002 interview with Gretchen Holbrook Gerzina. In this conversation, Zadie Smith admits to have done only minimal historical research on WWII. It is fiction's inherently deceitful

---

Zurich's Central Library in the same year ("James Joyce's *Ulysses*" 324). Since nobody involved with this issue appears to be immune from inconsistency, in another article of his, Senn affirms that Pokorny published his theory for the first time in 1923 (a year after *Ulysses* came out) and must have met Joyce in Dublin in 1912 ("No Trace of Hell" 256).

12. In the novel, weight is also measured in kilograms to describe the skinny archbishop Pendinelli (140).

13. In *L'ora di tutti*, tomatoes are mentioned six times, at pages 70, 187, 214 (twice), and 232 (twice).

14. Molly Thompson argues that the novel "reveals the frequent slippages that can occur between history and truth, indicated by Archie's awareness of the possibility of discursive falsifications" (132). As an example of this inaccuracy, Thompson cites the omission of Archie's achievement (tied for thirteenth place in track cycling) from the official record book of the 1948 Olympics.

nature, she argues, that makes serious research unnecessary: "Novels are a huge con job, because it's not like academic work; you don't have to prove anything. You just have to mention something and everybody's convinced that you must know everything about it and that's not the case" (269). As a consequence of this view of novelistic writing, when the narrative in *White Teeth* deals with historical facts, the goal of creating a compelling fictional story trumps the truth of the historical record.[15] Samad and Archie's lifelong friendship was wanting of a mythical beginning. Nothing could better satisfy this want than situating the origin of their friendship in a dangerous, remote area during a decisive time in world history such as the final days of WWII. As a final touch, the fallacious reference to the liberation of the work-camps shrewdly spices up the myth with an ethical component, by reminding the reader of what was ultimately at stake in the military effort that Samad and Archie had voluntarily joined. The unmotivated reference to the liberation of the concentration camps may also increase the market value of the book, as everybody feels better about buying and reading novels situated on the right side of history. This exploitation of the reader's gullibility, however, brings about structural problems in *White Teeth*. In particular, it translates into a historically ignorant narrator, poorly equipped to convey the experiences of characters whose situation is deeply historical.[16]

The manipulation of the historical truth in the Bulgarian episode assumes a particular importance in light of the fact that no character in the novel possesses enough knowledge of life to transcend the limits of his/her individual situation. As Paul Dawson persuasively maintains, *White Teeth* is told by "an all-knowing, heterodiegetic narrator

---

15. As she maintains that "Smith forces us to reconsider what we deem to be History and how it gets recorded as such," Supriya Nair argues that *White Teeth* deconstructs hierarchical history through the deliberate mixing of trivial, individual historical narratives (3). I believe that Nair's argument does not bear on my criticism of the narrator's dubious handling of the historical record in *White Teeth*. The historical record can be deconstructed by adding or eliminating events as well as by subverting the way in which these events coalesce into a sequence. Even the very fact that the historical record might have a meaning can be legitimately challenged. Falsification, however, remains outside of these deconstructive practices.

16. By choosing the Balkans and Italy as battlefields where fiction can run freely from the constraints of the archive, Smith displays an Anglo-centric bias: such mishandling of the historical record would never have been possible with the Battle of Britain or D-Day.

who addresses the reader directly, offers intrusive commentary on the events being narrated, provides access to consciousness of a range of characters, and generally asserts a palpable presence within the fictional world" (143). Unlike many of her nineteenth-century omniscient counterparts, this narrator does not outsmart the novel's characters due to her superior technological expertise: there is no room in *White Teeth* for elaborate disquisitions like the description of the Paris sewers in Victor Hugo's *Les Misérables*. In *White Teeth*, the narrator does not need to mastermind technology, because the field of knowledge where she excels is life itself: she knows the vicissitudes of life immensely better than the characters whose lives she recounts. Let us consider, for example, a declaration such as "Generally, women can't do this, but men retain the ancient ability to leave a family and a past. They just unhook themselves, like removing a fake beard, and skulk discreetly back into society, changed men" (18).[17] What separates the narrator from her characters is exactly her knowledge of what "generally" occurs, her self-assured ability to speak not as an individual stuck in her private life but as an analyst of humankind's behavior. As Dawson remarks, in *White Teeth*, overt commentary projects a narratorial self and demonstrates "the omniscient narrator's superior knowledge to the characters in terms of his or her moral sagacity, intellectual breadth and psychological and social insight" (149). Dwarfed by such a powerful voice, characters lose agency and ultimately life itself. They "are not really alive, not fully human," as occurs in other "big ambitious novels" at the end of the last millennium, according to James Wood (42).

Exceeded by an oversized narrator who happily disregards historical truth, characters find themselves unable to read their own situation in historical terms. For, given the gap in intelligence and agency that separates narrator from characters, the former's historical agnosticism inevitably translates into the latter's inability to understand history. Historical understanding, however, is exactly the faculty that the novel's characters would desperately need as individuals defined by a historical event of gigantic proportions: the migration of millions from the poor countries of Asia, Africa, and the Americas to the rich metropolitan areas of the West in the second half of the twentieth cen-

---

17. Commentaries of the same kind (the list is far from exhaustive) can be found on pages 161, 193, 212, 244, 306, 326, 439, and 462.

tury. If we consider the oft-cited passage in *White Teeth* that defines the last century as that of "the great immigrant experiment," then we realize that the novel is not at all helpful in understanding the reasons for the mass migration that shapes its characters' lives (326). This passage surely represents a lively and accurate description of certain effects of immigration (from the hybridization of names and cultures to the growth of racism among young whites), but escapes dealing with crucial issues. In particular, the description of the great immigration in *White Teeth* does not answer the following questions: Who benefits from the immigrant experiment? Who are the winners and the losers in immigration? And, above all, if immigration is an experiment, then a scientist of sorts must be in charge of it: who is the scientist carrying out the experiment of immigration? Those pondering these questions will not find a single clue, let alone an answer, in Smith's description of "the great immigrant experiment," nor in the novel as a whole, for that matter. This lapsus occurs because of the novel's overall stance toward the historical past, a fact that Jonathan Sell has correctly noted. Historical time, Sell argues, is flattened in Smith's novel: "*White Teeth* feels its way towards a demotion of the past from a position of causal pre-eminence with respect to the present and the future. No longer are present and future inevitably historically determined; any relationship obtaining between past and present may be simply coincidental, rather than necessarily causal" (29). Altering the truth of events that occurred in 1945 in order to enliven the narrative of a friendship taking place in the 1980s indeed represents a case of flattened historical time. It is a past that becomes an extension of the present.

Ironically, the historical accuracy that the omniscient narrator discharges in order to tell a compelling story informs, instead, the deep underlying structure (aka the unconscious) of the novel. The very epistemic gap that yawns between the narrator and the characters—whereby the narrator masters a uniquely panoramic knowledge of life while the clueless characters merely go on with their private existences—introduces into the novel's form the deep epistemic dualism that distinguishes the age of global capital. Even in this case, however, as the novel mirrors the larger sociopolitical context in which it is located, characters end up being shortchanged. The defining trait of this context, which still obtains in our own present day, is the existence of a mass of powerless subjects deprived of the cognitive tools they need in order to understand their historical situation. In *White Teeth*, characters dwarfed by the novel's omniscient narrator come to represent the fictional counterparts of these subjects, with historical illiteracy being their shared trait. In any case, history, be it vandalized by the narrator or mirrored by the novel's narrative structure, remains the great unknown for *White Teeth*'s characters.

Spatial Displacement in *White Teeth*: The Public Space

In Smith's novel, historically ignorant characters are left stranded in urban territories shaped by historical processes. If the urban space is based, as Bertrand Westphal maintains, on the accumulation of temporal strata, and if these strata provide the city with its historicity, then characters deprived of historical understanding lack the tools for decoding the spatial configuration that surrounds them (ch. 4). Only the kind of historical awareness that characterizes Lukácsian (and Hegelian) heroes—"world historical individuals" who are "conscious bearers of historical progress . . . in the sense of granting consciousness and clear direction to a movement already present in society"— could allow Smith's characters to situate themselves in the world as mindful, empowered agents (*Historical Novel* 39). Yet, this awareness is exactly what characters lack in a narrative in which all the instruments for understanding the challenging world in which their daily lives unfold belong to a patronizing narrator, the very same narrator who downgrades the account of history to the composition of a fictional drama.

The forbidding environment Smith's characters face is the global metropolis, a historical product of global capital through "the combination of spatial dispersal and global integration" (Sassen, *Global City* 3). In the global metropolis, spaces are partitioned according to their function in the production and circulation of goods, information, and financial assets. In *White Teeth*, the narrative conforms to this partition by representing greater London as a territory dissected along the lines of the social division of production. The suburb—Willesden Green, where the Joneses, the Iqbals, and the Chalfens live—is the site where reproduction, both physical (generating and raising children) and cultural (the education of the young generation through family, school, and religious institutions), coexists with small but significant pockets of material production: Alsana, Samad's wife, for example, works at home sewing plastic outfits for a Soho shop called Domination. By contrast, downtown London is the space dedicated to the production of goods and services: both Archie and Samad work there, the former folding paper for a printing firm, and the latter waiting tables in a restaurant. Troubles loom in both areas. The type of cultural reproduction that Samad envisions for his family, whereby parents smoothly hand their children a set of values defined by tradition and guaranteed by religion, cannot occur in the deterritorialized spaces of the global city, open to the influx of global media and periodically swept by cultural waves that defy localization. As he fails to transmit a certified package of traditional values to Millat and Magid, his troubled children, Samad experiences the type of difficulty Appadurai observes: in our time, "standard cultural reproduction" has become an "endangered activity that succeeds only by conscious design and political will, where it succeeds at all" (54). As for the spaces assigned to productive activities, they are the sites in which characters experience alienation at its worst. Archie is excluded from the company's social events for being married to a woman of Caribbean descent, while Samad is bullied by his boss and humiliated by ignorant and arrogant customers. As for Alsana, she produces items that mean nothing to her: "Many were the nights Alsana would hold up a piece of clothing she had just made, following the pattern she was given, and wonder what on earth it was" (55). Finally, the metropolis also comprises spaces for socialization: the O'Connell's Pool House, a diner that provides its male customers with both a shelter from and a substitute for their families, and the common areas of the Glenard Oak School, which carry out the same functions for teenagers of both genders. Repetition appears to characterize human behavior in both of these spaces. While Samad and Archie enjoy ordering the same meals for two decades, their children and peers revel in repeating their favorite rituals: smoking, sharing cigarettes, and using a formulaic language as a connecting medium.

There is nothing extraordinary in the above organization of urban spaces. What matters in *White Teeth* is the fact that these urban spaces never coalesce into a readable unit. London suffers from the inability to come together, the very same disparateness that turns Glenard

Oak School into a patchy aggregate of disconnected territories. The school has "a complex geography" that results from the lack of integration between a former workhouse, built in 1886, and a scholastic building, built in 1963. Hence, "the school contained and sustained patches, hang-outs, disputed territories, satellite states, states of emergency, ghettos, enclaves, islands" (290). Significantly, "there were no maps" that could provide a comprehensive image of this chaos. Both the metropolis and its synecdoche, Glenard Oak School, are lacking a readable form.[18] To grasp the importance of the city's (un)readability, the following consideration by Lynch appears to be extremely helpful: "If the environment [of a city] is visibly organized and sharply identified, then the citizen can inform it with his [sic] own meaning and connections. Then it will become a true *place*, remarkable and unmistakable" (92, emphasis in the original). Characters are not given this opportunity in *White Teeth*, as their experience of the city never moves past the fragment, be it one of the spaces allocated for (re)production or one of the few, preestablished paths that allow for inter-space mobility. Ryan Trimm, who nevertheless praises Smith's decentered representation of London as the mirror of its diverse population, notes that "*White Teeth* inhabits spaces of displacement: major scenes transpire on the street, in cars, in tube stations, on trains, and on buses" (156). As characters move across these spaces, they draw lines that fail to combine into a network, however limited it may be. Inter-space paths, in *White Teeth*, amount to just three bus routes (52, moving west-east, 17, moving north-south, and 98, from Willesden to downtown London) and an Underground line (Jubilee, from Willesden to Charing Cross). Since the dawn of modernism, the movement of characters is indeed crucial to the readability of the urban space in a novel. Barring outdated, meticulous descriptions à la Balzac or Dickens, it is the characters' movements that make their city readable: the walking hero is the modernist tool for making sense of, and indeed creating, the urban space. Fittingly, what functions for fictional characters also obtains for human beings in the real world. As Michel De Certeau wrote, "Pedes-

---

18. Susie Thomas argues that despite its London setting, *White Teeth* has "little sense of place." As such, like the fiction of Foster Wallace, Wolfe, Eggers, and Rushdie, it belongs to postmodern, transatlantic literature. To support her argument, Thomas adds that in *White Teeth* "it is difficult to think of an atmospheric description of a single specific locality" (para. 17).

trian mobility cannot be localized: it is this mobility that spatializes" (147). Walking, in other words, does not occur in a container, because walking creates the container. In *White Teeth*, however, walking is confined to the immediate surroundings of the home, as if the human intelligibility of space had to stop at the threshold of the domestic fragment. Within the entire novel, we read of a walk by Alsana, who tours the area around her new house, and one by Irie, who travels back and forth from the Chalfens' house and the Iqbals' house (62–66, 458–63). As Laurent Mellet rightly notes in her analysis of London in *White Teeth*, "However multicultural the city maybe, it is a failure in the way it traps the individual in a single overdetermined neighborhood" (188). Trapped in a sliver of the fractured global city, the novel's characters experience a type of displacement that stems from their inability to transcend their own situation and see themselves as part of a larger picture: it is these characters' incapacity to understand their historicity that weakens their comprehension of their own spatial circumstances and ultimately determines their displacement. The presence of the immigrant in the global metropolis could be explained only in historical terms, as it results from long-standing processes that have accelerated quickly in the last fifty years. In *White Teeth*, however, characters are constructed in a way that prevents them from producing historically informed explanations for their situation in the world; this, in turn, is the reason why they are lost. The historical ignorance of Smith's characters translates into their lack of cultural tools needed for creating what Lynch calls "the environmental image" of the space people inhabit: "the generalized mental picture of the exterior physical world that is held by an individual" (4). The environmental image is the link that can turn a space into a place: without this image, the global city can be experienced only as a site for displacement.

Spatial Displacement in *White Teeth*: The Domestic Space

If the public space in *White Teeth* is unreadable, the domestic space is broken. Molly Thompson has written about the unlikelihood of feeling "at home" in the novel's multicultural world. This sense of unease occurs as a result of the characters "belonging to different generations and holding a diversity of cultural beliefs" (123). The Iqbals' home represents a case in point. As occurs with the city, a readable image of the house is missing from the narrative. In its place, the novel identifies three distinct, noncommunicating spaces, with the execution of a precise task assigned to each. The kitchen is Alsana's territory: there she spends long hours at a Singer machine sewing clothes for the Soho shop. Samad's space is located upstairs, in a "little bedroom on top of the house," where he sleeps alone after coming back from work at three in the morning. Above all, this is the room for masturbation, the solitary pleasure which a sexually dissatisfied Samad practices, despite feeling ashamed for his sinful behavior (139–41). And then there is the garden, the third space, where Alsana and Samad fight over the numerous issues—from the role of religion in their lives to more mundane domestic disputes—that punctuate their conjugal life (200). In the Iqbals' house, an unconventional utilization of place emerges. The garden becomes a wrestling ring, the kitchen a factory floor, and a bedroom a place for autoerotic vigils. Familiar objects are refashioned to be used in uncanny ways, bringing to mind the great Edward Said's statement about Mona Atoum's installations: "Domesticity is thus transformed into a series of menacing and radically inhospitable objects whose new and presumably non-domestic use is waiting to be defined" (108).

Emblematic of the cracks running through the domestic space is the outcome of a gathering of the Iqbal and Jones families in the latter's house to watch the Fall of the Berlin Wall on television. Despite the chance of seeing history in the making, arguments arise between generations and genders, until only Samad and Archie remain in front of the screen. At this point, there is nothing for the two fathers to do but to move to the O'Connell's Pool House, their male-only refuge from their families (237–42). As Trimm aptly argues, in *White Teeth*, "even seemingly solid domestic spaces are subject to disruption and change, as with the hurricane's damage to both the Iqbal and Jones households. This sense of nonpermanent places, of transitional sites and houses that cannot shelter, only accentuates the peregrinations and rootlessness of the novel's characters" (156).

What takes place during the Fall of the Berlin Wall demonstrates how the disruption of the domestic space has a precise target in *White Teeth*: the territory of the patriarchal family. Both Samad and Archie are clearly unable to exercise that kind of despotic, pervasive control over the familial territory that was the duty of the nineteenth-century husband in Balzac's *Physiologie du mariage*. In *White Teeth*, domestic displacement shatters the structures of patriarchy, thus indirectly confirming Massey's argument about the inherently gendered nature of place when the latter coincides with home. However positive, this outcome alone is not enough to turn displacement, as narrated in the novel, into a fully liberating process. It is true that the self-empowerment of the subjectivities historically oppressed by patriarchy is one of the forces that generate displacement in *White Teeth*: Samad and Archie, for example, are displaced at home because they cannot behave as the patriarchs they would like to be. This emancipating movement, however, occurs in territories saturated by global capital's ability to penetrate all the interstices of our dwellings. Alsana regularly beats up her husband in their garden fights, but remains absolutely helpless against the capitalistic command embedded in the Singer to which she is handcuffed day and night. She experiences a uniquely acute type of displacement that stems from alienation, from being forced not out of but into a place where none of her actions has any bearing on the development of her own subjectivity.

In *White Teeth*, as characters fail to understand that their situation in the global city results from historically determined processes, they become strangers to themselves. This sense of displacement grows as the migrants' children approach adulthood: "The new generation moves toward an increasingly rootless situation. In fact, displacement and homelessness increase over the course of the novel, a line initiated when the stability of the children is broken by Magid being shipped to Bangladesh" (Trimm 157). Displaced subjectivities cannot figure out their own situation in the world, because even their own bodies remain unknown to them. It is a condition that Millat's cousin, Neena, vividly describes: "He [Millat] doesn't know his arse from his elbow. Just like his father. He does not know who he is" (284). As the novels proceeds, the narrative focuses increasingly on the characters' failed attempts to orient themselves in the alienating environment where they live. The depth of the displacement experienced by Smith's characters can be appreciated by taking into consideration the solutions they find to their disorientation. As the years go by, Samad comes to rely more heavily on religion for guidance in his life. As for his children, Millat joins KEVIN (Keepers of the Eternal and Victorious Islamic Nation), a fundamentalist Islamic group, while Magid absolutizes scientific rationalism: "I have converted to Life. I see his god in the millionth position of *pi*, in the arguments of the Phaedrus, in a perfect paradox" (429). Joshua Chalfen, finally, teams up with FATE (Fighting Animal Torture and Exploitation), a militant animalist group. Faith, science, and animal rights, however, are just pretexts. Smith's characters turn to religion, unconditional rationalism, and animal advocacy to answer a personal, practical need: that of finding a way to orient themselves in the world. Samad, for example "has never been a devoted Muslim. Rather, Islam is a facade he adopts to protect the roots that he is so afraid to lose" (Mirze 193). In the turbulent times in which they live, characters believe that orientation can only come from values that withstand change and maintain their validity in different situations and time periods. These values are not contextual, but essential; as such, they do not follow but precede experience. Thus conceived, values become life-orienting tools immune from empirical verification: in other words, they become metaphysical.

In their search for metaphysical answers to their worldly problems, Samad, Millat, Magid, and Joshua tread a well-known path in Western philosophy. In "History of an Error," an oft-quoted chapter in the *Twilight of the Idols,* Nietzsche argues that metaphysical speculation helped "the wise man, the pious man, the virtuous man" to build a "real world," the site for those ideal, moral values that exist only as pale imitations within the "apparent" world (20). The latter, as Nietzsche spells out in *Ecce Homo,* signifies nothing other than our empirical reality.[19] After centuries in which the "real world," in its various forms, has occupied humankind's dreams and thoughts, Nietzsche maintains, we moderns have decided to discard it as a useless, superfluous idea. Upon disposing of the "real world," however, we discover that "*with the real world we have also done away with the apparent one!*" (20, emphasis in the original). How can empirical, "hard" reality vanish simply because a set of ideal principles is proven false? It can, indeed, because metaphysical principles are needed precisely to aid humans in making sense of the puzzling reality of their lives. It is these systems of values that make reality "hard": without them, the world would soften into

---

19. "Reality has been robbed of its value, its sense, its truthfulness insofar as an ideal world was faked up. . . . The 'real world' and the 'apparent world'—in plain words: the fake world and reality" (*Ecce Homo* 3).

an incomprehensible pulp. As a consequence, when metaphysical values crumble, reality becomes unreadable and turns into a battlefield in which individuals' wills to power clash. If we reverse the progression of Nietzsche's argument and relate it to Samad, Millat, Magid, and Joshua's attempts to achieve orientation, then we can understand the reason for their choices and gauge their displacement. Smith's characters hope that metaphysics can provide them with the categories necessary for making the world understandable, and thus visible. They hope for such guidance because they are lost in the unreadable landscape of the global city, like ancient philosophers facing the mystery of the universe.

The same elusive path out of an unreadable landscape also characterizes the life experience of another character, Irie Jones, Archie's daughter. Her story appears particularly significant because Irie initially does not seek guidance from metaphysical principles. Her journey toward transcendence begins by chance. While Irie is living temporarily at her grandmother's house, she comes across a family archive of photos and other memorabilia. This discovery leads Irie to the obvious search for her roots, a search that rapidly evolves into the cult of origin: "*Homeland* is one of the magical fantasy words like *unicorn* and *soul* and *infinity* that have now passed into the language. And the particular magic of *homeland*, its particular spell over Irie, was that it sounded like a beginning. The beginningest of beginnings. Like the first morning of Eden and the day after apocalypse. A blank page" (402, emphasis in the original). Hence, after starting on solid, empirical ground (the storage of records as a conduit to the past), Irie comes to seek a quintessentially metaphysical entity: the origin. The pure origin for which she longs is the ἀρχή, the original event that precedes the archive but, because of its very anteriority, eludes any attempt to be recorded and brought to domestication.

The fact that Smith's characters need metaphysical solutions for their worldly problems demonstrates both the extent of their displacement and the lack of viable answers to their demands for orientation in the sublunar world. Because Irie initially rejects the metaphysical tools that other characters enthusiastically embrace, her ultimate turn to metaphysics remains the most powerful sign of the uprootedness that defines the characters' lives in *White Teeth*. The very ending of Irie's story, and of the novel—on a Jamaican beach along with her grandmother Hortense, Joshua Chalfen, and her fatherless daughter—

speaks volumes regarding her displacement. With her journey to her ancestors' land, Irie replaces the territorial displacement of living the daily alienation of a London suburb with the absolute displacement of those who jump out of their own time.[20] As discussed in this chapter, *White Teeth* frames the fictional narrative within an account of historical facts. Key among these events is the "great migration," or the journey of millions from the former colonies of the British Empire to the metropolis in the four decades that followed WWII. Differently from what occurs to Irie, however, for migrants, "migration is a one-way trip. There is no 'home' to go back to. There never was" (Hall, "Minimal Selves" 44). By settling down in Jamaica with her unconventional family, Irie performs an action that neither migrants nor their children—nor any of us, for that matter—can do: swim upstream in the river of history. Hence, in the episode that seals *White Teeth*, the fictional narrative once again contradicts historical truth. This time, the contradiction results from the novel's attempt to translate an experience of absolute displacement, Irie Jones's, into a narrative form. However, the antihistorical character of the solution adopted in the text opens a conflict between narrating displacement on the one hand and the novelistic discourse's vocation to tell the truth on the other. Here, we are close to what happens at the end of *Porque parece mentira*. While Sada's narrative conveys the novel's undermining of its own representational tools through the metaphor of the inexorable self-effacing of a message's words, *White Teeth* achieves the same result by placing personal and historical destinies on two diverging roads.

---

20. See also Nair: "Irie's flight to the homeland . . . might undermine any chance of overcoming the paradoxical stasis of the migrant condition in its endless game of catch-up" (10).

CHAPTER 6

Symptoms

Mathias Énard's *Zone*

Ideology, Symptoms, and the Novel of Displacement

Globalized society has one ideology: unbounded mobility. In our time, any observer may note that capitals, individuals, data, and signs all appear to be constantly on the move. This perpetual motion wins the approval of the public opinion through an ideological twist: mobility is to be seen as both beneficial to humankind's well-being and necessary for the progress of human civilization at large. Contemporary civilization is inspired by what Cresswell calls "nomadic metaphysics," or an approach to human geography that considers place "as stuck in the past, overly confining, and possibly reactionary" (26). Since nomadic metaphysics does not take into consideration the context of nomadic movements, it appears to suffer from abstract universalism. Furthermore, it often overlooks the colonial power relations that produced the images (infected by Orientalism) of the nomad invested with desire and romance (55). To understand the environment in which the ideology of mobility is rooted, Lussault's meditation is once again helpful. Our urbanized and globalized world, he argues, follows the logic of *mobilisation,* or of "putting every entity in motion." In this context, "the word 'mobility' stands for all the movements that facilitate the creation of connections among entities, whatever they may be: material entities (human beings, goods, as well as viruses, microorganisms, animals, and so on . . .) or immaterial entities (analog or digital data transmitted through technological networks)" (ch. 1).

As a defining trait of our age, mobility inevitably takes a central place in the considerations of an advocate of globalization such as Thomas L. Friedman. The world is now flat, Friedman maintains, meaning that all the barriers which in the past hindered the movements of material and intellectual resources have now been leveled for good. After the demolition of these barriers, "we are now connecting all the knowledge centers of the planet together into a single global network" (8). The world has also become smaller, mirroring Harvey's space-time compression, or "the processes that so revolutionize the objective qualities of space and time that we are forced to alter, sometimes in quite radical ways, how we represent the world to ourselves" (*Postmodernity* 240). The world shrank from size large, at the time of Columbus's voyage in 1492, to medium, around 1800. Then, it became size small in 2000 and size tiny today (Friedman 10). The world has been shrinking because the speed at which we move and communicate has continued to increase. The flattening and the shrinking of the world have been made possible by vectors of mobility, such as developments in telecommunications and other technologies for connecting the various areas of the planet to one another: while mobility has grown exponentially as a consequence of the flattening of the world, the actual distances traveled by individuals, commodities, or signs on the move have grown dramatically. Ten "flatteners" have given the world its present flat configuration: the Fall of the Berlin Wall, Netscape, Work Flow Software, Uploading, Outsourcing, Offshoring, Supply-Chaining, Insourcing (UPS), In-forming (Google, Yahoo, MSN Web Search), and the Steroids (universal connectivity through smart phone and high-speed Internet) (Friedman 48–172). The ideological crux of Friedman's analysis consists in its considering mobility as both inevitable and inherently good. It partakes of both the classical concept of fate and the Christian notion of love and, like the latter, combines with free will: we move around because we want to do so.

As occurred with other ideologies that shaped their own epoch, in the age of global capital, mobility draws its strength from its being at one with technology; examples of this coupling may be found in twentieth-century Fordism and the assembly line, Renaissance humanism and the printing press, as well as classical liberalism and the steam engine. Today mobility, too, has its technological partner: electronic writing.

The written word has always appeared to be phenomenologically distinct from the spoken word. The reason for this distinction lies in the ability of the written word to convey meaning even during temporal segments that differ from the one in which it was created. As Walter Ong argues, writing establishes context-free language, a kind of discourse that "cannot be directly questioned or contested as oral speech can be because written discourse has been detached from its author" (78). On the contrary, the spoken word can carry a message only at the time it is uttered by a human voice.[1] Electronics have further decontextualized the written word. Since the invention of the Colossus, the code-breaking electronic machine used by British Intelligence in 1944–45, computers have been particularly well suited to manipulating written language (Ceruzzi, ch. 1). This manipulation has given the written word a kind of fluidity that it did not possess in the paper age. In electronic form, the written word increases its autonomy from its original frame of reference by breaking free even from the paper page. The "omnipresent copy, cut and paste commands" available in word processing programs have unshackled the written word from the constraints inherent in its inscription on a material support (Manovich, ch. 1). A well-known Latin proverb states, "*Verba volant, scripta manent*": spoken words fly away, written words remain. As Hayles maintains, "The stubborn fact remains . . . that once ink is impressed on paper, it remains relatively stable and immovable" (*My Mother*, ch. 4). In the last three decades, however, written words have been able to transcend their stubborn impression on paper and have learnt how to fly: "Words on a printed page are irradicable: text on a video display terminal (VDT) is readily altered" (Nichols 631). As Ernst convincingly argues,

---

1. Since the invention of the gramophone, the spoken word can also be recorded, thus gaining independence from the speaker. However, the recorded word represents a different medium from the human voice: it reproduces the voice but does not coincide with it.

"The constant dynamic flow of information in cyberspace" contradicts the printed culture's goal of "freezing, for all time, that which has been thought and said" (part 2, ch. 6).[2] By moving from one Word document to another, or jumping from an email to an HTML page, each time changing font, size, and style, the written word becomes increasingly independent from that particular context which was coextensive to its inscription on a medium. As it enjoys unfettered mobility, the written word closes the ideological circle: the signs carrying the ideology of mobility also become the embodiment of how that very ideology functions. In situationist style, the ideology of mobility turns into the mobility of ideology.

In *The Sublime Object of Ideology*, a discussion of how ideology works in relation to subjectivity, Slavoj Žižek maintains that "the last support of the ideological effect (or the way an ideological network of signifiers 'holds' us) is the non-sensical, pre-ideological kernel of enjoyment" (140). This kernel is organized as a fantasy; that is to say, as "an overlooked, unconscious illusion" that structures our actual, effective relationship to reality (30). In the case of present-day dominant ideology, our illusion of being in control of our mobility, of being able to combine agency and mobility, is fantastical. In our fantasy, we see ourselves as nomads who move through physical as well as virtual spaces at will. Thus, we still live and operate in a place, which is simply larger and, at the same time, richer in possibilities than the bounded places of the paper age. When this fantasy is pushed to the extreme, the flattened space of the planet becomes one immense place for us to enjoy: from those who negotiate the hyper-lieux of the global city to the migrants embarking on the routes to the metropolis, we are all part of a happy-to-be-on-the-move species.

If, however, we take a sober look at the reality of globalized society, we find a picture that actually contradicts the fantasy described above. Refugees fleeing from wars, brutal power practices, and natural calamities surely provoke the most dramatic spatial movements in our time. Far from being Deleuzian nomads who freely roam through spaces smoothed out by the demise of the State's sovereignty, today's refugees are forced to leave their homes in order to follow the risky routes of

---

2. Ernst quotes from Rowdes and Sawday, *The Renaissance Computer*, at page 10 and not 11, as appears erroneously in Ernst's bibliographic footnote ("Notes," "6 Discontinuites," note 31).

emigration. And the same is true for the economic migrants who seek dignified living conditions in the wealthier areas of the globe. In both cases, the agency that ultimately determines these spatial movements resides with political and economic powers whose capacity to act far exceeds that of the subjects moving (or moved) on the ground. What occurs in our time is a reenactment of events that have punctuated the course of human history. Indeed, in most of the *diasporas* reported in the historical record, people were compelled to scatter themselves around the world, with little to no hope of returning to their homeland.

In the metropolis, forced mobility represents a common, everyday experience for those low-income workers who, ironically, appear to be stuck in their place of residence. As the epitome of their condition, I want to consider once again the Uber drivers: formally, they are free contractors driving their cars at will; in actuality, they are driven by the combined action of software (the Uber application) and their own material needs, aka how to make ends meet. The separation of Uber drivers from the location of their operations (the area of the city where they work) is absolute. This location could even be the neighborhood where they grew up, but, as subjectivities deprived of agency, these drivers would still remain displaced at home.

If we climb the income ladder, so as to consider the condition of the white-collar workforce employed by financial corporations, we come across subjects submitted to the same mix of technologically embedded commands and economic incentives squeezing the life out of the workers employed in the gig economy. In his illuminating "Il general intellect del capitale" (Capital's general intellect), Franco Fratini describes how white-collar workers' days are structured by their company's poisonous gift, a Blackberry. This smartphone starts receiving its earliest emails at 6:00 am and works late into the night, when messages continue to arrive from the other side of the Atlantic Ocean (Fratini depicts the working environment of a company set in Europe). The biopolitical seizure of workers' time through digital gadgets couples with the company's policy of linking bonuses to hyperbolic budgets (a budget is the level of revenue that an office must reach in a given period of time) and setting unreasonable targets for each employee. This system of relentless interpellation, calculated incentives, and unreachable goals functions from the top down so as to structure the workday (by now expanded to cover all the time that is not dedicated to sleep) of the entire company's workforce, from well-paid managers down to low-ranked employees: "In the age of financial capital, the culture of *budgets* is mere abstraction turned into a material practice. In the long run, it shapes people's bodies. It is an intoxicated production of work by means of work" (Fratini 97, emphasis in the original). This state of permanent mobilization has actually spilled out of the workplace and flooded the spaces of private life. "The nonstop live-world of twenty-first-century capitalism," as Crary convincingly argues, is characterized by "a generalized inscription of human life into duration without breaks, defined by a principle of continuous functioning" (8).[3] Present-day humans are permanently inscribed in a cycle of production and consumption: "Since no moment, place, or situation now exists in which one can not shop, consume, or exploit networked resources, there is a relentless incursion of the non-time of 24/7 into every aspect of social or personal life" (Crary 30). McKenzie Wark puts it more succinctly: "When information in turn becomes a form of private property . . . [t]ime itself becomes a commodified experience" ("Class," Section 030).

In this context—the state of affairs represented by the Cloud/earth metaphor in chapter 1—the fantasy of being free, nomadic subjectivities in total control of our movements allows us to start two mutually supporting processes, concerning identification and separation. Key to the former is the fact that our image as self-determining, empowered individuals cannot stand alone: it is incomplete without the regard of the other. The latter is the Cloud-dweller, as we fancy him/her in the act of casting his/her benevolent gaze on earth. Representing ourselves as we would like the Cloud to see us is key to our "symbolic identification, identification with the very place *from where* we are being observed, *from where* we look at ourselves so that we appear to ourselves likeable, worthy of love" (Žižek 116, emphasis in the original). In sum, our self-representation as the happy nomads whom the Cloud contemplates

---

3. Already in 1893, Paul Lafargue noticed that the shift from the Ancien Régime to the bourgeois State had been accompanied by a law that encroached on areas of individual freedom that until then had been protected from the dictates of production: "Under the Ancien Régime the Church's laws guaranteed workers 90 days of rest (52 Sunday and 38 holidays) in which working was strictly prohibited. . . . Once in power, the Revolution abolished the holidays and replaced the seven-day week with a ten-day week. The Revolution freed workers from the Church's yoke in order to better submit them to the yoke of working" (36).

from above (the happy Uber drivers described in the company's website) allows us to identify with the source of that contemplation. We do not imitate the Cloud: we do not ape Mark Zuckerberg or Warren Buffett—this would make no sense—but we symbolically feel at one with them: "In symbolic identification we identify ourselves with the other precisely at the point at which he is inimitable, at the point which eludes resemblance" (121). This symbolic identification structures our subjectivity by allowing us to occupy a key position in the intersubjective symbolic network: the elevated place from which we can look down at the small folks below.

Furthermore, our fantasy of being in control of our spatial movements situates us on the winning side of the divide separating agency from disempowerment and place from displacement. Beyond the border that cuts through these oppositional pairs, gig economy workers, refugees, and migrants live. This line, of course, is movable: we can situate it wherever it suits our position in the symbolic network, provided it does not separate us from the Cloud. In other words, an Uber driver will probably see him/herself as an independent actor operating freely on the market and will pity the unfortunates who do not enjoy the same freedom. At work here is the same mechanism whereby many people consider themselves to be part of the middle class while not actually belonging there.[4] As Žižek argues, "The notion of social fantasy is . . . a necessary counterpart to the concept of antagonism: fantasy is precisely the way the antagonistic fissure is masked" (142). Through our fantastic, symbolic identification with the elites running the world, we mask the split cutting through the body social (the split I represent through the Cloud/earth metaphor) and transform it into a manageable contradiction. What is masked, in other words, is not social antagonism per se, but its location along a fault line whose position damages our self-esteem. By pretending that the boundary separating the powerful from the powerless runs between us and the

---

4. In addition to functioning as an adjustable tool for symbolic identification, the fantasy of seeing oneself as a subject endowed with free mobility creates the framework within which we can experience desire: fantasy "provides the co-ordinates of our desire—which constructs the frame enabling us to desire something" (Žižek 132). In a capitalist society, as our desires are mediated through the market, the possession of freedom constitutes the sine qua non for becoming a consumer of goods and services: it is on individual freedom that the membership in the free-market economy rests.

marginalized, rather than between us and the elites managing the big finance and software corporations, our social fantasy provides us with full membership in society.

As Žižek reminds us, anti-Semitism functions similarly under Fascism. Within that context, social antagonism is inconceivable since Fascist ideology hinges on the fantasy of Fascist society as an organic and homogeneous body. However, since social antagonism appears instead ineliminable, it is portrayed as a conflict between society as a whole and an enemy coded as alien to the body social: "The basic trick of anti-Semitism is to displace social antagonism into antagonism between the sound social texture, social body, and the Jew as the force corroding it, the force of corruption" (140). The divide that runs through conflicting social groups is moved to the outskirts of society so as to exclude an ostracized, scapegoated minority. In anti-Semitism as a "disfigured representation of social antagonism," the Jew becomes a symptom of the fissure that cuts through the Social (141). But the kind of Fascism discussed by Žižek, essentially the regime in power in several European states in the 1920s and 1930s, operated in the paper age, where ideologies were elaborated within a kind of hub (the party headquarters, the big university, the national newspaper) and then passed along to followers positioned along its spokes, so to speak. In our software-informed age, each of us possesses the tools necessary for operating as an ideological micro-hub and recycling the dominant ideology according to our individual needs. Thus, we need not converge on one single scapegoat functioning as the symptom of all the cracks that disrupt the social edifice. Instead, we can enjoy greater flexibility in choosing the symptom (anyone who lives beyond the divide that cuts through the Social in our fantasy) best suited to our process of symbolic identification.

In order to discover the actual fissures that run deep within the body social, Žižek argues, symptoms are to be turned upside down. To do so, we must recognize that the properties we attribute to symptoms are indeed our own: "In 'going through the fantasy' we must in the same move identify with the symptom: we must recognize in the properties attributed to the 'Jew' the necessary product of our very social system; we must recognize in the 'excesses' attributed to 'Jews' the truth about ourselves" (144). To get to the bottom of an ideology, we must identify with the subjects our fantasy marginalizes as symptoms and assume the kernel of their condition as our own symptom; for, had this symptom not been ours, we would have had no reason to banish it beyond a wall. In present-day society, the marginalized subjects are the worker employed in the gig economy, the refugee, and the migrant: the core of their condition is their lack of agency. This, then, is our symptom: our depleted or nonexistent agency. Far from being an exclusive condition of the marginalized, the lack of agency that we would like to move to society's periphery is our own.

Having recognized our symptom, we are presented with two options. On the one hand, we can continue to exclude it from our existence by erecting fences around the places we inhabit. Alternatively, we can bring our symptom to the fore, as a Lacanian contingency that "stops not being written" (*Encore* 183). The former choice corresponds to Freud's "acting out," or the patient's compulsive repetition of a behavior related to an unpleasant experience that he/she "reproduces . . . not as a memory but as an action" ("Remembering, Repeating and Working-Through" 150). The latter alternative corresponds, instead, to Freud's "working through," or the patient's ability to identify the impulses that feed his/her resistance (155). In the case of the present-day, extensive lack of agency, acting out means building barriers, be they the real walls erected on the borders of States, communities, and private residences, or the cultural borders created in the name of nativism, muscular nationalism, machismo, and/or religious fundamentalism. Working through, instead, means becoming "conversant" with our condition, as patients in the process of overcoming their resistance should do according to Freud's discussion of symptoms, repression, and memory ("Remembering, Repeating and Working-Through" 155).

Novels of displacement are to be viewed as an articulation of this conversation. In global capital's discursive field, they counter the ideological narrative that describes the global, digitized society as an open territory crisscrossed by autonomous, empowered subjects joyously competing to reap the benefits of the worldwide free market. Through this posture, novels of displacement align themselves with a key practice in novelistic discourse, whereby the novel, "in the discursive totality of a given epoch," occupies "a place opposite to its ideological authoritative core" (González Echevarría, *Myth and Archive* 8). In our time, this core is the neoliberal economic theory as a rational, all-encompassing explanation of human behavior and actions. The three novels I have discussed so far sabotage the neoliberal apprehension of the human being as a free agent on the market by pointing to the depleted agency of displaced subjectivities in the age of global capital. They do so in a literary way; that is to say, by speaking of their actual content and, at the same time, gesturing toward something else: displacement in the social environment in which they are written. In other words, in the novels discussed in this study, "the literary subject . . . points behind itself," to borrow a line from Charles S. Singleton's commentary on Dante's *Commedia* (1). These three novels narrate events that are by and large consistent with the historical record. In other words, they are true. It is their very truthfulness that allows them to gesture toward something that appears equally true: displacement in the age of their own writing. The truth-to-truth association structures the relationship between the text's diegesis and the outer world in novels of displacement.

This study endeavors to examine both present-day displacement as the defining mood in our age and its fictional rendition in novelistic form. The novel with which I shall conclude my textual analysis, Mathias Énard's *Zone*, narrates a story in which both types of displacement discussed so far—epistemic displacement and spatial displacement—converge to haunt the hero's experience of living in our age.

Thematic and Structural Displacement in Mathias Énard's *Zone*

In Énard's *Zone*, displacement not only constitutes a key theme at the content level but also acts as an unsettling force that destabilizes both the novel's narrative structures and its language. A gargantuan work, *Zone* mixes fiction and history to depict an incredibly vast array of characters, events, and locations. To provide these materials with a narrative form, Énard creates a fictional frame story: a train journey from Milan to Rome, during which the first person narrator of the novel, Francis Servain Mirković, recalls hundreds of stories buried within his memory. This narrative, which constitutes the conventional present of the novel, gestures toward both the narrator's recent past, a journey from Paris to Milan after missing a flight at the Charles De Gaulle airport, and his immediate future, a short trip from Termini (Rome's train station) to the Fiumicino airport. As for the stories Francis recalls from his memory, they can be divided into approximately three blocks. This division makes sense only a posteriori, as the novel follows the meanderings of Francis's memory through sudden flashes, interruptions, and repetitions in a manner that randomly mixes narrative fragments taken from different stories and distinct temporal layers so as to prevent the reader from immediately identifying the novel's main storylines.

The first narrative block comprises stories regarding Francis's own past, notably his military experience as a voluntary fighter on the Croatian side in the wars in former Yugoslavia (in Croatia, Herzegovina, and Bosnia), his work as an analyst for France's Secret Service, and his love affairs with Marianne, Stephanie, and Sashka. The second and by far the largest block includes stories of war crimes committed in the Mediterranean basin, the "Zone" of the novel's title. The bulk of these crimes is carried out in the twentieth century, even though the novel makes several incursions into the ages before 1900. Indeed, violence appears to be so deeply ingrained in human behavior that its practice transcends a specific time in history: violence defines the human experience on earth as such. Through repeated references to Homer's poems and Greek mythology, the text points to the Battle of Troy as the event in which the exercise of violence first achieves a historical dimension in the context of Mediterranean civilization.[5] Within this historical framework, war is a strictly male business. It is the very upbringing of young men, "educated to violence, accustomed to the idea of weapons since childhood, primary school and cartoons, schooled in the cult of God and the nation," which leads them to carry an assault weapon in adulthood (115). These are men very like Francis: in his own words, a "former warrior . . . who embodies all the clichés of an absolute machismo" (354). Fittingly, the war criminals mentioned in the novel are all males, and there is not a single war crime narrated in *Zone* that does not also involve the perpetration of a sexual crime. As a consequence, throughout the history of the Mediterranean peoples, violence is invariably gendered. Itself the offspring of displaced subjectivities, in *Zone*, male violence is historically responsible for the uprooting of enormous segments of the population, from antiquity

---

5. Elodie Coutier maintains that "the entire novel is placed under the sign of the *Iliad* that informs its structure and precedes its reading" (sect. 2).

to modernity: male displacement generates universal displacement. At the root of this vicious loop lies a primordial, gendered manifestation of the dualism of power that is characteristic of our time. The third narrative area comprises biographical fragments concerning several English language writers of the twentieth-century, such as James Joyce, Ernest Hemingway, Malcolm Lowry, and William S. Burroughs, all of whom spent part of their lives in the Mediterranean. As these writers seem to follow a pattern of self-destructive behavior, drunkenness, and troubled masculinity, they display disturbing similarities with the soldier-butchers who crowd the pages of *Zone*. The emblem of this way of living is Joyce, "who could not admit his secret desires, the violence he kept inside, and his guilty love for his own daughter; Joyce who had to disguise himself through his writing" (Énard 425). Finally, mixed with the debris of Francis's memory, a completely different narrative—both in formal and thematic terms—also emerges: the story of Intissar, a female Palestinian fighter during the Lebanese Civil War in the early 1980s. Francis reads Intissar's adventures in a book he bought in Paris, a collection of short stories by Rafaël Kahla. Entirely fictional, Rafaël Kahla does not exist in the real world, Intissar's story is the only narrative in the novel that displays a plot in the Aristotelian sense. As Intissar's story displays a crucial difference from the rest of *Zone*—it is the only episode in the novel in which characters are not displaced, but rooted, albeit temporarily, in the territory where they live—it deserves a specific analysis, which I will provide later in this chapter.

Through its rendition of an endless stream of violence, what the novel actually narrates is displacement. Even though *Zone* recounts stories set in the Mediterranean, an area in which, for millennia, people have established deep roots in the territories they have inhabited, displacement hegemonizes the narrative. Accordingly, in the novel, rather than being characterized by the deeply rooted cultures it hosts, the Mediterranean becomes just a "zone," that is to say an administratively defined area. In the language of bureaucracy, a zone is a territory that is identified and delimited with the purpose of allocating specific responsibilities among the employees of an administrative unit. In Énard's novel, this unit is the Secret Service branch where the narrator worked. The first time Francis uses the term "zone," he does so with reference to Algeria, the first sector assigned to him as an analyst. Then, as he narrates the progression of his career, the term—at times in the form of "my Zone"—comes to designate the entire Mediterranean basin (230). Periodically swept by waves of blind, disruptive barbarity, the Zone becomes the stage for crimes against humanity, vendettas, and atrocities. Throughout the three millennia of historical time covered by the novel, it occurs over and over again that entire populations are chased from their homes and scattered around the world:

> I thought about all those movements in the Zone, flows, counterflows, exiles driving away other exiles, according to the victories and defeats, the strength of weapons and the outlines of the borders, a bloody dance, an eternal, endless vendetta, . . . the defeated with their city destroyed want to destroy other cities in turn, rewrite their history, turn it into a victory. (234)

The history of the Mediterranean peoples amounts to an incessant ebb and flow of murderous violence, in which victims and persecutors cyclically change position. Francis finds the perfect example of this senseless cycle in his own family's history: his father, the son of a resistance fighter during the German occupation of France from 1940 to 1944, tortured helpless prisoners during the Algerian war. He administered torture "with the same zeal shown by the Gestapo who tortured his father" (462).

As society is hit by waves upon waves of brutal cruelty, the practice of place becomes impossible. People may reside in territories rich in cultural heritage, enclosed within political borders, and protected by the power of the nation-state. None of these factors, however, can guarantee them the minimum of safety needed to call the location they inhabit a place in Malpas's sense: an open region in which one can live and operate through a fruitful relation with other living beings and things. In the "Zone," neither the hard power of the nation-state nor the soft power of cultural traditions appears able to shield national and local communities from the periodical outbursts of the destructive, uprooting rage to which male warriors are prone.

While displacement defines *Zone* at the content level (the stories of ethnic cleansing, deportations, and forced migrations narrated in the text), it also affects the novel's narrative structures. In particular, displacement destabilizes the text in the narrative space delimited by the novel's frame story, the sole structuring tool operating in

Zone. With the notable exception of Intissar's adventure—a second-degree narrative told by Francis as an intradiegetic narrator—what is recounted within this frame story amounts to a chaotic accumulation of fragments. As this pile results from the random operations of Francis's troubled memory, it proceeds without following any recognizable order. In this magma, only a loose circular pattern emerges; it is created by Francis's habit of repeating the narration of the same events. Repetition and circularity characterize the operation of memory in traumatized subjects haunted by their experience of events that overcome their capacity for comprehension. As Cathy Caruth convincingly maintains, trauma is a "wound of mind" that "is experienced too soon, too unexpectedly, to be fully known and is therefore not available to consciousness until it imposes itself again, repeatedly, in the nightmares and repetitive actions of the survivor" (4). The traumatized subject is split between the urge to reclaim his/her past and the imperative to shut it down, the impulse to remember and the refusal to come to terms with the past. Subjects in this condition are affected by the urge to narrate and, at the same time, the sheer impossibility to verbalize their experience. If they talk about the events at the source of their troubles they become peculiar narrators: both unrestrained and reluctant. Francis Servain Mirković, as Claudia Jünke correctly argues, is precisely this sort of narrator: "traumatized by his own wartime experiences during the Yugoslav Wars, by what he has witnessed and what he has done" (76). Fragmented memories and inchoate narratives are the traces left behind by his attempts to reclaim experiences that, for the sake of his sanity, he should keep buried in the deepest recesses of his psyche. An unstructured narrative stems from this congenitally split narration. It results from the accumulation of the pieces randomly produced by the narrator, their repetition, and the sheer impossibility of arranging them into a cohesive plot. Displacement runs deep within this jumbled novel, as Francis's memory functions through a chain of association that continually displaces the narrative rendering of Francis's past. This time, displacement assumes the meaning it conveys in Freud's theory:

> The multitude of *other* accounts of war and violence provides an opportunity to avoid a confrontation with his *own*. The temporal and spatial delimitation and transgression on the level of internal action

is therefore the basis for the novel's staging of a *Verschiebung* ['displacement'] in the Freudian sense: Francis fixates compulsively on the crimes of others in order not to acknowledge his own. (Jünke 79, emphasis in the original)[6]

As Francis narrates the crimes he witnessed in order to postpone the account of those he perpetrated himself, his own wrongs will emerge only toward the end of the novel. This combination of unstructured storytelling and narrative procrastination creates within *Zone* a restless narrative that comprises more than five hundred pages of pure action, without ever pausing for a moment of textual reflection, be it a comment, a summary, or a description: *Zone*'s narrative restlessness embodies in structural form the displacement that its narrator has experienced in his own life and has observed in the lives he narrates.

The linguistic surface of Énard's novel is stirred by the same displacement that disrupts its narrative structure. In *Zone*, just as the content is part of a stream of endless violence that had actually begun even before the Battle of Troy, language, too, is comprised of a linguistic flow that is already in motion when the text begins. As is known, Francis's narrative amounts to a five-hundred-page-long sentence, one breathless run that begins with a lowercase word and ends with the period that concludes the novel. Before the end of the last sentence, no other full stop interrupts the flow of the narrator's words. Language never rests, never finds a place where it can pause to allow readers to assess the message they have received and the ambiguities yet to be spelled out. Swept by this linguistic frenzy, temporal connections between events disappear: as Elodie Coutier aptly notes, "The lack of full stops until the end of the narrative compels novelistic writing to juxtapose the actions it narrates, thus erasing most of the novel's chronology" (sec. 9).

Within this linguistic stream, one exception stands out: the short story by the fictitious writer Rafaël Kahla (the recounting of Intissar's adventure during the Lebanese Civil War) that Francis reads on the train (63–72; 293–313; 439–44). It is a story written according to the

---

6. In the dream work, Freud argues, *displacement* is "a shifting of accent"; it takes the form of a passing of accent, that is to say significance, "from important elements to indifferent ones" (*New Introductory Lectures* 20). In Francis's narrative, the accent shifts from important (his crimes) to less important elements (others' crimes).

established rules of mainstream fictional writing: content divided into typographically delimited sections; a storyline running through a beginning, middle, and end; dialogues realistically represented in reported speech; and an intrigue that leads to a final resolution. As for the language, albeit characterized by a prevalence of paratactic structures, it displays all the features of a text written according to the conventions of good grammar: use of punctuation marks, capitalization of the initial word in sentences, division into paragraphs, and correct syntax. As Intissar's story represents an exception in the linguistic fabric of *Zone*, it comes to constitute a revealing difference. It is the only war narrative in *Zone* in which a woman, Intissar, is the hero as well as a warrior, and a weapon is used not for perpetrating a sexual crime, but for preventing it. Intissar's story also constitutes the sole narrative in the text not resulting from the workings of Francis's guilt-ridden memory. Furthermore, as anticipated earlier in this chapter, although Intissar's adventure involves military defeat and exile, it is not a narrative of displacement. The hero and her comrades-in-arms do not operate in a zone, but in a place, that is to say a region identified by the network of their relations (which go beyond the war) as well as by its cultural, historical, and geographical features.[7]

Characters like Francis—who epitomizes the male warriors who have wreaked havoc on the Mediterranean since the beginning of history—will never be able to entertain productive relations with a territory in order for it to be called a "place." Their situation in the world is determined by their lack of "a substantial community," according to Paolo Virno's clever definition of what is missing in the lifestyle of those—essentially all of us—who today share a common sense of "not feeling at home" (19–21). Deprived of a place, Francis and those like him must settle for a "zone." As said, this displacement translates into a narrative defined by the continuous postponement of the narration

---

7. *Zone* would appear to conceptualize space and time in a way that squarely matches Massey's theory. In Western thought, Massey argues, space is coded feminine and time masculine. *Zone* would confirm this pattern by confining Intissar into a bounded space and representing History as a male affair. However, in Massey's argument, time is coded masculine in that it is a productive dimension fittingly represented as progress and civilization. Space, is instead seen as aligned with "stasis, passivity and depoliticization" (6). Here *Zone* differs starkly from Massey's theory, since Intissar's active presence makes her space productive, while the male warriors' destructive violence deprives historical time of sense.

of its key story (Francis's war crimes) and by a never-ending flow of language that delays stability (the completion of a sentence) until its very end. Appropriately, in *Zone,* the end of the narrative, of language (represented by the period that finally concludes Énard one-sentence novel), and of male warriors' world, all coincide. "One last smoke before the end of the world," reads the last line of *Zone* (517).

Both the epistemic displacement and the spatial displacement I have discussed in this study are part of the life experience of *Zone*'s narrator and hero. As for the former type of displacement, the test treats it through the narrative of Francis's professional life. Back in Paris, after two years in the Balkans and a few months in Venice, Francis the warrior becomes an archivist. He lands a job as an information agent with the Secret Service, a bureaucratic position in which he displays a true passion for secret dossiers, along with an uncanny ability to carry out archival research. It is not by working in his office, however, that Francis shows his talent as an archivist, but by arranging a personal, secret archive of war crimes and war criminals. This repository takes five years to complete: it is "a sad piece of the past" housing thousands of records (77). It carries out two functions. To begin with, it provides the documentary evidence for the memories Francis narrates in the novel. With the exception of literary or historical episodes, such as the siege of Troy or the battle of Lepanto, Francis recounts stories that constitute the narrative interface of the documents he has stored. As a consequence, Énard's novel becomes an archive in and of itself: a monumental record-series in which every single record achieves its meaning as part of a sequence of documents. Through their century-long experience of senseless violence, the Mediterranean peoples have created these documents. Secondly, Francis's documentation on war criminals helps him to create his personal line of flight, to paraphrase Deleuze and Guattari, from the existential morass in which he is mired. After carefully arranging his documents in a suitcase, Francis plans to sell them to the Vatican for 300,000 dollars: his journey to Rome is part of this plan.

From the sale of his archive, Francis clearly hopes to obtain the money necessary for a fresh start in his life. What does it mean, however, in historical terms, to deliver crucial documentation on the history of the twentieth century to "the great Archivist," the Catholic Church (284)? It certainly means that *Zone* delivers an utterly skeptical message on the epistemic value of the writing of history. Since the establishment of its academic status in early nineteenth-century Germany, history has become the discipline that carries out a precise task: making sense of archival records by turning them into readable, meaningful narratives. History, however, cannot achieve sense, and archives remain substantially illegible, if both become the byproduct of a human civilization steeped in savage violence. Historical meaning vanishes when three millennia of Mediterranean history amount to a senseless repetition of acts of brutality, by which their perpetrators aim at procuring power, wealth, and sexual satisfaction. A novel structured like *Zone*—a sheer accumulation of fragmented reports framed by a narrative that never attempts to arrive at their explanation—becomes the only possible interface to an archive of repeated madness. At the end of the day, it makes sense to trust archival records to "the specialist in eternity," or the Catholic Church (382). The Church's authority supposedly exceeds human power, just as eternity transcends history: the mind of the Church, hopefully, will be able to make sense of the documents of human mindlessness. Yet, even this plan is ultimately discarded when Francis throws his suitcase into the Tiber (516). This gesture of ultimate archival skepticism appears consistent with a key motif in the novel, the "end of the world" (the novel's last four words).[8] Indeed, in *Zone*, the world ends not only when the novel reaches its conclusion, but twenty-one other times, all occasions in which the text mentions "the end of the world"; and if the world is ending, what use is there for the archive?[9] As Jacques Derrida taught us, we store records for the future: the question of the archive "is a question of the future, the question of the future itself, the question of an answer, of a promise and of a responsibility for tomorrow" (59). When the world is coming to a close, the future is not an option, and neither is the archive: Francis's suitcase and the records it contains can sink into the Tiber.

In *Zone*, as the future vanishes, the past becomes opaque. "History is a story of ferocious beasts, a book with wolves at each page," Fran-

---

8. Coutier claims that the end of the world mentioned in *Zone* is ecological in kind: "Only a natural catastrophe can break the eternal cycle of human violence" (sect. 17).

9. "The end of the world" (*la fin du monde*) is mentioned in chapter 1 (12, 15 [twice], and 17), chapter 2 (22), chapter 3 (59), chapter 5 (87), chapter 6 (130), chapter 7 (161), chapter 9 (190), chapter 11 (249), chapter 15 (332 and 345), chapter 16 (382),

cis says while commenting on the atrocities committed in the Balkans since the outbreak of WWI (401). Beasts do not evolve, but behave in the same way now as they did when they set foot on the surface of the planet for the first time; meaning that the human species is stuck at day one of its existence. In particular, Mediterranean civilization is condemned to go through cycles of endless ferocity. As Jünke notices, the vision of the past conveyed in *Zone,* "which is founded on the idea of a basic constellation of violence and vengeance that determines the history of all times," is mythical rather than historical (83). Put another way, since the past amounts to continuous waves of compulsive violence, it makes no sense to conceive of it as History or to place Reason at its helm, as in the case of the Hegelian philosophy of history. Since myths ignore change, the passing of the centuries does not determine any progression whatsoever within the Mediterranean narrated by Énard. The events of the twentieth century further reinforce the idea that history is completely immobile: the continuous state of war that took place at the end of our immediate past is a plain and simple repetition of what occurred at its beginning. Since 1914, Francis's Zone has been one of endless conflict: the war "is still going on, almost a century past Gavrilo Princip's Balkanik shot" (146). It is this mythical conception of the past that discredits the cognitive value of the archive (why store records if the same events repeat themselves through the centuries?) and sidelines history itself.

Berardi argues that Modernity, the age that believes in the future, came to a conclusion in the twentieth century (14). Moderns are those who experience time as a progress toward perfection. In our age, Berardi argues, as we doubt that future and progress coincide, we have ceased to be modern (15). By doing away with the correspondence between Reason and History that lies at the foundation of modern thought and, at the same time, by erasing the future from its horizon, *Zone* is a deeply antimodern novel. It is the novel of a displaced humanity, unable to read the past, skeptical about the very idea of a future, and forced to hold onto a directionless present.[10]

---

chapter 17 (385), chapter 18 (402), chapter 19 (424), chapter 21 (462), chapter 22 (484), and chapter 24 (510 and 517 [twice]).

10. Crary also discusses the end of the future in our time. He argues that the unsustainable speed of technological change represents the ultimate reason for the present-day disappearance of the future as a time differing from the present: as "the acceler-

Spatial Displacement in *Zone*

Francis's journey from Paris to Rome epitomizes the spatial displacement that has marred his entire life. Francis is a lost hero, much like Trinidad and Cecilia González, Buell Quain, and Samad Iqbal. His memory travels in time, but what he recalls are his endless moves through space. In particular, Francis's movements through the Zone follow the same pattern that characterizes the attempts of his traumatized memory to dig up the fragments of his past: continuous and directionless repetition. This compulsive mobility comes to an end in the garden of the French embassy in Beirut, where he gets lost once again, but is still able to meet with the papal nuncio in Damascus. This is the prelate who will put Francis in touch with the Church leaders interested in his archive of war crimes (190, 514). The direct consequence of this meeting in Damascus is Francis's journey from Paris Charles De Gaulle to Rome Fiumicino, from one airport to another. Augé would probably argue that Francis travels between two nonplaces, while Lussault would counter that he moves between two hyper-places, but this discussion would miss the point: in the narrative space of the novel, what matters is the event that repeats itself in the two airports. In Paris, Francis fails to catch (a Freudian slip?) his flight to Rome, while in Rome he intentionally misses a second flight, this time headed for an unknown location (outside the Zone, in any case). Francis's case is peculiar. As a displaced subject, he looks for a line of flight that might deliver him not from his territorialization (as in Deleuze and Guattari's theory), but from his deterritorialization, which makes sense given the negative character of the latter, forced upon him rather than chosen in an exercise of personal freedom. This line of flight that Francis seeks, however, cannot be. Francis himself proves to be aware of this impossibility by missing two airplanes in a row and finding himself stranded in the Rome airport at the end. As Francis utilizes airports for the act of missing rather than embarking on planes, he essentially moves from one non-airport to another non-airport, thus making any discussion on the nature of airfields moot. The only place he manages to inhabit

---

ated tempo of apparent change deletes any sense of an extended time frame that is shared collectively, . . . the future is so close at hand that it is imaginable only by its continuity with the striving for individual gain or survival in the shallowest of presents" (40).

throughout the novel is his seat on the train to Rome, an uncomfortable accommodation to say the least.[11] During this journey, Francis states, his "life is in parentheses," in a literary reference to *In Parenthesis,* David Jones's poem on WWI (129).[12] At the end of this parenthesis, he is stranded in Fiumicino. There he faces the end of history and geography, or the end of the human writing of time and space; that is to say, "the end of the world" as we are able to represent it.

The Literary Subject and the Outer World in *Zone*

As he ponders the circumstance of his journey to Rome on the train traversing Italy, Francis realizes the ultimate truth regarding his story: "I am being carried around . . . without maybe being really aware of the game I am playing, of the strings that are pulling me as surely as the train that is carrying me to Rome" (31). Behind the endless sequence of violence that the novel narrates, there lies an obscure power that moves human beings around as if they were puppets. A drifter like Francis, involved in an interminable sequence of local and international conflicts, becomes the perfect subject for suffering the might of this power. At the end of his experience as a soldier and secret agent, Francis is entirely aware of the network of power relationships in which he was involved: "I was a pawn like any other in the arguments between Zeus, Hera, Apollo, and Pallas Athena, a pawn utilized for executing a plan as obscure as the clouds amassed over the inaccessible Olympus" (283). Francis's chiefs, "the gods of the Boulevard," remain in the shadows and tower above even his direct, visible superior, the quiet bureaucrat Lebihan: they have "abused, manipulated, and used" Fran-

---

11. Jünke argues that "the train compartment is a very abstract, transitory, and functional space—an archetypal 'non-lieu' [nonplace] in the words of Marc Augé (1992)—that offers no opportunities for individual and collective identification" (75).

12. In addition to treating war as their subject matter, Jones's and Énard's works connect on a deeper level: both texts associate the war fought in the present with archetypal battles fought in the past, such as the Celtic defeats at Camlam and Catraeth (in Jones's poem) and the fall of Troy (in *Zone*), the "ur-catastrophe of western culture" (Dilworth 97).

cis (283).[13] They even knew of his secret archive of war crimes and have probably facilitated his theft of classified files. In short, Francis is not even in control of the "line of flight" he has imagined for himself: no agency is possible in *Zone*, apart from that which is exercised by the opaque powers who shift their pawns around the Mediterranean. As a powerless foot soldier who does not control his own destiny, Francis finds himself in the same condition as the unfortunate populations and individuals who crowd his memory. What is more, the democratic institutions of the Modern Age have not shortened the unmeasurable distance that separates power from its subjects in the Zone. We can verify this fact by considering the cases in which democratic authority carries out acts of sheer brutality in the novel: two Italian policemen viciously abuse a young black man at the Milan train station in one of the initial episodes of the novel; the CIA partners with Middle Eastern dictatorships in the torture of prisoners; and during the war for Algerian independence, the soldiers, judges, and policemen of the French Republic commit crimes against humanity that go unpunished after an ad hoc amnesty (16, 193, 207).

Inscrutable, overwhelming power is the literary subject that points behind itself in *Zone*. It points, I argue, to the top of the dualistic power structure that defines the age of global capital, the time in which the novel is written and in which several of the historical facts it narrates occur. What allows the "fact to fact" relation to function particularly well in *Zone* is the absolute truthfulness of its narrative. Under the thin veil of Francis's fictional journey to Rome, all the events narrated in the novel are historically true. As these facts constitute the greatest part of the novel's content, *Zone* represents the ultimate example of the truth-to-truth association that relates literary subjects to the outer world in novels of displacement.

---

13. *Zone* appears to be a novel informed by "oneworldedness," Emily Apter's neologism for a kind of perverted globalism that "envisages the planet as an extension of paranoid subjectivity vulnerable to persecutory fantasy, catastrophism, and monomania" (part 1, ch. 4). In Énard's Mediterranean, which substitutes for the planet as a bounded totality of sorts, "everything is connected" as in the nightmares of Apter's paranoid subjectivities, while Francis lives through his fantasy of being persecuted by an anonymous, almighty, and omniscient power (part 1, ch. 4).

POSTSCRIPT

On Records and Errors

The four novels discussed in this book share a common epistemic trait: they uphold as true the type of knowledge provided by the historical record and/or everyday, sensible experience. In these four texts, this true knowledge frames the fictional narrative. In our time, however, the very idea of true knowledge must be related to our software-saturated age and, in particular, to its regime of truth. The latter, as Foucault taught us, consists of "the mechanisms and instances which enable one to distinguish true from false statements, the way in which each is sanctioned; the techniques and procedures which are valorized for obtaining truth; the status of those who are charged with saying what counts as true" (*Power, Truth, Strategy* 46). Today fictional texts, in particular, operate within a regime of truth that is strictly connected to the technology utilized for communicating and storing information. In this respect, an initial consideration appears necessary: in our epoch, novels (all of them, be they about displacement or not) have become technological hybrids, electronic files created through word processing software and converted to print texts only in the final stage of their composition: "Except for a handful of books produced by fine letter presses, print literature consists of digital files throughout most of its existence" (Hayles, *Electronic Literature* 159). Key to my argument here is the fact that print and software gesture toward two distinct manners of managing information and ultimately proving its truth. As paper books, contemporary novels display their affinity with the bureaucratic archive, while, as electronic files, they belong to the universe of the digital database. This twofold allegiance obviously affects novels of displacement, as occurs with every narrative committed to telling the truth about our age. Indeed, today's novelists retrieve records substantiating their claim to textual truth from both archives and databases. In these repositories, however, the storage of records takes place according to protocols informed by different notions of stability.

Rudi Laermans and Pascal Gielen argue that if one applies the "wisdom of the archivist" to the observation of the records stored in a digital database, "one will not observe a profound change but only mourn a profound loss, i.e. of stability. The classical archival paradigm indeed privileges the stable storage of information and therefore relegates its flexible use to the realm of interpretation" (sect. 2). On the contrary, databases appear plagued by "the instability of the sources or records themselves." As databases are continually renewed, they privilege "the active user above the stable source, the need for present information or information that is also (re-)usable within the present above a more or less accurate representation of the past within that very same present" (sect. 2). Because of their diverse relations to stability, archives and databases lead to distinct approaches to truth.

The archive of the paper age belongs to a context that favors a practice of truth based on correspondence. A modern, bureaucratic archive informed by the Principle of Provenance (first established in Germany in 1881) must place each individual record in just one location. In turn, the order of the items on the shelves must correspond to the internal structure (divisions, departments, offices) of the originating record agency. In novels written in the paper age, a trusted method for claiming narrative truth occured through reference to archival records that supported the text's truthfulness. Whether the text alluded to actual records the novelist located in an archive or to fictional papers retrieved by imaginary characters, the novel symbolized the establishment of truth by means of correspondence. In the practice of the archive, correspondence takes the form of an accord between records and facts. The archive makes this accord possible by adopting tested protocols for the appraisal and the storage of records as well as for their arrangement in meaningful, uninterrupted series. In novels composed within this epistemic framework, a chain of correspondence links the author's initial judgment about certain developments within society and/or an individual to the documentation which proves that judgment to be reasonably founded and to the narrative whose truthfulness those very papers support. Beneath this chain of correlation runs the conviction, backed by a widespread trust in archival procedures, that the papers stored in the archive are tethered to the pillars of the real world.

In the paper age, truthful narratives indexed themselves to the archive. Think, for example, of Assia Djebar's *L'amour, la fantasia* (1985), a novel encompassing postmodernist suspicions toward the very notion of truth. In Djebar's work, the novel's first person narrator transcribes a series of written reports on the French conquest of Algeria and then her own dialogues with several women who joined the struggle against the French occupation during the Algerian War of Independence. These transcriptions confirm both Djebar's view of the French colonization as a kind of sexual violence and her recognition of the role played by women in the anti-French Resistance. Finally, as the novel describes the narrator in the act of recording written and oral testimonies, the fictional text becomes a peculiar archive, one that exhibits its own *mise en archive* (archivization), as Paul Ricœur calls the practice of establishing documentary proof (*La mémoire* 209). In *L'amour, la fantasia,* in short, an authorial judgment on society is validated by a record-backed narrative, while the mediation of signs allows for the correspondence between thoughts, records, and, ultimately, facts. In our software-informed age, however, this kind of indexing appears increasingly difficult, because the digital database floods the novel with a profusion of data deprived of context: nowadays, the chain of correspondence of the paper age dangles precariously in the void. Hayles argues that in this situation, narratives become "more and more infused with data," which multiplies opportunities both for the emersion of truth and for the creation of errors (*How We Think* 182). The fact that these data are part of digitized networks, where each point can connect to all others, complicates our search for truth in this environment.

Underlying our current epistemic debates is what Clay Shirky calls a question of philosophy: "Does the world make sense or do we make sense of the world?" (21). If the world makes sense, then it becomes imperative for the learning subject to produce categories that encapsulate the ontology of the universe: in order to be true, all the knowledge that follows will need to correspond to these categories. If, on the other hand, making sense of the world is a task incumbent upon the learning subject, then ours is a "probabilistic world" in which we "try to find ways that the individual sensemaking can roll up to something which is of value in aggregate, but [we] do it without an ontological goal" (21). As hybrids produced in our time, novels of displacement partake in both of the epistemic methods mentioned in Shirky's question: they oscillate between the commitment to grasp the sense of a world instilled with meaning and the attempt to attribute meaning to the world by transforming clusters of propositions into meaningful assemblages. While the former method gives rise to a practice of truth based on correspondence, the latter leads to a practice of truth based on probability.

In investigating novels that are technological hybrids, fact-checking—the procedure I have followed, for example, in the analysis of *White Teeth*—becomes a helpful heuristic practice. Fact-checking can assist in identifying the position of a text within today's epistemic field, which is characterized, as discussed above, by the coexistence of the paper archive and the digital database. Empirical considerations suggest that in the database's "probabilistic world," the less strict criteria of correspondence between narrative and records, allows for a greater amount of errors to go unchecked and end up on the written page. More factual mistakes, in other words, hint at a text that gravitates toward the epistemic framework of the digital database. No discussion, however, about error and truth in the in the age of software-driven, global capital can mean anything if one does not take into account the regime of truth that operates in Google, the portal that grants access to universal knowledge. A key tenet in this regime consists in the principle that what makes a piece of information valuable is not its correspondence to either our trusted records or the state of affairs in our worldly experience, but its capacity to establish connections to and from other similar entities. I now want to apply the theoretical concepts I have just clarified to the study of a text that appears particularly fertile for an investigation on error and truth: *Zone*, the last of my case studies.

Truth in the Age of the Search Engine

In *Zone,* the narrative of past events appears to be remarkably faithful to the historical record. This accuracy vanishes when the text deals with facts situated in the novel's present; that is to say, at the time of Francis's journey from Milan to Rome. Readers cannot pinpoint the date of this trip because the text makes contradictory references to events reported in the news. To begin with, on the basis of conflicting textual elements, Francis could conceivably have taken the train to Rome in three different years: 2001, 2004, and 2005. The first option, 2001, is determined by adding ten years to the date of Slovenia's Declaration of Independence (June 25, 1991), an event Francis recalls while he is traveling to Rome. Slovenia became independent, he remembers, at the time in which he was taking a vacation in Istanbul with his girlfriend Marianne (54). Francis then adds: "Ten years later I find myself in this overheated wagon" (55). Hence, the year of his trip to Rome should be 2001 (1991+10). The second year, 2004, is inferred from the suicide of Al Khatib Muannad Shaliq Ahma, a Jordanian national who blew himself up in Modena on December 11, 2003 (Meletti). As the train passes by Modena, Francis ponders over the fact that, "exactly a year ago, on Thursday, December 11, Mohammad el-Khatib [*sic*] blew himself up at five o'clock in the morning," just a few steps away from the synagogue (200). Accordingly, the journey to Rome should be taking place in 2004 (2003+1). Finally, the third year, 2005, is obtained by checking the date of Lapo Elkann's emergency admission to the Mauriziano Hospital in Turin, following a cocaine overdose. The incident, which made news because Lapo Elkann is the scion of the Agnelli, the owners of the biggest carmaker in Italy, occurred on October 11, 2005 (Aspesi). Twice on the train, Francis catches sight of the news regarding Lapo's ordeal in newspapers his fellow travelers are reading (22, 489).[1] The mention of Lapo Elkann's overdose is the first of three references to the year of Francis's journey appearing in the text. It is also the only reference that is repeated twice. Most importantly, it originates in a written text (a newspaper article that is not the subject of a memory, but a tangible object in the novel's present) rather than in the narrator's memory, as

---

1. In *Zone,* Elkann's first name is erroneously spelled as Lupo (the Italian for wolf) (22).

do the two previous references. For these reasons, I shall make an educated guess and consider 2005 as the year in which Francis takes his train to Rome, all of which prompts another question, this time regarding the day of his journey.

Still in Milan, Francis states that the date is December 8, the Day of the Immaculate Conception in the Catholic Calendar, a holiday the Pope will celebrate that evening in Rome's Spagna Square. December 8 is consistent with the wintry weather—fog and rain—of the day, which could also be read as a metaphor for the narrator's gloomy mood. As stated above, however, Lapo Elkann's overdose took place on October 11, which suggests October 12 as the day of Francis's journey to Rome. To add further to the confusion, later in the novel Francis mentions a "shaking and infallible Polish Pope," clearly Saint John Paul II (né Karol Wojtyła, born in Wadowice, Poland), who "has just finished his sermon in Spagna Square" (333).[2] Saint John Paul II, however, died on April 2, 2005. In short, having accepted 2005 as the year in which Francis's journey occurs, what, then, is the date for this trip? Is it December 8, October 12, or any day in between Jan 1 and Apr 1, 2005? Since no answer can be found in the text, it makes more sense to ask how a novel built on historical accuracy and narrated by a fictional archivist can make such sloppy references to information anyone could check with just a couple of clicks on the Internet.

The insertion of factual mistakes into *Zone* can be ascribed to our obsession with maximizing the networking capability of our media objects, be they novels, films, video clips, or blog entries. While handling one of these objects, we behave as if the number of connections to and from it were a value in and of itself. As I will discuss in depth a little later in this postscript, the downside of this "Google mentality" consists in a cavalier handling of the factual details conveyed through this working style. This occurs because a media object's potential for networking becomes more valuable than the truthfulness of its factual details. In the case of a novel, this factual indifference has formal consequences, in that it clashes with a key feature of the novel form, as firstly defined by Clara Reeve in 1785: "The Novel is a picture

---

2. Another allusion to Saint John Paul II occurs earlier in *Zone* when the text mentions "the dying Saint Peter" who is preaching in Rome. This Pope is described as a sick man who is suffering from Parkinson's disease and Alzheimer's disease, as indeed was the ailing Saint John Paul II in the last years of his life (189).

of real life and manners, and of the times in which it is written. The Romance, in lofty and elevated language, describes what never happened nor is likely to happen" (111). Consistency with sensible experience as well as with the facts reported in the historical record defines the novel, while unrestrained imagination belongs to the romance. As narratives dedicated to the depiction of the key mood in our time, novels of displacement represent precisely that minority in present-day fiction that holds to the tradition of the novel, as a genre committed to the representation of truth. Globalized novels, instead, embody a different trend, defined by a less careful (to say the least) handling of truth. To locate an example of this carelessness, we can once again turn to *The Da Vinci Code*. In this novel, we come across a character, Sophie Neveu, who is introduced as a direct descendant of Jesus Christ and Mary Magdalene; and as if this were not enough, Jesus and Magdalene's marriage "is part of the historical record" (265). On the supposed historicity of Jesus' marriage, Bart D. Ehrman's argument is decisive:

> Most significant is a fact that cannot be overlooked or underestimated: in none of our early Christian sources is there any reference to Jesus' marriage or to his wife. This is true not only of the canonical Gospels of Matthew, Mark, Luke, and John but of all our other Gospels and all of our other early Christian writings put together. There is no allusion to Jesus as married in the writings of Paul, the Gospel of Peter, the Gospel of Philip, the Gospel of Mary, the Gospel of the Nazarenes, the Gospel of the Egyptians, the Gospel of the Ebionites—and on and on. List every ancient source we have for the historical Jesus, and in none of them is there mention of Jesus being married. (153)

Today, novels that approach truth in *The Da Vinci Code*'s manner constitute by far the bulk of the novelistic genre, at least from the point of view of circulation, which takes into consideration factors such as the number of translations and the amount of copies published and sold on the worldwide market. For novels that do not conform to the model of *The Da Vinci Code*, however, representing Reeve's picture of "real life and manners" is becoming an increasingly difficult operation. The new regime of truth that pervades our postarchival epistemic environment constitutes an adverse context for the truth-finding practice that novelists had adopted up to the inception of the digital age: backing the novel's truth with records. Even in truth-committed novels such as those I examine here, occasional factual mistakes not only substitute record-supported information but, more disturbingly, also take on their form. Under this disguise, erroneous statements cannot be separated from truthful propositions.

Behind the deceiving status of certain factual errors in contemporary fiction, there lies the altered status of truth in the age of software-enhanced, global capital. In the move from paper to bit, from a rarity to an overabundance of data, our practice of truth has changed: we no longer trust a proposition when it is supported by either the historical record or the data of our own experience, but only if it can be linked to a larger informational network. Oftentimes—and this is the key point—it does not matter at all whether this proposition is true or not. This is the regime of truth that Alessandro Baricco sees functioning in Google, our gateway to universal knowledge: "The value of a piece of information is given by the number of the websites that send you towards its site" (*I barbari* 90). The principle that informs this logic is connectivity, the discriminating factor I discussed in chapter 3. What matters in the evaluation of a piece of information is its being part of a sequence, its pointing to and being pointed to by other pieces: "There is almost no other criterion for quality and even for *truth*; a piece of information counts when *it can be put in a sequence with all the other pieces of information*" (*I barbari* 92, emphasis in the original). What is occurring here is not so much the notion that having more connections means speaking a greater truth (as Baricco seems inclined to suggest), but that proven, record-backed truth is simply not as important as it used to be.

The approach to truth described by Baricco also inspires *Zone*: it is indisputable that Saint John Paul II was already dead on December 8, 2005, but this fact counts for nothing. As a character in the story, the living Pope makes the novel truer, in the Google sense of the term, because so many websites refer to him: they can point to him as well as to the novel in which he is now included. Saint John Paul II, in turn, can help the novel to point to innumerable other pieces of information, in fields as diverse as religion, politics, history, and even medicine and popular culture. The dead Pope represents a multidirectional link for channeling heavy traffic to and from the novel.³ Of course, the link Saint John Paul II does not agree factually with the link Lapo Elkann, but this detail is irrelevant: together, they increase the number of pointers aiming at and initiating from the novel, thus raising the text's networking ability. In so doing, they augment the ranking (truth's newest form) of the novel in the sequence of news, chats, and reviews to which *Zone* belongs. In other words, they raise the informational capital of *Zone*.⁴ In the present reality, this type of capital is quickly supplanting Casanova's "literary capital," which, in the paper age, determined the success of a literary work and the reputation of its author (32).

In any epistemic context, individuals in positions of power can reasonably hope to be believed without seeing their propositions submitted to fact-checking. Since successful writers today find themselves in this position, Zadie Smith's claim—that novelists do not need to prove the truth of their narratives due to their readers' uncritical trust—no longer appears as a young author's naïve dissemination of a professional secret. Rather, it constitutes a rational assessment of the present situation in novelistic writing. Today's novelists cannot identify reliable rules for the production of truth with the same confidence that their colleagues enjoyed only forty years ago. Therefore, at times, they reserve the right to create their own truth, which does not mean that the novel becomes a fictional alternative (aka romance) to the accepted truth. Rather, today's novelists create substitutes for truth. The fabric of this surrogate cannot be distinguished from that of proven truth, unless it is submitted to scholarly fact-checking. Epistemically, this operation is closer to deliberate lying, or to "photoshopping" for that matter, than it is to creating fiction.⁵ Thus, the "fin du monde" that

---

3. In *White Teeth*, Zadie Smith carries out the same operation by including the narratively unmotivated and historically flawed reference to the liberation of the concentration camps in late May 1945. This reference places the novel within the huge sequence of media objects dealing with the Holocaust, thus making for an enormous increase in the traffic of information to and from the text.

4. Slovenia's independence and Mohammad el-Khatib's suicide carry out the same function as the mention of Saint John Paul II, albeit with an inferior capability to accrue the novel's informational capital.

5. For a discussion of how a fictional text can persuade its readers of the historicity of imaginary facts, see Mexal's clever analysis of Dan Brown's "three-tiered strategy" in *The Da Vinci Code*. Mexal demonstrates how, in Brown's novel, two initial layers of realistic, trivial details allow the text to assert the historicity of a third stratum of unproved, utterly false claims (1092–94).

haunts *Zone* must be understood not in an apocalyptic but in a historical sense. It refers to a literary type of displacement: the end of the epistemic context in which the novel has thrived for two centuries. In other words, it is the world of the modern novel as we know it—at least since Ian Watt's definition of the novel's purpose as the "production of what purports to be an authentic account of the actual experiences of individuals"—that ends with the last words of *Zone* (27).

Through factual errors camouflaged as reliable information, the novels I have analyzed in this study bespeak the fatigue weighing on truth in the stories they relate. These novels point to a problem looming over our epistemic horizon: the crisis of place entails a crisis of truth, as if our difficulty to establish a productive relation with place also involved a parallel strain in producing truthful propositions about the things and individuals we meet in the territories we inhabit. We would need a neologism like "*distruth*" to define the trouble with truth in our time, in particular in public discourse. It makes perfect sense that this problem arises in novels of displacement, narratives defined by their commitment to tell the truth about the hegemonic discourse in our age.

My research, which set out to explore what happens to place in our time, discovered an even larger issue at play: what happens to truth in our age. Discussing the status of truth today would require nothing less than adding another volume to this study. However, writing one book in order to bring another to fruition would make little sense; and, frankly, one book at a time is enough, if not too much.

WORKS CITED

Primary Sources

Achebe, Chinua. *Things Fall Apart*. New York: Doubleday, 1994. Print.

The Americans. FX, 2013–18. Writ. Joe Weisberg. Television.

Balzac, Honoré de. *César Birotteau*. Vol. 6 of *La Comédie humaine*. Ed. Pierre-Georges Castex. Paris: Gallimard, 1977. 37–312. Print.

———. *Physiologie du mariage*. Vol. 11 of *La Comédie humaine*. Ed. Pierre-Georges Castex. Paris: Gallimard, 1980. 903–1205. Print.

Blest Gana, Alberto. *Martín Rivas*. Santiago, Chile: Zig-Zag, 1961. Print.

Breaking Bad. AMC, 2008–13. Writ. Vince Gilligan. Television.

Brown, Dan. *The Da Vinci Code*. New York: Doubleday, 2003. Kindle.

Carvalho, Bernardo. *Nove noites*. São Paulo: Companhia de bolso, 2002. Print.

Corti, Maria. *L'ora di tutti*. Milan: Bompiani, 1991. Print.

The Departed. Dir. Martin Scorsese. Warner Bros, 2006. Film.

Djebar, Assia. *L'amour, la fantasia*. Paris: Albin Michel, 1985. Print.

Eco, Umberto. *Il nome della rosa*. Milan: Bompiani, 1980. Print.

Énard, Mathias. *Zone*. Arles: Actes Sud, 2008. Print.

García Márquez, Gabriel. *Cien años de soledad*. Madrid: Cátedra, 1997. Print.

Horowitz, Eli, Matthew Derby, and Kevin Moffett. *The Silent History*. New York: Farrar, Straus and Giroux, 2014. Kindle.

Jones, David. *In Parenthesis*. New York: New York Review Books, 2003. Print.

Joyce, James. *Ulysses*. New York: Oxford UP, 1993. Print.

Marechal, Leopoldo. *Adán Buenosayres*. Buenos Aires: Editorial Sudamericana, 1967. Print.

McCarthy, Cormac. *No Country for Old Men*. New York: Vintage, 2005. Print.

Miéville, China. *The City & The City*. New York: Random House, 2009. Print.

Mr. Sunshine. TvN, 2018. Writ. Kim Eun-sook. Television.

Ngugi wa Thiong'o. *The River Between*. New York: Penguin, 2005. Kindle.

Sada, Daniel. *Porque parece mentira la verdad nunca se sabe*. Mexico City: Tusquets, 1999. Print.

Smith, Zadie. *White Teeth*. London: Penguin, 2001. Print.

Vinci, Simona. *Strada provinciale tre*. Turin: Einaudi, 2007. Print.

Woolf, Virginia. *Mrs. Dalloway*. Cambridge, UK: Cambridge UP, 2015. Print.

Secondary Sources

Adler-Bell, Sam. "Surviving Amazon." *Logic* 8. 3 Aug. 2019. <https://logicmag.io/bodies/surviving-amazon/>. Web.

Altamirano, Aldo-José. "La selva en el damero: la evolución del espacio urbano latinoamericano." *La selva en el damero: Espacio literario y espacio urbano en América Latina*. Ed. Rosalba Campra and Aldo-José Altamirano. Pisa: Giardini, 1989. 17–25. Print.

Anderson, Benedict. *Imagined Communities*. London: Verso, 1991. Print.

Appadurai, Arjun. *Modernity at Large: Cultural Dimensions of Globalization*. Minneapolis: U of Minnesota P, 1996. Print.

Apter, Emily. *Against World Literature: On the Politics of Untranslatability*. London: Verso, 2013. Kindle.

Aspesi, Natalia. "La notte brava dell'erede Agnelli." *La Repubblica*, 11 Oct. 2005: 1+. Print.

Augé, Marc. *Non-Lieux. Introduction à une anthropologie de la surmodernité*. Paris: Seuil, 1992. Kindle.

Bachelard, Gaston. *La poétique de l'espace*. Paris: Quadrige, 1957. Print.

Bakhtin, M. M. *The Dialogic Imagination*. Trans. Caryl Emerson and Michael Holquist. Austin: U of Texas P, 1981. Print.

Baricco, Alessandro. *I barbari*. Milan: Feltrinelli, 2006. Print.

———. *The Game*. Turin: Einaudi, 2018.

Baudelaire, Charles. *Le peintre de la vie moderne*. Paris: Fayard, 2010. Print.

Beal, Sophia. "Becoming a Character: An Analysis of Bernardo Carvalho's *Nove noites.*" *Luso-Brazilian Review* 42.2 (2005): 134–49. Print.

Beistegui, Miguel de. *Thinking with Heidegger: Displacements.* Bloomington: Indiana UP, 2003. Print.

Berardi, Franco (Bifo). *Dopo il futuro. Dal Futurismo al Cyberpunk. L'esaurimento della modernità.* Roma: DeriveApprodi, 2013. Print.

Berger, John. *And Our Faces, My Heart, Brief as Photos.* London: Bloomsbury, 2005. Print.

Berman, Marshall. *All That Is Solid Melts into Air.* New York: Penguin, 1982. Print.

Bhabha, Homi. *The Location of Culture.* London: Routledge, 1994. Print.

boyd, danah. *It's Complicated: The Social Lives of Networked Teens.* New Haven: Yale UP, 2014. Print.

Brown, Wendy. *Walled States, Waning Sovereignty.* New York: Zone Books, 2010. Kindle.

Bulson, Eric. *Novels, Maps, Modernity: The Spatial Imagination, 1850–2000.* New York: Routledge, 2007. Print.

Bylaardt, Cid Ottoni. "Os discursos do etnólogo, do filósofo e do ficcionista na estrutura do romance *Nove noites.*" *Estudos de literatura brasileira contemporânea* 45 (2015): 223–37. Print.

Cardon, Dominique, and Antonio Casilli. *Qu'est-ce que le Digital Labor?* Bry-sur-Marne: INA Éditions, 2015. Print.

Caruth, Cathy. *Unclaimed Experience: Trauma, Narrative, and History.* Baltimore: The Johns Hopkins UP, 1996. Print.

Casanova, Pascale. *La république mondiale des lettres.* Paris: Seuil, 1999. Print.

Casey, Edward S. *Getting Back into Place.* Bloomington: Indiana UP, 1993. Print.

———. "Going Wireless: Disengaging the Ethical Life." Wilken and Goggin 175–80.

Celati, Gianni. *Finzioni occidentali. Fabulazione, comicità e scrittura.* Turin: Einaudi, 2001. Print.

Ceruzzi, Paul E. *Computing: A Concise History.* Cambridge, MA: The MIT Press, 2012. Kindle.

Chartier, Roger. "Languages, Books, and Reading from the Printed Word to the Digital Text." Trans. Teresa Lavender Fagan. *Critical Inquiry* 31 (2004): 133–52. Print.

Chun, Wendy Hui Kyong. "On Software or the Persistence of Visual Knowledge." *Grey Room* 18 (2004): 26–51. Print.

———. *Programmed Visions: Software and Memory.* Cambridge, MA: The MIT Press, 2011. Kindle.

Colebrook, Claire. *Gilles Deleuze.* London: Routledge, 2002. Print.

Coletti, Vittorio. *Romanzo mondo. La letteratura nel villaggio globale.* Bologna: il Mulino, 2011. Print.

Coutier, Elodie. "Un mémorial romanesque pour l'épopée. Fonctions de la référence homérique dans *Zone* de Mathias Énard." *Revue critique de fixxion française contemporaine*. Jun. 2017. <http://critical-review-of-contemporary-french-fixxion.org/rcffc/article/view/ fx14.11>. Web.

Crampton, R. J. *A Concise History of Bulgaria*. Cambridge, UK: Cambridge UP, 1997. Print.

Crary, Jonathan. *24/7: Late Capitalism and the Ends of Sleep*. London: Verso, 2013. Print.

Credit Suisse Research Institute. *Global Wealth Databook 2015*. 20 Oct. 2015. <http://publications.credit-suisse.com/tasks/render/file/index.cfm?fileid=C26E3824-E868-56E0-CCA04D4BB9B9ADD5>. Web.

Cresswell, Tim. *On the Move: Mobility in the Modern Western World*. New York: Routledge, 2006. Print.

Crispi, Luca. "Some Textual and Factual Discrepancies in James Joyce's *Ulysses*: The Blooms' Several 'First Nights.'" *Variants. The Journal of the European Society for Textual Scholarship* 12–13 (2016): 104–24. Print.

Crowley, Dustin. "'A Universal Garden of Many-Coloured Flowers': Place and Scale in the Works of Ngũgĩ wa Thiong'o." *Research in African Literatures* 44.3 (2013): 13–29. Print.

Dardot, Pierre, and Christian Laval. *La nouvelle raison du monde. Essai sur la société néolibérale*. Paris: La Découverte, 2009. Print.

Davidson, Donald. "Agency." *Essays on Actions and Events*. Oxford: Clarendon Press, 1980. 43–61. Print.

Dawson, Paul. "The Return of Omniscience in Contemporary Fiction." *Narrative* 17.2 (2009): 143–61. Print.

Debenedetti, Giacomo. *Il romanzo del Novecento*. Milan: Garzanti, 1971. Print.

Debord, Guy. *La société du spectacle*. Paris: Gallimard, 1992. Print.

De Certeau, Michel. *L'invention du quotidien*. Paris: Gallimard, 1990. Print.

Deleuze, Gilles. "Post-scriptum sur les sociétés de contrôle." *Pourparler*. Paris: Les Éditions de Minuit, 1990. 240–47. Print.

Deleuze, Gilles and Félix Guattari. *Anti-Œdipus. Capitalism and Schizophrenia*. Trans. Robert Hurley, Mark Seem, and Helen R. Lane. New York: The Viking Press, 1977. Print.

———. *Kafka. Pour une littérature mineure*. Paris: Les Éditions de Minuit, 1975. Print.

———. *A Thousand Plateaus: Capitalism and Schizophrenia*. Trans. Brian Massumi. London: Bloomsbury, 2013. Print.

Derrida, Jacques. *Mal d'archive. Une impression freudienne*. Paris: Galilée, 1995. Print.

De Souza e Silva, Adriana. "Interfaces of Hybrid Spaces." *The Cell Phone Reader: Essays in Social Transformation*. Ed. Anandam Kavoori and Noah Arceneaux. New York: Peter Lang, 2006. 19–43. Print.

Dilworth, Thomas. *The Shape of Meaning in the Poetry of David Jones*. Toronto: U of Toronto P, 1988. Print.

Do Ho Suh. "'Seoul Home/L. A. Home'—Korea and Displacement." Interview. *Art 21*. 11 Nov. 2017. <https://art21.org/read/do-ho-suh-seoul-home-la-home-korea-and-displacement/>. Web.

Donnarumma, Raffaele. *Ipermodernità*. Bologna: il Mulino, 2014. Print.

Dreyfus, Hubert L. *Being-in-the-World: A Commentary on Heidegger's* Being and Time, *Division I*. Cambridge, MA: The MIT Press, 1991. Print.

Ehrman, Bart. D. *Truth and Fiction in* The Da Vinci Code: *A Historian Reveals What We Really Know About Jesus, Mary Magdalene, and Constantine*. Oxford: Oxford UP, 2004. Print.

Ek, Richard. "Topologies of Human-Mobile Assemblages." Wilken and Goggin 39–54.

Entrikin, J. Nicholas. *The Betweenness of Place*. Baltimore: The Johns Hopkins UP, 1991. Print.

Erber, Pedro. "Contemporaneity and Its Discontents." *Diacritics* 41.1 (2013): 28–49. Print.

Ernst, Wolfang. *Digital Memory and the Archive*. Ed. Jussi Parikka. Minneapolis: U of Minnesota P, 2013. Kindle.

Espinoza, Alejandro. "Tradición y ruptura en *Porque parece mentira la verdad nunca se sabe*, de Daniel Sada." *Revista de literatura mexicana contemporánea* 23 (2004): 65–73. Print.

Formenti, Carlo. *Utopie letali*. Milan: Jaca Book, 2013. Print.

Foster, Hal. "An Archival Impulse." *October* 110 (2004): 3–22. Print.

Foucault, Michel. "Governmentality." Ed. Graham Burchell, Colin Gordon, and Peter Miller. *The Foucault Effect: Studies in Governmentality*. Chicago: The U of Chicago P, 1991. 87–104. Print.

———. *Michel Foucault: Power, Truth, Strategy*. Sidney: Feral Publications, 1979. Print.

———. *Sécurité, territoire, population*. Paris: Gallimard Seuil, 2004. Print.

Frank, Joseph. "Spatial Form in Modern Literature." *The Widening Gyre: Crisis and Mastery in Modern Literature*. New Brunswick, NJ: Rutgers UP, 1963. 3–62. Print.

Fratini, Franco. "Il general intellect del capitale." *Quaderni di San Precario* 4. 8 Mar. 2013. <http://quaderni.sanprecario.info/wp-content/uploads/2013/03/>. Web.

Freud, Sigmund. *New Introductory Lectures on Psycho-Analysis*. Vol. 22 of *The Standard Edition of the Complete Psychological Works of Sigmund Freud*. London: The Hogarth Press, 1964. 1–182. Print.

———. "Remembering, Repeating and Working-through." Vol. 12 of *The Standard Edition of the Complete Psychological Works of Sigmund Freud*. London: The Hogarth Press, 1958. 145–56. Print.

Friedman, Thomas L. *The World Is Flat: A Brief History of the Twenty-first Century*. New York: Farrar, Straus and Giroux, 2005. Print.

Galloway, Alexander R. *The Interface Effect*. Cambridge, UK: Polity Press, 2012. Kindle.

Genette, Gérard. *Narrative Discourse: An Essay in Method*. Trans. Jane E. Lewin. Ithaca, NY: Cornell UP, 1980. Print.

Gibson, Chris, Susan Luckman, and Chris Brennan-Horley. "(Putting) Mobile Technologies in Their Place: A Geographical Perspective." Wilken and Goggin 123–39.

Gikandi, Simon. *Ngugi wa Thiong'o*. New York: Cambridge UP, 2000. Print.

Golumbia, David. *The Cultural Logic of Computation*. Cambridge, MA: Harvard UP, 2009. Print.

González Echevarría, Roberto. *Myth and Archive: A Theory of Latin American Narrative*. Durham, NC: Duke UP, 1998. Print.

———. *The Voice of the Masters: Writing and Authority in Modern Latin American Literature*. Austin: U of Texas P, 1985. Print.

Gordon, Eric, and Adriana de Souza e Silva. "The Urban Dynamics of Net Localites: How Mobile and Location-Aware Technologies are Transforming Places." Wilken and Goggin 89–103.

Gramsci, Antonio. *Selections from the Prison Notebooks of Antonio Gramsci*. Ed. and trans. Quinton Hoare and Geoffrey Nowell Smith. New York: International, 1971. Print.

Hall, Stuart. "Minimal Selves." *The Real Me: Post-Modernism and the Question of Identity: ICA Documents 6*. Ed. Lisa Appignanesi. London: Institute of Contemporary Arts, 1987. 44–46. Print.

———. "New Cultures for Old." *A Place in the World? Places, Culture, and Globalization*. Ed. Doreen Massey and Pat Jess. Oxford: Oxford UP, 1995. 157–213. Print.

Hardt, Michael, and Antonio Negri. *Empire*. Cambridge, MA: Harvard UP, 2000. Print.

Harley, J. B. *The New Nature of Maps*. Baltimore: The Johns Hopkins UP, 2001. Print.

Harrison, Thomas. *1910: The Emancipation of Dissonance*. Berkeley: U of California P, 1996. Print.

Harvey, David. *The Condition of Postmodernity: An Enquiry into the Origins of Cultural Change*. Oxford: Blackwell, 1990. Print.

———. "Space as a Key Word." *Spaces of Global Capitalism*. London: Verso, 2006. 119–48. Print.

Hauser, Arnold. *The Social History of Art. From Prehistoric Times to the Middle Ages*. Vol. 1. New York: Vintage, 1957. Print.

Hayles, Katherine N. *Electronic Literature*. Notre Dame, IN: U of Notre Dame P, 2008. Print.

———. *How We Think: Digital Media and Contemporary Technogenesis*. Chicago: U of Chicago P, 2012. Print.

———. *My Mother Was a Computer: Digital Subjects and Literary Texts*. Chicago: U of Chicago P, 2005. Kindle.

Hegel, G. W. F. *Phenomenology of Spirit*. Trans. A. V. Miller. Oxford: Oxford UP, 1977. Print.

Hobsbawm, Eric. *The Age of Revolutions: 1789–1848*. New York: Vintage, 1962. Print.

Hungerford, Amy. *Making Literature Now*. Stanford: Stanford UP, 2016. Print.

Hunt, Lynn. "Révolution française et vie privée." Trans. Françoise Werner. *De la Révolution à la Grande Guerre*. Ed. Michelle Perrot. Vol. 4 of *Histoire de la vie privée*. Ed. Philippe Ariès and Georges Duby. Paris: Seuil, 1987. 19–46. Print.

Jackson, William, and T. P. Gleave. *The Mediterranean and Middle East*. Vol. 6 of *Victory in the Mediterranean*. Part 3 of *November 1944 to May 1945*. London: Her Majesty's Stationery Office, 1988. Print.

Jünke, Claudia. "Trauma and Memory in Mathias Énard's *Zone*." *Journal of Romance Studies* 17.1 (2017): 71–88. Print.

Kant, Immanuel. "What Does It Mean to Orient Itself in Thinking?" *Religion within the Boundaries of Mere Reason and Other Writings*. Ed. and Trans. Allen Wood and George Di Giovanni. Cambridge, UK: Cambridge UP, 1998. 1–14. Print.

Kay, Alan, and Adele Goldberg. "Personal Dynamic Media." Ed. Noah Wardrip-Fruin and Nick Montfort. *The New Media Reader*. Cambridge, MA: The MIT Press, 2003. 393–404. Print.

Koltun, Lilly. "The Promise and Threat of Digital Options in an Archival Age." *Archivaria* 47 (1999): 114–35. Print.

Kula, Witold. *Measures and Men*. Trans. R. Szreter. Princeton: Princeton UP, 1986. Print.

Lacan, Jacques. *Encore*. Ed. Jacques-Alain Miller. Paris: Seuil, 1975. Print.

———. *Le Séminaire. Livre VII: L'éthique de la psychanalyse*. Paris: Seuil, 1986. Print.

La Cecla, Franco. *Perdersi. L'uomo senza ambiente*. Rome: Laterza, 2011. Print.

Laermans, Rudi, and Pascal Gielen. "The Archive of the Digital An-archive." *Image & Narrative* 17. Open Humanities Press. 25 Apr. 2016. <http://www.imageandnarrative.be/inarchive/digital_archive/laermans_gielen.htm>. Web.

Lafargue, Paul. *Le droit à la paresse*. Paris: Allia, 2016. Print.

Lapenta, Francesco. "The Infosphere, the Geosphere, and the Mirror." Wilken and Goggin 213–26.

Leyshon, Andrew, and Nigel Thrift. "The Capitalization of Almost Everything: The Future of Finance and Capitalism." *Theory, Culture, and Society* 24 (7–8): 97–115. Print.

Liddell Hart, B. H. *History of the Second World War*. New York: G. P. Putnam Sons, 1971. Print.

Lukács, Georg. *Goethe and His Age*. Trans. Rober Anchor. London: Merlin Press, 1968. Print.

———. *The Historical Novel*. Lincoln: U of Nebraska P, 1983. Print.

———. *The Theory of the Novel*. Cambridge, MA: The MIT Press, 1971. Print.

Lussault, Michel. *Hyper-lieux. Les nouvelles géographies de la mondialisation.* Paris: Seuil, 2017. Kindle.

Lynch, Kevin. *The Image of the City.* Cambridge, MA: The MIT Press, 1960. Print.

Malabou, Catherine. *Que faire de notre cerveau?* Paris: Bayard, 2004. Print.

Malpas, Jeff. *Place and Experience: A Philosophical Topography.* Cambridge, UK: Cambridge UP, 1999. Print.

———. "The Place of Mobility: Technology, Connectivity, and Individualization." Wilken and Goggin 26–38.

Manovich, Lev. *Software Takes Commands.* New York: Bloomsbury, 2013. Kindle.

Marx, Karl. *Capital: A Critique of Political Economy.* Trans. Ben Fowkes. New York: Vintage Books, 1977. Print.

———. *The Civil War in France.* Peking: Foreign Languages Press, 1970. Print.

———. *The Communist Manifesto.* New Haven: Yale UP, 2012. Kindle.

Massey, Doreen. *Space, Place and Gender.* Minneapolis: U of Minnesota P, 1994. Print.

Mazzoni, Guido. *Teoria del romanzo.* Bologna: il Mulino, 2011. Print.

Mazzucato, Mariana. *The Value of Everything. Making and Taking in the Global Economy.* New York: Public Affairs, 2018. Kindle.

McCann, Willis H. "Nostalgia: A Review of the Literature." *Psychological Bulletin* 38 (1941): 165–82. Print.

McKeon, Michael. *The Origins of the English Novel: 1600–1740.* Baltimore: The Johns Hopkins UP, 1987. Print.

Meletti, Jenner. "È un attentato alla sinagoga l'ultimo atto di un suicida." *La Repubblica,* 12 Dec. 2003: 12. Print.

Mellet, Laurent. "'Just keep on walking in a straight line': Allowing for Chance in Zadie Smith's Overdetermined London (*White Teeth, The Autograph Man* and *On Beauty*)." *(Re)Mapping London: Visions of the Metropolis in the Contemporary Novel in English.* Ed. Vanessa Guignery and François Gallix. Paris: Publibook, 2008. 187–200. Print.

Mexal, Stephen J. "Realism, Narrative History, and the Production of the Bestseller: *The Da Vinci Code* and the Virtual Public Sphere." *The Journal of Popular Culture* 44.5 (2011): 1085–101. Print.

Meyrowitz, Joshua. "The Rise of Glocality: New Senses of Place and Identity in the Global Village." *A Sense of Place: The Global and the Local in Mobile Communication.* Ed. János Kristóf Nyíri. Wien: Passagen Verlag, 2005. 21–30. Print.

Mezzadra, Sandro. "Fuori dal perimetro dei propri confini." *Euronomade.* 12 Dec. 2018. <http://www.euronomade.info/?p=11355>. Web.

Mirze, Z. Esra. "Fundamental Differences in Zadie Smith's *White Teeth.*" *Zadie Smith: Critical Essays.* Ed. Tracey L. Walters. New York: Peter Lang, 2008. 187–200. Print.

Moretti, Franco. *Atlas of the European Novel: 1800–1900.* London: Verso, 1998. Print.

Muir, Richard. *Modern Political Geography.* London: Macmillan, 1975. Print.

Nair, Supriya. "Dented History in Zadie Smith's *White Teeth*." *Anthurium: A Caribbean Studies Journal* 7.1 (2010). 23 Aug. 2015. <https://scholarlyrepository.miami.edu/anthurium/vol7/iss1/12/>. Web.

Negroponte, Nicholas. *Being Digital*. New York: Vintage, 1996. Print.

Nesci, Catherine. *La Femme mode d'emploi: Balzac de la Physiologie du mariage à La Comédie Humaine*. Lexington, KY: French Forum, 1992. Print.

Nichols, Bill. "The Work of Culture in the Age of Cybernetic Systems." Ed. Noah Wardrip-Fruin and Nick Montfort. *The New Media Reader*. Cambridge, MA: The MIT Press, 2003. 627–41. Print.

Nietzsche, Friedrich. *Ecce Homo: How to Become What Your Are*. Trans. Duncan Large. Oxford: Oxford UP, 2007. Print.

———. *The Twilight of the Idols*. Trans. Duncan Large. Oxford: Oxford UP, 1998. Print.

Ong, Walter. *Orality and Literacy: The Technologizing of the World*. London: Routledge, 1988. Print.

Perrot, Michelle. "La famille triomphante." *De la Révolution à la Grande Guerre*. Ed. Michelle Perrot. Vol. 4 of *Histoire de la vie privée*. Ed. Philippe Ariès and Georges Duby. Paris: Seuil, 1987. 81–92. Print.

Piketty, Thomas. *Le capital au XXIe siècle*. Paris: Seuil, 2013. Print.

———. *Capital et idéologie*. Paris: Seuil, 2019. Print.

Pred, Allan. "Place as Historically Contingent Process: Structuration and the Time-Geography of Becoming Place." *Annals of the Association of American Geographers* 74.2 (1984): 279–97. Print.

Ratcliffe, Matthew. "Why Mood Matters." *The Cambridge Companion to Heidegger's Being and Time*. Ed. Mark Wrathall. Cambridge, UK: Cambridge UP, 2013. 157–76. Print.

Reeve, Clara. *The Progress of Romance and the History of Charoba Queen of Egypt*. New York: The Facsimile Text Society, 1930. Print.

Renan, Ernest. "Qu'est-ce qu'une nation?" *Œuvres de Ernest Renan*. La Bibliothèque Digitale. Kindle.

Ribeiro, Marília Scaff Rocha. "Fiction as Deception: Anthropology, Journalism, and Narrative Traps in Bernardo Carvalho's *Nove Noites*." *Bulletin of Hispanic Studies* 91.3 (2014): 307–16. Print.

Ricœur, Paul. *L'intrigue et le récit historique*. Vol. 1 of *Temps et récit*. Paris: Seuil, 1983. Print.

———. *La mémoire, l'histoire, l'oubli,* Paris: Seuil, 2000. Print.

Robins, Kevin. "Tradition and Translation: National Culture in Its Global Context." *Enterprise and Heritage: Crosscurrents of National Culture*. Ed. John Corner and Sylvia Harvey. London: Routledge, 1991. 21–44. Print.

Roncayolo, Marcel. *La Ville et ses territoires*. Paris: Gallimard, 1990. Print.

Rosenblat, Alex, and Luke Stark. "Algorithmic Labor and Information Asymmetries: A Case Study of Uber's Drivers." *International Journal of Communications* 10 (2016): 3758–84. Print.

Rowdes, Neil, and Jonathan Sawday, ed. *The Renaissance Computer: Knowledge Technology in the First Age of Print*. London: Routledge, 2000. Print.

Sack, Robert David. *Human Territoriality: Its Theory and History*. Cambridge, UK: Cambridge UP, 1986. Print.

Sada, Daniel. "Una conversación con Daniel Sada." Interview by Raúl Silva. *Revista Replicante*. 11 Dec. 2015. <http://revistareplicante.com/una-conversacion-con-daniel-sada/>. Web.

——. "Daniel Sada." Interview by José Manuel Prieto. *Bomb* 94 (2005): 56–59. Print.

Said, Edward W. "The Art of Displacement: Mona Hatoum's Logic of Irreconcilables." *Mona Hatoum: The Entire World as a Foreign Land*. Mona Hatoum, Edward W. Said, Sheena Wagstaff, and Tate Britain (Gallery). London: Tate Gallery, 2000. 7–17. Print.

Sanders, Rickie. "The Triumph of Geography." *Progress in Human Geography* 32.2 (2008): 179–82. Print.

Sassen, Saskia. *The Global City: New York, London, Tokyo*. Princeton: Princeton UP, 1991. Print.

——. *Territory, Authority, Rights: From Medieval to Global Assemblages*. Princeton: Princeton UP, 2006. Print.

Scheiber, Noam. "How Uber Uses Psychological Tricks to Push Its Drivers' Buttons." *New York Times*, 2 Apr. 2017. Print.

Schlosser, Markus. "Agency." *Stanford Encyclopedia of Philosophy*. 10 Aug. 2015. <http://plato.stanford.edu/archives/fall2015/entries/agency/>. Web.

Schmitt, Carl. *Political Theology*. Trans. George Schwab. Chicago: U of Chicago P, 1985. Print.

Sell, Jonathan P. A. "Chance and Gesture in Zadie Smith's *White Teeth* and *The Autograph Man*: A Model for Multicultural Identity?" *A Journal of Commonwealth Literature* 41.3 (2006): 27–44. Print.

Senn, Fritz. "James Joyce's 'Ulysses': Hell, Purgatory, Heaven in 'Wandering Rocks.'" *Hungarian Journal of English and American Studies (HJEAS)* 19.2 (2013): 323–28. 9 Dec. 2017. <https://www.jstor.org/stable/44789681>. Web.

——. "No Trace of Hell." *James Joyce Quarterly* 7 (1970): 255–56. Print.

Sesay, Kadija, ed. *Write Black, Write British: From Post Colonial to Black British Literature*. Hertford, UK: Hansib, 2005. Print.

Shirky, Clay. "Ontology Is Overrated: Categories, Links, and Tags." *Clay Shirky's Writings about the Internet*. 2 Sept. 2014. <http://www.shirky.com/writings/ontology_overrated.html>. Web.

Singleton, Charles S. *Dante Studies. Commedia: Elements of Structure.* Cambridge, MA: Harvard UP, 1965. Print.

Sini, Carlo. *Etica della scrittura.* Milan: il Saggiatore, 1999. Print.

Smith, Marquard. "Theses on the Philosophy of History: The Work of Research in the Age of Digital. Searchability and Distributability." *Journal of Visual Culture.* 10 Dec. 2013. <http://journals.sagepub.com/doi/abs/10.1177/1470412913507505>. Web.

Smith, Zadie. Interview by Gretchen Holbrook Gerzina. *Writing Across Worlds: Contemporary Writers Talk.* Ed. Susheila Nasta. Oxford: Routledge, 2004. 266–78. Print.

Soja, Edward W. *Postmodern Geographies: The Reassertion of Space in Critical Social Theory.* London: Verso, 1989. Print.

Sommer, Doris. *Foundational Fictions: The National Romances of Latin America.* Berkeley: U of California P, 1991. Print.

Srnicek, Nick. *Platform Capitalism.* Cambridge, UK: Polity Press: 2017. Print.

Sturani, Maria Luisa. "Cartography and Territorial Change in the Building of the Italian Nation: Some Reflection on the Production and Use of Small Scale Maps during the 19th Century." *Per le vie del mondo.* Ed. Piero de Gennaro. Turin: Trauben, 2009. 349–57. Print.

Tally, Robert T., Jr. *Spatiality.* London: Routledge, 2013. Print.

Thomas, Susie. "Zadie Smith's False Teeth: The Marketing of Multiculturalism." *Literary London: Interdisciplinary Studies in the Representation of London* 4.1. 11 Mar. 2016. <http://www.literarylondon.org/london-journal/march2006/thomas.html>. Web.

Thompson, Molly. "'Happy Multicultural Land'? The Implication of an 'excess of belonging' in Zadie Smith's *White Teeth.*" Sesay 122–40.

Trimm, Ryan. "After the Century of Strangers: Hospitality and Crashing in Zadie Smith's *White Teeth.*" *Contemporary Literature* 56.1 (2015): 145–72. Print.

Turchi, Peter. *Maps of the Imagination: The Writer as Cartographer.* San Antonio: Trinity UP, 2004. Print.

Urry, John. *Mobilities.* Cambridge, UK: Polity Press, 2007. Print.

Vieira, Yara Frateschi. "Diante do espelho: refração e iluminação em Bernardo Carvalho." *Portuguese Studies* 21 (2005): 210–23. Print.

Virno, Paolo. *Grammatica della moltitudine.* Rome: DeriveApprodi, 2002. Print.

Walkowitz, Rebecca. *Born Translated: The Contemporary Novel in an Age of World Literature.* New York: Columbia UP, 2015. Print.

Wark, McKenzie. *A Hacker Manifesto.* Cambridge, MA: Harvard UP, 2004. Kindle.

Watt, Ian. *The Rise of the Novel.* Berkeley: U of California P, 1962. Print.

Wellman, Barry. "Physical Place and Cyberplace: The Rise of Personalized Networking." *International Journal of Urban and Regional Research* 25 (2001): 227–52. Print.

Westphal, Bertrand. *La Géocritique. Réel, fiction, space.* Paris: Les Éditions de Minuit, 2011. Kindle.

Wilken, Rowan, and Gerard Goggin, ed. *Mobile Technology and Place.* New York: Routledge, 2012. Print.

Williams, Raymond. *Marxism and Literature.* Oxford: Oxford UP, 1977. Print.

Wood, James. "Human, All Too Inhuman: The Smallness of the 'Big' Novel. *White Teeth* by Zadie Smith." *The New Republic* 223.4 (2000): 41–45. Print.

Yeginsu, Ceylan. "If Workers Slack Off, the Wristband Will Know (And Amazon Has a Patent for It)." *New York Times,* 1 Feb. 2018: B3. Print.

Zavala, Oswaldo. "La genealogía *otra* de la modernidad latinoamericana: Daniel Sada y la literatura mundial." *Latin American Literary Review* 79 (2012): 23–44. Print.

Zelinsky, Wilbur. *Nation into State: The Shifting Symbolic Foundations of American Nationalism.* Chapel Hill: U of North Carolina P, 1988. Print.

Žižek, Slavoy. *The Sublime Object of Ideology.* London: Verso, 1989. Print.

INDEX

absolute displacement, 147–48
Achebe, Chinua, *Things Fall Apart*, 49, 56
achrony, Genette's definition of, 124
Adichie, Chimamanda Ngozi, *Half of a Yellow Sun*, 21
Adler-Bell, Sam, 7
agency: and dualisms of power, 59–60; in experience of displacement, 98, 108; hyper-places and depletion of, 106; and intentionality, 8n5; relationship with subjectivity and place, 92, 104; and social fantasy of individual freedom, 154–57, 158; under global capitalism, 7–8; under negative deterritorialization, 7–8, 108; of youth, 104–5, 105n7, 105n9. *See also* invisibility; migrants and migration; mobility; nation-state; *Nove noites*; place; subjectivity; *White Teeth*; *Zone*
airports, 107
Altamirano, Aldo-José, 127n4

Álvarez Diestro, Manuel, *Displacements*, 24n18
Alyan, Hala, *Salt Houses*, 21
Amazon, 41, 42, 44, 60
Amazon wristband, 6–7
Americans, The (Weisberg, FX), 23, 67n13
anagnorisis as literary tool, 84
analepses, 121, 123
ancien régime: affinity of government and heads of households in, 14n9; description of, 50–51; individual freedoms under, 154n3; and nation-states, 19; power of, 51n5; wealth in, 61
Anderson, Benedict, 38, 57
Anderson, Sean, *Insecurities*, 24n18
anthropology: schizophrenia in, 73n1; vertical gaze in, 75, 75n4
anti-Semitism, 156
app novels, 59
Appadurai, Arjun, 34, 141

193

Apple, 41, 42, 44, 60
Apter, Emily, 170n13
archival records: immobility of, 165–67; and truthful narratives, 172. See also *Nove noites*; truth; *Zone*
artist-as-archivist, 80
Atoum, Mona, 144
Augé, Marc, 168, 169n11
Austen, Jane: marriage in novels of, 49; *Pride and Prejudice*, 17n13; territoriality of landed gentry in novels of, 18–19, 19n14

Bachelard, Gaston, 112
Bakhtin, M. M., 53
Balzac, Honoré de: globalized novels as parallel with, 65–66; similarity of family and state governance, 14n9; and territoriality of the novel, 9–10, 16; and ties between historical change and spatial transformations, 18; transformation of the novel by, 16; as witness to reterritorialization following French Revolution, 10. See also *Comédie humaine*; *Physiologie du mariage*
Balzac, Honoré de, writings of: *César Birotteau*, 54; *Le dernier Chouan ou la Bretagne*, 10–11n8; *Le lys dans la vallée*, 57; *Splendeurs et misères des courtisanes*, 15. See also *Comédie humaine*; *Physiologie du mariage*
Baricco, Alessandro, 23, 178
barroquismo, 118, 126, 127–28, 130
Baudelaire, Charles, 99, 101
Beal, Sophia, 75n4
Beistegui, Miguel de, 112
Benedict, Ruth, 77
Benjamin, Walter, 99
Berardi, Franco, 34, 106n10, 167
Berger, John, 112
Berman, Marshall, *All That Is Solid Melts into Air*, 4
Bhabha, Homi, 8n7; *The Location of Culture*, 8–9

Blackberry, 95, 153
Blanchot, Maurice, 68
Blest Gana, Alberto, *Martín Rivas*, 17
BNP Paribas, 60
borders and boundaries: border walls, 35–37, 35n3, 157; cartography and, 38; delimitation of, 36n4; and flatness of the world, 150; as horizons, 93; porosity of, 38–39, 92
Bourdieu, Pierre, 24
bourgeois family: and Balzac's understanding of territoriality in novels, 10; emergence of, 51; gender politics and sexuality in, 15–16n11, 16; and national context for thriving, 52
boyd, danah, 104–5, 105nn7–8
Braschi, Giannina, *United States of Banana*, 21
Brazilian National Museum, 78
Breaking Bad (Gilligan, AMC), 23, 67n13
Brennan-Horley, Chris, 92n1
Brown, Dan, *The Da Vinci Code*, 25, 63–66, 67, 177, 179n5
Brown, Wendy, 32, 34, 35n3
Bulson, Eric, 111n15
Burroughs, William S., 159
Bylaardt, Cid Ottoni, 74, 79

capitalism: deterritorializing power of, 39n7; flexible accumulation engineered by, 37n5; and homogenization of space, 40n8; national capitalism, 33; nature of, 32–33; oppositional tendencies in, 5, 5n3
cartography and maps, 37–38, 38n6, 126. See also *Porque parece mentira la verdad nunca se sabe*
Carvalho, Bernardo: and fiction as mix of canonical devices and imagination, 84; giving Quain a place in history, 73–74; research archive of, 78. See also *Nove noites*
Casanova, Pascale, 179
Casey, Edward S., 94n2, 95n3, 113n16
Catholic Church, in *Zone*, 165–66

Celati, Gianni, 19n14
Certeau, Michel De, 142
Cervantes, Miguel de, and territoriality of the novel, 110
Chun, Wendy Hui Kyong, 30, 30n1, 44, 59
Cloud/earth metaphor, 58, 62, 65, 154–55
Colebrook, Claire, 5n3
Coletti, Vittorio, 63, 64
Comédie humaine (Balzac): as archetype of novels' territoriality, 9–10; female desire in, 15–16n11; key mood of lust in, 66; male subjectivity and pleasure in, 15; spatial consciousness in, 18. See also *Physiologie du mariage* (Balzac)
commodities: digitized world as commodity, 45; relational nature of digitized, 43; and social relations of value, 30–31; and theory of the spectacle, 62, 65
computers. See databases; electronic information; software
Concordia University, 78
contemporary ideology, 27, 42, 65
Coppola, Francis Ford, *The Godfather Part III*, 118n3
corporations, rise of transnational corporations, 41–42. See also supranational corporations
Corti, Maria, *L'ora di tutti*, 135–36, 136n13
Coutier, Elodie, 159n5, 163, 166n8
Crary, Jonathan, 68, 105, 154, 167–68n10
Credit Suisse, 61
Cresswell, Tim, 97, 149
Crispi, Luca, 135
Crowley, Dustin, 56
cultural identity: and cultural reproduction, 141; in globalized and traditional novels, 63–65; novels as representative of, 53–55; place in, 93–94

Dardot, Pierre, 6, 34n2
data mining, 43–44, 62n11, 107–8, 108n11
databases: and crumbling of Westphalian order, 37; instability of, 172; reliability of, 82; and search for truth in, 173
Davidson, Donald, 104, 105
Dawson, Paul, 137, 138
Dean, Tacita, *Girl Stowaway*, 80
Debenedetti, Giacomo, 64n12
Debord, Guy, 35, 62, 65
Declaration of the Rights of Man and of the Citizen, 50
Deleuze, Gilles: capitalism and deterritorialization, 39n7; on centers of internment, 41; character of territoriality, 53; concept of deterritorialization, 4–5, 7; definition of minor literature, 20; and Empire, 39; on global capital, 33; paraphrasing of, 165; "Post-scriptum sur les sociétés de contrôle," 103n6; territoriality and the bourgeois family, 51–52
Departed, The (Scorsese), 23n17
Derby, Matthew, *The Silent History* (with Horowitz and Moffett), 59
Derrida, Jacques, 166
detective stories, 75, 87
deterritorialization: and borders, 36–37; capital as agent of, 39; concept of, 4–5; human experience of, 46; negative deterritorialization, 5–9; tensions with reterritorialization, 58; through the Web, 39; and weakening of nation-states' sovereignty, 31
Deutsche Bank, 60
Dick, Philip K., *The Man in the High Castle*, 124
Dionne-Krosnick, Arièle, *Insecurities*, 24n18
displacement: absolute displacement, 128–30; artistic representation of, 23–24, 23–24nn17–18; concept of, 1; created by negative deterritorialization, 8; and diminishment

of human agency, 1; disappeared persons and, 131–32; and modern subjectivity, 26; as outsideness, 9; radical forms of, 67–68; scope of effect of, 21. *See also* information communication technologies (ICTs); mobility; place; subjectivity

Djebar, Assia, *L'amour, la fantasia*, 173

Do Ho Suh, *Seoul Home/L. A. Home/New York Home/Baltimore Home/London Home/Seattle Home*, 24

Donnarumma, Raffaele, 50n3

dual allegiance, 23, 23n17, 67n13

dualism in society, 25, 50, 58–59, 100–101. *See also* Cloud/earth metaphor

eBay, 41

Eco, Umberto, 84; *Il nome della rosa*, 63

Ehrman, Bart D., 177

Ek, Richard, 95

electronic age, ideology and identity in, 156

electronic information: and electronic communication, 59–60, 79, 95–96; flattening and shrinking of the world through, 150–51; and place, 95–97, 95n3; and truth, 171–72; and the written word, 151–52

Empire: in Latin America, 120; as ultimate sovereign, 39

empirical reality: and apparent reality, 146–47, 146n19; literary language's liberation from, 123

emplacement, 128

Énard, Mathias. See *Zone*

entrepreneurs, 42–43

Entrikin, J. Nicholas, 106

epistemic environment for novels, 28

Erber, Pedro, 73n1

Ernst, Wolfgang, 152

Espinoza, Alejandro, 117, 118, 131n6

European debt crisis, 33–34

exclusion, place as instrument of, 93

Facebook, 41, 42, 43, 44, 60, 105–6, 108

fact-checking, 174–78, 179

Fall of the Berlin Wall, 150

Fascist ideology, 156

Faulkner, William, 57

finance, internationalization of: effect of software on, 29; foundation for, 33; role of software in, 6

flânerie and *flâneurs*, 99, 101, 111

Ford, Henry, 41, 41n9

Fordism, 37n5, 41, 41n9, 42n10, 44, 151

Formenti, Carlo, 60

Foster, Hal, 80

Foucault, Michel: on family and state governance, 14n9, 15n10; on the regime of truth in modern society, 171; on the state, 37; on supranational corporations and customers, 42

Frank, Joseph, 125

Frankish Empire, 36

Frantzen, Ed, 103

Fratini, Franco, "Il general intellect del capitale," 153

French Revolution, 10, 16, 50, 51, 51n5, 154n3

Freud, Sigmund: acting out and working through, 157; displacement in theory of, 162–63, 163n6; use of middle name of, 84

Friedman, Thomas L., 150

GAFA (Google, Amazon, Facebook, and Apple), 42, 42n10. *See also individual companies*

Galloway, Alexander R., 58n9

García Márquez, Gabriel, *Cien años de soledad*, 55, 57

gender politics and sexuality: in bourgeois family, 15–16n11; in the home, 112; in marriage, 11–13

General Electric, 41

General Motors, 41

Genette, Gérard, 74n2, 121, 124
Geographical Information Systems (GIS), 108n11
geopower, 99–100, 101, 103
ghosts, 131, 131nn6–7
Gibson, Chris, 92n1
Gielen, Pascal, 172
gig economy and gig workers, 106, 155, 157
Gleave, T. P., 134n9
global capital, era of: altered state of truth in, 178; from Being to Becoming in, 40, 40n8; capitalism compared to cerebral functioning, 40; computer software's contribution to, 2–3; culture of budgets in, 153–54; directional center of global capitalism, 3; flattening and shrinking of the world in, 150–51; future in, 167–68n10; and move to hyper-places, 109–10; polarization and fragmentation in, 57–63; and territory, 37–46; threat to human's relation to place in, 3–4; universal mobilization in, 3. *See also* data mining; deterritorialization; displacement; mobility; nation-states; place; reterritorialization; software; spatiality; subjectivity; truth
Global Wealth Databook 2015, 61
globalization: and cultural reproduction, 141; as distinct from *mondialisation*, 99n5; as driven by software, 29–30, 42; dynamics of, 2n2; of economic and political decision making, 30; ideology of mobility in, 149–50; of the metropolis, 140–41, 153; states' submission to, 6. *See also* mobility; supranational corporations
globalized novels, 21, 25, 63–67, 177
Goethe, Johann Wolfgang von, 49, 49n2
Goldberg, Adele, "Personal Dynamic Media" (with Alan Kay), 2
Goldman Sachs, 60

Golumbia, David, 58
González Echevarría, Roberto, 88
Google: as flattener of the world, 150; inner workings of, 44; overabundance of data available through, 80–81, 108; relationship with customers, 42–43; search functionality in, 80–81; as supranational corporation, 41–42; value of information in, 174, 176, 178
Gordon, Eric, 95n3
Gramsci, Antonio, 42
Guattari, Félix: capitalism and deterritorialization, 39n7; on centers of internment, 41; character of territoriality, 53; concept of deterritorialization, 4–5, 7; definition of minor literature, 20; and Empire, 39; on global capital, 33; paraphrasing of, 165; territoriality and the bourgeois family, 51–52

Hall, Stuart, 93
Hardt, Michael, 9, 39, 120
Harley, J. B., 38, 126
Harrison, Thomas, 60
Harvey, David: absolute space of, 127n5, 150; on Fordism, 41n9; on homogenization of space, 40n8; on maps and sense of place, 38; on relationality of space, 94–95; on shift from Fordism, 37n5; on working class movements and space, 103n6
Hauser, Arnold, 8–9n7
Hayles, N. Katherine, 102, 151, 173
Head, Tim, *Displacement*, 24n18
Hemingway, Ernest, 159
Hemon, Aleksandar, *The Lazarus Project*, 21
hidden manuscripts, 78
historical novels, 18
historical record: and correspondence with reason, 167; as immobile, 165–67; novels and truth of, 171,

179n5; novels' errors and inconsistencies with, 135–36, 135–37nn11–15, 173, 174, 177–78; spatial displacement through ignorance of, 27. *See also* archival records; *White Teeth* (Smith)

Hofer, J., 109n13

home: contested territoriality in, 112; and homelands, 147–48, 148n20; and homesickness, 109, 109n13; and subjectivity, 112. See also *Porque parece mentira la verdad nunca se sabe* (Sada)

Homer: *Iliad*, 159, 159n5; *Odyssey*, 69

Horowitz, Eli, *The Silent History* (with Derby and Moffett), 59

Hugo, Victor, *Les Misérables*, 138

Hungerford, Amy, 59

hyper-places and hyper-spatiality, 98–101, 103–4, 109–10, 168

immateriality, cultivation of, 44

income inequality, 60–61, 61n10

information communication technologies (ICTs), 59–60, 79, 95–96

informational capital, 179, 179n4

informational economy: and customer's lives, 42–44; and decentralization of production in, 41; immateriality in, 44–45

Instacart, 106

Instagram, 105–6

intentionality, 8n5, 104

International Monetary Fund (IMF), 33, 34

Internet, 60; oligarchic structures and polarization in, 60; searches using, 27–28. *See also* Amazon; Apple; Facebook; Google; informational economy

invisibility: control through, 30–31, 50; in finance corporations, 45; and human agency, 45; of power and knowledge, 30, 68; relationship with visibility in global era, 44–45; in software, 3, 25, 30, 31, 59; in software corporations, 44

Jackson, William, 134n9

Jones, David, *In Parenthesis*, 169, 169n12

Joyce, James, 110–11, 159; *Ulysses*, 135, 135–36n11

Jünke, Claudia, 162–63, 167, 169n11

Kant, Immanuel, 112–13

Kay, Alan, "Personal Dynamic Media" (with Adele Goldberg), 2

Kerouac, Jack, *On the Road*, 69

Kushner, Rachel, *The Flamethrowers*, 21

La Cecla, Franco, 36

labor and labor management: algorithmic, 102, 103, 106; and Fordism, 41; technological control in, 6–7. *See also* workforce

Lacan's notion of the Real, 44, 70

Laermans, Rudi, 172

Lafargue, Paul, 154n3

Lapenta, Francesco, 59–60, 91, 108n11

Latin America: imperialism in, 120; urban planning in, 127n4

Latin American literature: contribution to nation-state project in, 17; representation of power in, 119

Laval, Christian, 6, 34n2

Leyshon, Andrew, 29

linguistic space, novels as guardian of, 53–55

literary canon, genres of, 47

literary capital, 179

literary cartography, 56–57

literary devices: anagnorisis, 84; exchange of identities, 84; flashbacks and flashforwards, 121; hidden manuscripts, 78; parallel worlds, 124; spatial indicators, 125; temporal markers, 123, 125

Lowry, Malcolm, 159

Luckman, Susan, 92n1

Lukács, Georg, 47, 58, 66, 140
Lussault, Michel: and geopower, 99–100, 103; hyper-places of, 26, 107, 109, 168; hyper-spatiality of, 98, 104; on mobility in globalized world, 149–50; on *mondialisation*, 99n5; and networked publics, 104–5; on Times Square's rebound, 98n4
Lynch, Kevin, 142, 143

Machiavelli, Niccolò, 11
Malabou, Catherine, 40
male privilege and masculinity: machismo in war, 159; and pleasure, 11–12. *See also* marriage
Malpas, Jeff: and horizons, 93; and openness of space, 92; *Place and Experience*, 109; and relationality of place, 94, 127n4, 161; subjectivity and place in theory of, 104, 108
management: and asymmetry of power, 106–7; automated and algorithmic, 102; centralization of, 45
Manovich, Lev, 40–41, 49
Marechal, Leopoldo, *Adán Buenosayres*, 57
marginalization, insight from, 8–9n7
marriage: gender politics and sexuality in, 11–13; similarity to governance of the nation-state, 13–15
Marx, Karl, 30–31, 37, 58
Massey, Doreen, 6, 93, 94, 97–98, 145, 164n7
Mazzoni, Guido, 47, 52, 61, 69
Mazzucato, Mariana, 60–61
McCarthy, Cormac, *No Country for Old Men*, 129
McKeon, Michael, 48n1, 52n6
McLuhan, Marshall, 38
media objects, networking capabilities of, 176
Mediterranean civilization, gendered violence in, 159–60, 165–66
Mellet, Laurent, 143
metadata, 43–44

metamedia, 2
metaphysical principles, need for, 146–48
Métraux, Bernard, 77
Mexal, Stephen J., 63, 179n5
Meyrowitz, Joshua, 91, 95
Mezzadra, Sandro, 109n12
Microsoft, 41
middle station in life, 25, 47, 61
Miéville, China: *The City & The City*, 21, 67–68, 67n13
migrants and migration: agency in, 109, 109n12, 153; and experience of displacement, 22, 145, 148, 157; and fantasy of mobility, 152; handling in *White Teeth*, 138–39, 148
mobile phones, 95, 153
mobility: agency in, 27, 109n12, 153; benefits and human suffering from, 4; as ideology of globalized society, 149–52; refugees and ideology of, 152–53; relationship with place, 97; and sociopolitical contexts, 98, 109. *See also* written word; *Zone*
minor fiction: and narration of displacement, 20, 20–21, 25; *Nove noites* as, 82, 85, 88, 89
modernism: novels and place in, 110–11; readability of urban space in, 142
modernity: description of, 4; ideology of, 167; temporality and spatiality in cultural products of, 124–25
Moffett, Kevin, *The Silent History* (with Horowitz and Derby), 59
mondialisation, 99, 99n5, 100
Moretti, Franco, 17n13, 18, 19, 54
Mr. Sunshine (Kim, tvN), 23
Muir, Richard, 35
multinational organizations, 39

Naimark, Michael, *Displacements*, 24n18
Nair, Supriya, 137n15
Napoleon's Code, 52

narrative genres: temporal order compared to story order in, 121–24; tools of, 56–57
narrators, 74n2
nation, hegemonic narrative of, 9
nation-states: in Austen's and Balzac's time, 19; Balzac's understanding of territoriality in novels, 10; crisis for, 25, 35; cultural space of, 53–54, 54n7; marriage as metaphor for political governance of, 14–15; relationship with international capital, 32; sovereignty of, 31–32, 33, 34, 35–36, 50–51; territorial agency of, 19, 19n14; transformation of, 34n2
"National Romances," 17
negative deterritorialization: agency in, 7–8; concept of, 5–6; and human subjectivity, 108–9; in informational economy, 46; and lack of agency, 108; and place, 9
Negri, Toni, 9, 39, 120
Negroponte, Nicholas, 57
neoliberalism, 2, 29, 35, 157–58
Nesci, Catherine, 11–12, 15
networked publics, 104–5
Nietzsche, Friedrich: *Ecce Homo*, 146, 146n19; *Twilight of the Idols*, 146
nomadic metaphysics, 149, 152
North Dakota Historical Society, 78
nostalgia, 35, 93, 109n13
novel, genre of: affiliation with the nation-state project, 16–17, 17n13, 19n14, 53–54; capture of essence of life in, 49–50; to convey changes in practice of place, 110; definition and goals of, 47–48, 180; displaced persons in context of territoriality in, 21n15; favorability of sociocultural environment to, 48–49, 61–63; key feature of form, 176–77; and middle station in life, 25, 47; nineteenth-century paradigms of, 57; in nomadic paradigm, 68–69; stabilization of, 52, 52n6; technological hybridity of, 171; territoriality of, 9–13, 17, 20, 24, 53–58; as truthful narrative, 27–28, 48–50, 48n1, 50n3, 82, 173; uniqueness of form to address displacement, 25. *See also* Austen, Jane; Balzac, Honoré de; *Comédie humaine*; globalized novels; novelistic writing; novels of displacement

novels of displacement: absence of place in, 70; complication of the novelistic canon by, 20–21; components of, 70; and continuing connections with territoriality, 25–26; and crisis in place, 108–11, 112–13; displacement of form, 20; key epistemic mood of displacement in, 67–70; narration of sadness in, 110; as part of larger cultural trend, 23; reasons to study, 21–22; refinement of form in, 22–23; similarities in case study novels, 22; telling the truth in, 70–71, 74, 158, 170, 173–74, 180. *See also* historical record; *Nove noites*; *Porque parece mentira la verdad nunca se sabe*; *White Teeth*; *Zone*

Nove noites (Carvalho): anthropological research and politics in Brazil in, 77–78; archive of documents in, 77–79, 80; as case study, 21; conclusion of, 83–85, 83–84n6; discourses in, 75–76, 85, 87n7; displacement of characters in, 86, 87; displacement of the novel in, 85–86, 88–89; dying American in, 83; factual inconsistencies in, 84; incompleteness and missing center in, 78–79, 80, 81–82; Journalist's agency in, 87; Journalist's failure in, 87n7; Journalist's interest in writing a novel in, 79–80, 82–83; levels of displacement in, 88; multiple fictions in, 86–87; overview of, 26, 73, 79n5; Perna's letter in, 75, 76, 78, 82; role of Journalist in, 74n2; subjectivity of characters in, 92; truth as issue in, 22, 74–75,

75n3, 82; world of archive and fiction in, 85

novelistic writing: authorial decision and narrators in, 134; displacement's impact on, 25, 88; identification of key epistemic mood and, 67–68; and opposition to ideological authoritative cores of an age, 157; resilience of territoriality in, 55–56n8, 55–57; standard expectations of, 69; standard rules followed in Intissar's story in *Zone*, 163–64; and substitutes for truth, 179

Ong, Walter, 151
online socialization, 104–5
overabundance of data, 80–81, 82

panopticism, 12–13, 107
paper-based technologies: archives in, 172; and crumbling of Westphalian order, 37; as emplaced technologies, 96; establishing truth under, 172–73; written word in, 151
patriarchal families, 144–45
patriarchy/gender in Balzac, 11
Peace of Westphalia (1648), 31–32, 34
Philip II, "*Leyes de Indias*," 127n4
Physiologie du mariage (Balzac): definition of marriage in, 14; as epilogue to *Comédie humaine*, 10–11, 10–11n8; male-dominated marriage in, 11–12; marriage as metaphor for political governance in, 13–15; panopticism in, 12–13; relationship with *Comédie humaine*, 10–11n8; spatial consciousness in, 18
Piketty, Thomas, 32, 60–61, 61n10
Pirandello, Luigi, *Il fu Mattia Pascal*, 64n12
place: and agency, 101–8; crisis of, 108–11; deprivation of sense in, 9; destabilization of, 108; detachment of residency from, 67–68; and erosion of connections with subjectivity, 3–4; familiarity and, 111, 111n15; gendered nature of, 145, 164n7; and maps, 38; materiality and experience of, 24; meaning and connection in, 142; openness and, 92–93, 107; orientation in human experience of, 112–13, 113n16, 145–46, 147; placelessness of male Mediterranean warriors, 164; relational theory of, 91–98, 92n1, 94n2; removal from, 109, 109n13. *See also* deterritorialization; hyper-places and hyper-spatiality; reterritorialization; subjectivity; territoriality

Pokorny, Julius P., 135–36n11
polarization and fragmentation, 57–63
Porque parece mentira la verdad nunca se sabe (Sada): anonymous power networks in, 118–19; Cartesian spatiality in, 125–28; as case study, 21; circles as metaphor in, 117–18, 130; context of, 22; deconstruction of home in, 128–29; displacement in, 120, 121, 128–30; the ghost and *desaparecido* in, 130–32; helplessness in, 118; lack of finality in, 117–18, 130, 132, 132n8; main elements in study of, 111–12; overview of, 26–27; sociopolitical contexts of, 115–16, 120, 131–32; storylines and characters in, 116–17, 116n1; structure of, 118n3; supranational power links in, 120; temporal disorder and *achrony* in, 121–25

post-Westphalian order in international politics, 35–37
power: asymmetry of, 102–3, 104, 106–7; in era of global capital, 119; mapping as practice of, 126; and violence in *Zone*, 170. See also *Porque parece mentira la verdad nunca se sabe*
production: 24/7 and loss of spatiality and temporality in, 68; flows of, 5–6
prolepses, 121, 123
Proust, Marcel, *À la récherche du temps perdu*, 124–25

provenance, principle of, 172

Quain, Buell, 73–74, 73n1, 75n4, 77
quantitative relationality, 127n4

realism, novels and place in, 110
Reeve, Clara, 176; *The Progress of Romance*, 52
refugees, 97, 152, 155, 157
Renan, Ernest, 51
reterritorialization: in Balzac's oeuvre, 66; in France, 16; and global brands, 40–41; oppositional forces of, 40; as reformulation of components of deterritorialization, 5–6; on software, 42; through software, 6–7
Ribeiro, Marília Rocha, 76
Ricoeur, Paul, 74, 173
Robins, Kevin, 42
Roman Empire, 36
romances, 17, 17n12, 48n1, 52–53, 177
Roncayolo, Marcel, 37
Rosenblat, Alex, 102
Rousseau, Jean-Jacques, 14n9
Rulfo, Juan, *Pedro Páramo*, 131n7

Sack, Robert David, 13, 36n4, 56n8, 112
Sada, Daniel: background to writing *Porque parece mentira*, 116nn1–2; literary language's liberation from empirical reality, 123. See also *Porque parece mentira la verdad nunca se sabe*
Said, Edward, 144
Sanders, Rickie, 96
Sassen, Saskia, 29, 44–45; *Territory, Authority, Rights*, 2n2
Scheiber, Noam, 103, 106
Schmitt, Carl, 34
Sebald, G. W., *Austerlitz*, 21
Sell, Jonathan, 139
Senn, Fritz, 135–36n11
sensemaking in the world, 173–74

seventeenth century, cultural displacement in, 130
Shirky, Clay, 173–74
Singleton, Charles S., 158
Sini, Carlo, 80
Smith, Marquard, 43
Smith, Zadie: *On Beauty*, 57; and the historical record, 137–38n16; novelistic writing and strategy of, 136–37; on truth in narratives, 179. See also *White Teeth*
Snow, John, map of London, 124
social antagonism, 155–56
social fantasy, 152, 154–57, 155n4
social media, power of, 105–6
social networks, 107
socialization in the global metropolis, 141
software: binary code and duality in society, 58–59, 58n9; and capitalism, 2–3, 25, 30n1; compared to commodity form, 30–31; and global capitalism, 29–31; as labor management tool, 102–3; and reterritorialization, 6
Soja, Edward W., 128
Sommer, Doris, 17, 17n12
de Souza e Silva, Adriana, 95n3, 102
spatiality: of 24/7 world, 68; absolute space, 127n5; dualism in, 61–63; as feminine, 164n7; global capital era's distinctive traits of, 104; of grids, 127, 127nn4–5; and meaning in urban spaces, 142–43; relationship with temporality in modern fiction, 124; and unbounded space, 38. See also hyper-places; place
spectacle: self-exhibition and voyeurism in, 107; theory of the, 62, 65
Srnicek, Nick, 108
Stark, Luke, 102
Stone, Oliver, *Natural Born Killers*, 78
Sturani, Maria Luisa, 37–38

subjectivity: effect of displacement on, 1–2, 8; emplacement in, 8; humans as embodied subjectivities, 96; identity and self-representation in nomadic subjectivity, 154–56; paranoia in, 170n13; relationship with ideology, 152; relationship with place, 92, 104, 110; under negative deterritorialization, 108–9
supranational corporations, 41–44, 48, 58, 60
supranational financial institutions, 3, 3, 33

Tally, Robert, 56–57, 111
taxes: nation-states' prerogative to levy, 34; worldwide tax on capital, 32
temporal order in fiction, 121, 123–24
temporality: of 24/7 world, 68, 154; as masculine, 164n7; relationship with spatiality in modern fiction, 124–25
territorial motifs, 53
territoriality: Balzac's capture of, 12–14, 18; and boundaries, 36; defining tendencies in, 13; nation-state as symbol of territorialization, 37. *See also* bourgeois family; Fordism; hyper-places and hyper-spatiality; nation-state; place
Thiong'o, Ngugi wa, *The River Between*, 55–56, 56n8
Thomas, Susie, 142n18
Thompson, Molly, 136–37n14, 143
Thrift, Nigel, 29
Times Square, 98, 98n4, 107
Tolkien, J. R. R., 111
Torfs, Ana, *Displacement*, 24n18
Torres, Heloísa Alberto, 77
tourist guidebooks, 25, 64, 64n12
trauma and traumatized subjects, 162
Trimm, Ryan, 142, 144
truth: crisis in, 180; and erroneous information in novels, 173, 174, 177–78; experience of displacement in pursuit of, 22; and fact-checking, 174–78, 179; pursuit of, 74 (see also *Nove noites*); status in digital age, 82. *See also* historical record; novel, genre of; novels of displacement
Turchi, Peter, 126
Twitter, 41, 43

Uber: algorithmic management of drivers by, 102, 103; data mining and, 108; exercise of geopower by, 103–4, 103n6; forced mobility of drivers, 153; relationship with Uber drivers, 101–4, 106
unhomeliness, 8–9
University of São Paulo, 78
urban space, readability of, 142
urbanization, 99n5. *See also* globalization
Urry, John, 33, 106, 109

Vieira, Yara Frateschi, 84
Vinci, Simona, *Strada provinciale tre*, 21, 69–70
Virno, Paolo, 164

Wachtel, Julia, *Displacement*, 24n18
Walkowitz, Rebecca, 67
war, and experience of displacement, 22
war and gendered violence. See *Zone* (Énard)
Wark, McKenzie, 154
Watt, Ian, 48, 180
wealth: and income-polarization of society, 60–61; as instrumental to male eros, 15
Wellman, Barry, 95
Westphal, Bertrand, 140
White Teeth (Smith): as case study, 21; cavalier handling of the historical record in, 132, 133–35, 136n12, 137, 136–38nn14–16, 148; characters' agency in, 138, 139–40; characters' understanding of history in, 132,

138, 143; context of, 22; displacement in the city in, 140–43; domestic displacement in, 143–48; historical time in, 139; main elements in study of, 111–12; narrator in, 132, 137–38, 139; networking ability of, 179n3; overview of, 26, 27; the real world and the apparent world in, 146–47; sense of place in, 142n18, 143; sociopolitical and spatial contexts for, 115; sociopolitical contexts for, 132–34; structural issues with, 137, 139

Williams, Raymond, 19

Wood, James, 138

Woolf, Virginia, 110–11; *Mrs Dalloway*, 57

Work Flow Software, 150

workforce: and algorithmic management, 102, 103; individual freedom and, 106n10, 153–56, 154n3; placelessness of, 39; software and shift in governance of, 6–7; split reality experienced by, 103–4; transformation of control over, 6; white collar worker's mobility and agency, 153–54

working class movements, 103n6

world economy, oligarchic structures and polarization in, 60

World War II, fact and fiction in *White Teeth* (Smith), 133–35, 134nn9–10

written word, decontextualization of, 151–52

Yahoo, 41

Yates, Richard, *Revolutionary Road*, 57

Yeginsu, Ceylan, 6–7

youth, agency of, 104–5, 105nn7–9

Zavala, Oswaldo, 118n3, 123, 132n8

Zelinsky, Wilbur, 38n6

Žižek, Slavoj, 27, 65, 155, 156; *The Sublime Object of Ideology*, 152

Zone (Énard): agency and power in, 169–70; as case study, 21; context of, 22; destabilization of novel itself, 158; "end of the world" in, 165, 166, 166nn8–9, 179–80; epistemic displacement in, 165–66; factual consistency in, 175–76, 178–79; informational capital of, 178–79, 179n4; informed by "oneworldness," 170n13; Intissar's story as exception in, 160, 163–64; linguistic and temporal markers in, 163; main character's archive in, 165–66, 167, 168, 170; Massey's concept of space and time in, 164n7; narrative blocks in, 159–60; overview of, 27; spatial displacement in, 168–69, 169n11; story frame in, 158–59; thematic displacement in, 159–61; unstructured narration and procrastination in, 162–63; vision of the past in, 167

www.ingramcontent.com/pod-product-compliance
Lightning Source LLC
Chambersburg PA
CBHW020332240426
43665CB00043B/448